THE GREATEST AIR BATTLE

D1432341

THE GREATEST AIR BATTLE

Dieppe, 19th August 1942

Norman L. R. Franks

GRUB STREET · LONDON

First published in paperback in 1997 by
Grub Street
4 Rainham Close
London
SW11 6SS

Copyright this new edition © 2010 Grub Street
Text copyright © Norman Franks

A catalogue record for this book is available from the British Library

ISBN 978-1-906502-70-6

Front cover painting by Peter Endsleigh Castle
Printed and bound in Great Britain by the MPG Books Group

Contents

When Canadian troops and British Commandos made their now famous 'reconnaissance in force' against the harbour town of Dieppe on 19th August 1942, they were supported and protected by the largest array of Royal Air Force aircraft ever seen in WWII until that time. Air Marshal Trafford Leigh-Mallory, AOC of Fighter Command's No.11 Group, was given command of the air operation and had 46 Spitfire, 8 Hurricane, 3 Typhoon and 4 Mustang squadrons under his direction, as well as 7 Boston and Blenheim squadrons of 2 Group and Fighter Command. On 19th August Leigh-Mallory commanded more squadrons than were available to Air Chief-Marshal Hugh Dowding at any one time during the Battle of Britain two years previously.

This book provides a detailed, minute by minute, hour by hour, blow by blow account of operations on a day which has become accepted as the one on which the Royal Air Force fought its greatest air battle.

The RAF flew nearly 3,000 sorties: the Luftwaffe 945. Air combat, ground attacks, bombing and smoke laying missions cost the RAF over 100 aircraft and the Luftwaffe nearly 50. All this happened in just 16 hours. In addition to the in-depth research into the RAF's activities on 19th August 1942, there are also many personal accounts from pilots who took part, adding colour to the story of this unique day in the history of the Royal Air Force.

Norman Franks is a full time author and air historian. His other books, published by Grub Street, are:

Above the Lines (with Frank Bailey and Russell Guest)
Above the Trenches (with Christopher Shores and Russell Guest)
Above the Trenches Updated Supplement (with Christopher Shores and Russell Guest)
Battle of the Airfields
Bloody April, Black September (with Frank Bailey and Russell Guest)
Fighter Pilot's Summer (with Wing Commander Paul Richey)
Over the Front (with Frank Bailey)
Search, Find and Kill
Spitfire Offensive (with Wing Commander R Sampson OBE, DFC & Bar)
Tempest Pilot (with Squadron Leader C J Sheddan DFC)
The Jasta Pilots (with Frank Bailey and Rick Duiven)
Under the Guns of the Red Baron (with Hal Giblin and Nigel McCrery)
War Diaries of Neville Duke
Who Downed the Aces in WW1?

List of Illustrations

Maps

Acknowledgements

During the research and writing of this book I have been privileged to meet and correspond with a number of men who flew at Dieppe. Each one in his own way has made a useful contribution and to each and everyone of them I am more than grateful. My sincere thanks, therefore, go to:

Air Chief Marshal Sir Harry Broadhurst, GCB, KBE, DSO, DFC, AFC (11 Group, Fighter Command)
Air Vice Marshal David Scott-Malden, DSO, DFC (North Weald Wing Leader)
Group Captain Myles Duke-Woolley, DSO, DFC (Debden Wing Leader)
Group Captain Denys Gillam, DSO, DFC, AFC (Duxford Wing Leader)
Mr Eric Beverley, DFC (13 Squadron)
Lieutenant Colonel Harold Strickland (71 Eagle Squadron)
Air Chief Marshal Sir Denis Smallwood, GBE, KCB, DSO, DFC (87 Squadron)
Mr Frank Mitchell (87 Squadron)
Mr Stuart Hordern (87 Squadron)
Group Captain James Pelly-Fry, DSO (88 Squadron)
Group Captain Desmond Griffiths, DFC (88 Squadron)
Flight Lieutenant T. H. J. Cairns, DFC, DFM (88 Squadron)
Wing Commander Minden Blake, DSO, DFC (130 Squadron)
Group Captain Peter Simpson, DSO, DFC (130 Squadron)
Group Captain Michael Pedley, DSO, OBE, DFC (131 Squadron)
Captain Richard L. Alexander (133 Eagle Squadron)
Mr John Brooks, DFC, DFM (174 Squadron)
Air Vice Marshal Graham Magill, CB, CBE, DFC (226 Squadron)
Air Commodore Peter Donkin, CBE, DSO (239 Squadron)
Air Commodore John Ellacombe, CB, DFC, MBIM (253 Squadron)

Major General Helge Mehre, DSO, DFC (331 Norwegian Squadron)

Major General Svein Heglund, DSO, DFC (331 Norwegian Squadron)

Lieutenant General Wilhelm Mohr, DFC (332 Norwegian Squadron)

Captain Per Bergsland (332 Norwegian Squadron)

Captain Marius Erikson, DFM (332 Norwegian Squadron)

Senator John Godfrey (412 Canadian Squadron)

Air Commodore Peter Brothers, CBE, DSO, DFC (602 Squadron)

Wing Commander Roland Beamont, CBE, DSO, DFC, DL, FRACS (609 Squadron)

Air Chief Marshal Sir Dennis Crowley-Milling, KCB, CBE, DSO, DFC, AE (610 Squadron)

Air Vice Marshal Johnnie Johnson, CB, CBE, DSO, DFC (610 Squadron)

I also thank the Ministry of Defence (Air), Staff of the Public Records Office, Imperial War Museum, Norwegian Forsvaramuseet, Oslo. Also to my friend Chaz Bowyer, for his continued confidence, Herr Hans Ring for his kind information, to Martyn Ford-Jones for his maps, to Amy Howlett of William Kimbers for her enthusiasm, and as always to my wife Kate for far more than her ability to spell. Finally to my two sons, Rob and Mike, for providing cups of coffee.

'So intense has been the battle that I have had to make far greater calls on all squadrons than I ever anticipated, or I would have imagined you could have undertaken. I thank you for your cheerfulness and keenness with which all sorties were carried out and congratulate you all most heartily upon the brilliant result of the day's fighting.'

Trafford Leigh-Mallory

Introduction

Much has been written about the Dieppe Raid which took place on Wednesday, 19 August 1942. The gallantry of the Canadians at Dieppe has been recorded in great detail as well as the raids by the Commando forces on the flanking gun positions. What is less well recorded or documented is the great air effort which took place on that day in direct support of Operation Jubilee. This book is an attempt to put the air side on record.

By the end of that August day in 1942, the Royal Air Force and the German Luftwaffe had fought what must be regarded as the greatest air battle of the war if only in terms of aeroplanes lost in combat on both sides in the space of just sixteen hours. Despite the tragic losses suffered by the Canadian troops on the ground, the RAF claimed a great victory that day.

*

The plan to launch a raid on the French coastal town of Dieppe was conceived early in April 1942, the thirty-second month of the war, at Combined Operations Headquarters. Following a long study of the practicability of such an enterprise, an outline plan was drafted and produced on 13 May. This plan was formally approved by the Chiefs of Staff.

In general terms the plan was to land a force of troops at Dieppe, supported by landings by Commandos on the flanks to knock-out gun positions overlooking the Dieppe beaches. Following much discussion it was decided not to precede the landings with either an air attack or heavy naval bombardment, nor was it agreed to use any form of airborne troops, although the landed troops would be given the support of a number of the new Churchill tanks.

Initially the raid was code-named 'Rutter' and it was to be launched towards the end of June 1942. However, due to an unsuccessful exercise and then bad weather, the raid was abandoned on 7 July and the troops dispersed. Political pressure by the Russians for the Allies to open a second front in the West in order to relieve pressure on the Russian front, brought the raid back to life at the end of July. A full-scale invasion against the French coast was completely out of the question at this time, but this strong attacking raid would, it was felt sure, help to keep the Germans guessing and on their toes.

On 27 July the Chiefs of Staff approved a new plan – which was code-named 'Jubilee'.

*

Two brigades of the 2nd Canadian Division and a Canadian Tank Regiment were chosen for the raid. Canadian troops, quick to come to the support of the Mother country when the war began, had been virtually unemployed in England for more than two years. They were bursting for action. Jubilee was to be theirs. They would be supported by British Commandos and 50 American Rangers. Total strength for Jubilee was approximately 6,100 troops – 5,000 of whom were Canadian.

In Dieppe itself was the garrison force of the German 302nd Infantry Division plus artillery. When Rutter was conceived the 302nd had been well under establishment but by August it had been brought up to strength. The Germans in France were well aware of and fully expecting some form of hostile move against the French coast during the summer of 1942. Exactly where, when, or in what form it would take they did not know. They did know, however, the most likely periods when tides and weather might be conducive for such an enterprise if mounted from the sea. In August 1942, the most favourable period would be between the 18th and 23rd.

*

Extracts from a communication from Combined Operations Headquarters dated 31 July 1942:

Object

1. Operation Jubilee is a raid on Jubilee[1] with limited air and military objectives, embracing the destruction of local defences and power stations, etc; in Jubilee, the capture of prisoners, the destruction of aerodrome installations near the town, and the capture and removal of German invasion barges and any other craft in Jubilee harbour.

Air Support

25. Air action in direct support of the landings will be provided as follows:

    (i) Two gun-positions south of Jubilee which threaten the landings at Red and White beaches will be attacked by Hurricane bombers and day bombers. These positions will be attacked approximately five minutes before the landing craft are due to touch down.

    (ii) If weather permits, aircraft will lay smoke on and bomb enemy gun-positions on the headland to the east of Jubilee harbour during the final approach of the landing craft to Red and White beaches.

    (iii) Close support fighters will attack the beaches (Red and White), the buildings overlooking these beaches and gun positions on the headland to the west of Jubilee as the landing craft finally approach and the first troops step ashore on Red and White beaches.

    (iv) A Spitfire squadron will attack the gun positions 4½ miles west of Jubilee in support of the attack on these positions made by Commando troops previously landed at Orange beach.

44. Air Support will be provided as follows during the withdrawal:

    (i) Fighter Cover will be increased to maximum strength.

[1] Code name for the harbour town of Dieppe. Gun positions and fortified headlands etc, were all coded by the Allied planning staff with names of German leaders.

    (ii)   Bomber and Fighter Squadrons will be maintained at 'Readiness' in maximum strength to engage targets to cover the withdrawal.

*

For the Allies, Dieppe was a necessary test for the future planning of future invasions, such as those which later took place in North Africa, Sicily and in particular the 'big' invasion in Normandy in June 1944. The Chiefs of Staff, their back-room boys and planning staffs, the Army and the Royal Navy all heeded lessons which later proved invaluable. The Royal Air Force too took notice, learned their lessons well and were ready when D-Day came. They also wanted a major confrontation with what had been mostly an elusive Luftwaffe since the middle of 1941 when Germany had invaded Russia. On 19 August 1942 they found the Luftwaffe and fought their greatest air battle.

CHAPTER ONE

Overture and Beginners

Once the decision to proceed with the raid had been made the complete air operation was put under the control of Air Vice-Marshal Trafford Leigh-Mallory CB DSO, Air Officer Commanding No 11 Group of Fighter Command. At fifty years of age, Leigh-Mallory had considerable experience of command, having joined the Royal Flying Corps from the Army in 1916, holding various commands in that war and during the inter-war years. When World War Two began he commanded No 12 Group, Fighter Command which he continued to lead during the Battle of Britain. His immediate superior in 1942 was Air Chief Marshal William Sholto Douglas KCB MC DFC, who had been knighted for his services the previous year.

Leigh-Mallory and his staff gathered together a formidable number of squadrons with which to carry out the Royal Air Force's assigned tasks for 19 August. In total he had 48 squadrons of Supermarine Spitfires, four of which were equipped with the latest Mark IX, two with Mark VI, the remaining 42 having Fighter Command's main fighter aeroplane, the Spitfire Mark Vb and Vc. With very few exceptions these units would provide the essential air cover to the raid, including escort cover for light bombers plus escort for a planned attack by American B17 Flying Fortresses. They would also have to provide continuous protection for the ships and boats during the raid and their subsequent return to England in the afternoon and early evening.

For attacks against light and heavy gun positions and troops in and behind Dieppe itself and on the two headlands to the east and west of the harbour which dominated the harbour and town, Leigh-Mallory had eight squadrons of cannon-armed Hawker Hurricane IIs, including two squadrons designated as fighter-bombers. These latter two units could carry either two 250 lb or two 500 lb bombs, one bomb carried under each wing. For heavier attacks, especially in use against well protected gun emplacements, and for initial smoke screening operations, he had three squadrons of Douglas Boston IIIs from 2 Group, Bomber Command, plus a handful of Intruder Bostons from 418 and 605 Squadrons of Fighter Command. In addition he had two squadrons from Army Co-operation Command flying Bristol Blenheim IV bombers.

Both Leigh-Mallory and the Chiefs of Combined Operations needed to know instantly of any hostile developments inland from Dieppe. To keep the immediate rear areas of Dieppe under surveillance, four squadrons of North American Mustang Is of Army Co-operation Command were made available. The last units of his main force which were brought in at the last moment were one Hawker Typhoon Wing of three squadrons. One 'Jim Crow' Spitfire squadron was also brought in plus the usual air-sea-rescue units.

In total Leigh-Mallory had approximately seventy squadrons available to him for the raid. With 48 squadrons of Spitfires, including three from the USAAF, he had a far greater fighter force available than Air Chief Marshal Hugh Dowding had at any one time when he commanded Fighter Command during the Battle of Britain in 1940.

By the beginning of August 1942, the fighter pilots in Fighter Command were being led by many experienced air fighters. Most of the leaders of Leigh-Mallory's Dieppe squadrons were veterans of the Battles of France and Britain and the summer offensive of 1941. In these conflicts most of them had been junior officers or NCO pilots. Having survived to 1942, approximately fifty of the squadron or flight commanders at Dieppe had seen action in the Battle of Britain alone. The wing leaders too were all experienced, seasoned pilots of 1940–41.

Pat Jameson DFC had gained famed with 46 Squadron during the Norway Campaign in 1940 and had been one of only two survivors of the squadron when the aircraft carrier HMS *Glorious* had been sunk. Now he led the West Wittering Wing. David Scott-Malden DFC led the North Weald Wing. He had been a classics under-graduate at Cambridge and had flown with two Auxiliary squadrons in 1940 winning the DFC in 1941. Commanding 54 Squadron he received a bar to his DFC in 1942. Minden Blake, like Jameson a

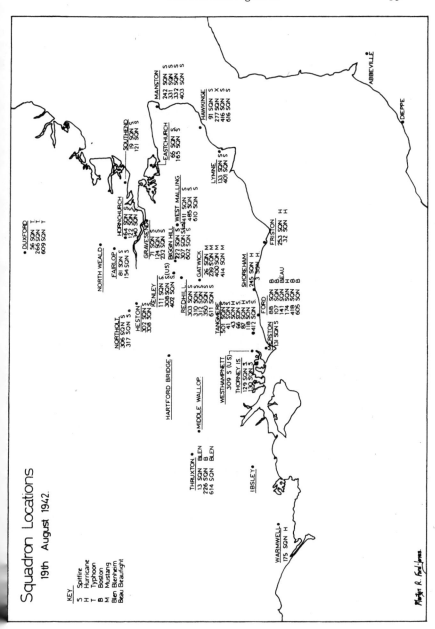

Squadron Locations
19th August 1942.

KEY
S   Spitfire
H   Hurricane
T   Typhoon
B   Boston
M   Mustang
Blen Blenheim
Beau Beaufight

• DUXFORD
56 SQN T
266 SQN T
609 SQN T

NORTH WEALD •

FAIRLOP •
81 SQN S
154 SQN S

• HORNCHURCH
64 SQN S
122 SQN S
340 SQN

GRAVESEND
71 SQN S
124 SQN S
232 SQN S

BIGGIN HILL
• WEST MALLING
• 222 SQN S 411 SQN S
307 SQN S 485 SQN S
602 SQN S 610 SQN S

• SOUTHEND
19 SQN S
121 SQN S

EASTCHURCH
65 SQN S
165 SQN S

MANSTON
242 SQN S
331 SQN S
332 SQN S
403 SQN S

HAWKINGE
91 SQN S
277 SQN X
416 SQN S
616 SQN S

LYMNE
133 SQN S
401 SQN S

NORTHOLT
306 SQN S
317 SQN S

HESTON •
302 SQN S
308 SQN S

KENLEY
111 SQN S
308 SQN S (US)
402 SQN S

REDHILL
303 SQN S
310 SQN S
312 SQN S
350 SQN S
611 SQN S

GATWICK
26 SQN M
239 SQN M
400 SQN M
414 SQN M

TANGMERE
501 SQN S
43 SQN S
41 SQN S
66 SQN S
87 SQN S
118 SQN S
412 SQN S

SHOREHAM
245 SQN H
3 SQN H

FORD
88 SQN B
107 SQN B
141 SQN BEAU
174 SQN B
418 SQN B
605 SQN B

FRISTON
253 SQN H
32 SQN H

MERSTON
131 SQN S

HARTFORD BRIDGE •

• MIDDLE WALLOP

WESTHAMPNETT
309 S (US)

THORNEY IS
129 SQN S
130 SQN S

THRUXTON •
13 SQN BLEN
226 SQN B
614 SQN BLEN

IBSLEY •

WARMWELL •
175 SQN H

ABBEVILLE •

DIEPPE •

Major R. Fred Jones

New Zealander, won his DFC in the Battle of Britain. By mid-1942 when he received the DSO he had claimed at least nine victories. He led the Portreath Wing where his usual task was to range long distances across the western end of the English Channel to Brest and Cherbourg. Petrus (Dutch) Hugo, a South African, had already won the DSO, DFC and bar, having seen action in France and in the Battle of Britain, commanding 41 Squadron in late 1941. By the time he took over the Hornchurch Wing in July 1942 he had claimed some ten victories.

Eric Thomas DFC was the Biggin Hill Wing Leader. A pre-war pilot he too had fought over England in 1940, becoming a squadron commander the following year. In early 1942 he led one of the Eagle Squadrons. R. M. B. Duke-Woolley was a graduate from the RAF Cadet College at Cranwell. Having initially been a Blenheim pilot he later went on to single-seaters to fight in the latter stages of the Battle of Britain, winning the DFC. A squadron commander in 1941–42, he was awarded a bar to his DFC before taking command of the Debden Wing, amongst whom were members of the first Eagle Squadron comprised of American volunteers. Denys Gillam DSO DFC was another Auxiliary pilot who fought in 1940 and had a string of victories by 1942 when he was given command of the first Typhoon Wing. Leader of the Tangmere Wing was P. R. 'Johnnie' Walker DFC. Another pre-war pilot he had seen action in France with 1 Squadron in 1940 gaining several victories. In 1941 he commanded 253 Squadron before becoming a Wing Leader. Included in his Wing was a Free French fighter squadron. Leading the first Polish Wing from RAF Northolt was Stefan Janus. He had gained several successes in 1941 and a DFC while a flight commander and later a squadron leader in two Polish squadrons.

These men, men from all over the world, and others like them were in evidence over Dieppe. In the air action that day would be Englishmen, Scots, men from Wales and Ireland, Australians, New Zealanders, Canadians, Americans, South Africans, and others from various British Colonies, including one from Ceylon and there was also a Maori. From Europe there were Free French, Free Belgians, Poles, Czechs; there were Norwegians and also a Danish pilot. All would contribute to the great air battle.

Trafford Leigh-Mallory grouped all his squadrons in southern England within a few days of 19 August. Those who were already strategically based in the extreme south were joined by others from either further north or from the west.

No 226 Boston Squadron of 2 Group, whose job it would be to lay smoke screens at Dieppe, was moved down from Swanton Morley, Norfolk to Thruxton near Andover on 14 August where it was joined by two Blenheim squadrons, 614 from MacMerry on the 15th, 13 Squadron from Odiham on the next day.

The other two 2 Group Squadrons, 88 and 107, moved from their Norfolk bases at Attlebridge and Great Massingham on the 16th in great secrecy.

No 88 Squadron was sent off from Attlebridge to be based at Ford on 16 August, so we had time to settle in. The night-fighter squadrons normally based at Ford were in some measure moved out to make room for us. The airfield commander, Wing Commander Gerald Constable Maxwell – a kinsman of the Duke of Norfolk – was kindness itself and most efficiently made every provision for our stay.

Upon arriving at the wartime officers' mess or rather the sleeping quarters element, I was curious to know just why all the house bells were ringing incessantly. Upon tackling one of my young men about it, he said, 'Have a look at the notice, sir.' The house, as I remember, was an erstwhile girl's boarding school. And the notice read: 'If you need a Mistress, ring the bell'!

No 88 Squadron was located somewhere at the furthermost point on the airfield from the hangars, control tower etc: and so we had to more-or-less play boy scouts. However, everything seemed to work although my time was more spent in being scout master than being a pilot.

Wing Commander James Pelly-Fry, O C 88 Squadron[1]

At Ford, near Littlehampton on the south coast of England, only a couple of crews remained of 605 Squadron who had just completed a move to RAF Hunsden on 14 and 15 August. The crews of two Bostons which remained, joined by two more who flew down from Bradwell Bay, would fly over Dieppe at dawn.

[1] All ranks are given as held in August 1942.

We of 226 Squadron were well prepared for our role. It was a good unit happily composed of aircrew from most parts of the Commonwealth plus one American whom we sadly lost at Dieppe. We considered ourselves something of experts in low level operations for which the Boston, at that time, was ideal. Squadron morale was high and not diminished by the fact that we were not particularly enamoured with the 'smoke' role.

Squadron Leader Graham Magill, 226 Squadron

For the Dieppe operation No 13 Squadron, which was based at Odiham in Hampshire, sent a detachment of aircraft, crews, maintenance personnel and catering staff to Thruxton in Wiltshire. This was necessary because the runways at Odiham were not long enough for a Blenheim IV to take off with a full load.

On the first occasion the detachment was very disappointed when the raid was called off at the last moment, but on the second occasion we were in position on 18 August and briefed that evening on the operational task which was to lay smoke along the cliffs of Dieppe to protect the attacking fleet from German coastal artillery.

Flight Lieutenant Eric Beverley, 13 Squadron

All eight Hurricane squadrons were grouped on the south coast. 175 Squadron stayed at its usual base at Warmwell but the other seven were all based right opposite Dieppe. 3 Squadron flew its machines down from Hunsden to Shoreham where it was joined by 245 Squadron from Middle Wallop. 32 Squadron moved to Friston, near Beachy Head, from West Malling where it was joined by 253 Squadron from Hibaldstone. 43 Squadron's home was already established at Tangmere but 87 Squadron joined them there from Charmy Down, the squadron doing one or two 'beat-ups' of the aerodrome upon their arrival to impress the locals! 87 Squadron was a night fighter and night intruder unit but spent several hours hurriedly repainting their Hurricanes in order to have day camouflage for the Dieppe show.

Squadron Leader Denis Smallwood, Commanding Officer of 87 Squadron, was initially informed that his squadron would be required to participate in an air exercise on Salisbury Plain and it was not until all unit commanders at Tangmere were called to a special briefing that he knew anything about the plan for Operation Jubilee. 87 were highly delighted at the prospect and at the chance of taking part in a daylight operation.

August 18 – spent the day, apart from briefing, in converting the black night fighters to daytime camouflage. Paint everywhere – very rushed job. The briefing told us of the raid and of the withdrawal, timed for 1300 hours. I remember thinking, 'It will be interesting to read how it all worked out, in the next day's papers – if I am still alive!' A hot summer's day and we worked on until well into dark.

Pilot Officer Frank Mitchell, 87 Squadron

The eighth squadron, 174, moved along from its usual base at Manston to Ford where it squeezed itself among the Bostons, the Hurricanes and the Bristol Beaufighters of 141 Squadron whose home base this was. 141 Squadron were merely spectators of the Dieppe Operation but one crew would become involved later in the day.

No 174 Squadron, which was often up against enemy shipping, had its detailed briefing, studying a model of Dieppe which showed the squadron's assigned targets. Then early to bed ready for an early start.

Every Spitfire unit was squeezed into the south. Tangmere received 41 Squadron from Llanbedr and all the squadrons of the Ibsley Wing, 66, 118 and 501, while 412 Canadian Squadron flew in from Merston. 412 Squadron were on an air firing exercise at Merston when they were suddenly recalled to their home base of Tangmere on the 14th. This in itself suggested some big operation was imminent. On Monday the 17th, 412 were briefed for an escort mission to American B17s who were to attack Rouen. As the Canadians came from the briefing room they saw outside Lord Louis Mountbatten, who was head of Combined Operations, plus several senior Army, Navy and RAF officers, waiting to hold a conference. This together with the fact that several other squadrons had begun to arrive at Tangmere only went to heighten everyone's suspicions and raise the general excitement. Other squadrons had similar experiences, and some like 412 were then busily engaged in Channel patrols on the 18th, ensuring that enemy aircraft should not spy out the naval activity at several south-coast ports.

Meanwhile, 130 Squadron moved on the 18th, from Perranporth to share Thorney Island with 129 Squadron.

As far as I can remember after the briefing, the evening before Dieppe, everyone was told to go to bed and get some rest before the early start next day. Sergeant Pilot X went to a phone box and rang his wife at Perranporth saying he was on a big thing the next day and that he might not return. (He) . . was either court martialled or something and reduced to the ranks on the squadron's return to Perranporth for breaking security regulations.

Squadron Leader P. J. Simpson, OC 130 Squadron

No 133 'Eagle' Squadron and 401 Canadian Squadron left Biggin Hill to operate from Lympne while 416 Canadian Squadron and 616 moved from Martlesham Heath and Great Sampford to invade the privacy of 91 'Jim Crow' Squadron's base at Hawkinge which they shared with 277 Air Sea Rescue Squadron. One pilot of 416 Squadron, Sergeant John Arthur Rae, 'Jackie' Rae to thousands of TV viewers in the 1960's, spent the 18th flying Air Training Corps cadets on Air Experience trips in the squadron's two-seater Magister. He made 21 such flights and was later to admit that had he known what was in store for him the next day he would not have been quite so keen.

RAF Manston was invaded by 242 Squadron and the two Norwegian Squadrons 331 and 332, all from North Weald and who comprised the North Weald Wing. They were joined by the Canadians of 403 Squadron who had been resting from operations at Catterick. Another squadron which was officially on rest was 602 at Peterhead in Scotland, but it flew down to Biggin Hill to join in the action. 303 Polish Squadron left its North Sea convoy patrol duties out of Kirton-in-Lindsay to move down to Redhill in Surrey where it was joined by the Czechs of 312 Squadron from Harrowbear and the Czech pilots of 310 Squadron, in from Exeter. Redhill was the base of 350 Belgian Squadron and 611 Squadron who made their visitors welcome.

West Malling was visited, on 16 August, by the Canadians of 411 Squadron from Digby in Lincolnshire, New Zealanders of 485 Squadron from Kingscliffe in Northamptonshire and 610 Squadron from Lydham in Norfolk.

At West Malling we found we were to form a 12 Group Wing with the New Zealand 485 Squadron and the Canadian 411 Squadron. Pat Jameson from Wittering was appointed wing leader; he told us that we would be based at West Malling until the big show was over. Jamie flew off to various conferences at 11 Group, and although we had no official news, the security of the proposed operation was exceedingly bad, for it was common knowledge that the Canadians were to assault a selected point on the French coast. We were about to take part in Operation Jubilee, the disastrous combined operation against Dieppe.

Squadron Leader J. E. Johnson, O C 610 Squadron[1]

No 610 had left their convoy patrols and Jim Crow missions to fly at Dieppe. The pilots were a trifle taken aback when they found that West Malling had not batmen but batwomen – WAAFS – who brought round the early morning tea. One enterprising pilot, on hearing the approach of his batwoman one morning, placed a 12 inch wooden ruler between his legs under the bedclothes, which formed quite a pyramid. The WAAF brought in his tea and appeared to take little notice before leaving the room. A few moments later, however, the door slowly opened slightly and *two* wide-eyed female faces gradually peered into the room!

Other squadrons came from further afield. 165 left Ayr in Scotland to fly to Eastchurch on 14 August while 222 also left Scotland, moving to Biggin Hill from Drem. 232 like 222 left its tedious convoy patrol duties and moved from Turnhouse to Gravesend.

Throughout the summer of 1942 No 131 County of Kent Squadron daily had been on operations over France so by 19 August the unit was at the peak of its efficiency. The squadron was located at Merston, a small grass airstrip and it comprised part of the Tangmere Wing then led by Johnnie Walker.

Wing Commander Michael Pedley, OC 131 Squadron

Other squadrons at Kenley, Biggin Hill, Gravesend, Southend, Fairlop, and North Weald stayed put. By the morning of the 18th all were more or less settled in even though some of the domestic

[1] *Wing Leader*, J. E. Johnson, Chatto & Windus 1956.

arrangements were a trifle strained. Despite this everyone was keyed up. All were certain that something big was in the air and when the pilots and aircrews were finally called into briefing huts or rooms all knew they were in for a big battle.

Eighty-one Squadron at Fairlop were called to their parent station, Hornchurch, where they were briefed for the morrow. They returned to Fairlop and like many others went 'to bed early to be on the top-line in the morning which is awaited with great eagerness.'

At RAF Manston Wing Commander David Scott-Malden DFC had all of his pilots, British and Norwegian, crammed into a briefing hut to give them a detailed run down on the raid. Scott-Malden recalls that it was the first operation where it was essential to know everything about what the Army – Canadians and Commandos – and the Royal Navy planned to do and where the RAF fitted into the scene of operations. For the first time it was truly to be a Combined Operation.

> The briefing contained that we were to maintain air superiority throughout the operation and regardless of opposition or cost to ourselves – ' . . . fight it out even if you are to remain there alone to the end.' Our Wingco, David Scott-Malden, was one of few words and tremendous authority. It is amazing how words like that can arouse enthusiasm.
>
> *Major Wilhelm Mohr, OC 332 Norwegian Squadron.*

This attitude reflects 332 Squadron's motto, *'Samhold I Strid Til Seier'* – 'Stick together and fight until victory.'

> The daring atmosphere about this particular operation, new to most of the air and ground crews I shall not try to describe. *This* was something *new*, a step into the future, a step of advance on the enemy, a step which demanded an all out effort on the ground and in the air. The briefing of the pilots followed its normal routine, but little was told to the ground crews until after the operations had started. However, the evening before, when all preparations had been done, I went round to the various sections of my squadron to see that they were all happy and to let them have an idea of what was coming. The ground crews were just as anxious as the pilots, and some of them too, not only

pilots, didn't sleep too long that night. I must have been rather confident in my squadron, because I did after all sleep most of the night!

Major Helge Mehre, OC 331 Norwegian Squadron

602 Squadron moved from Peterhead, whence it had been withdrawn for a rest exactly a month earlier, to Biggin Hill on 16 August, to participate in Operation Jubilee. In order to keep our hand in, we organised a Rodeo or fighter sweep on the 17th and 18th, the former proving somewhat abortive whilst the latter provoked enemy reaction and enabled me to destroy an FW190. Sadly we lost Flight Sergeant Gledhill, last seen going down in flames, but to our later joy heard that he was safe and well although a prisoner.

Squadron Leader Peter Brothers, OC 602 Squadron

At RAF Duxford, where the first Hawker Typhoon Wing was based, all three squadrons comprising the Wing, 56, 266 and 609, heard about the proposed raid on the 18th. They were called to briefing and addressed by the Duxford station commander, Group Captain John Grandy DSO.

He told us in his usual blunt and cheerful style that a major operation was about to begin which would take our forces back to France for the first time since our hurried withdrawal in May 1940. For some of us who had taken part in that battle and the subsequent Battle of Britain this was a tremendous moment, but he went on to say that in view of the prevailing technical problems with our new Typhoons which were suffering engine failures and tail breakages at the time, all he would do on this occasion was to tell us that we could go on this operation if we wanted to, but if we thought the Typhoon wasn't ready he would go along with that.

The Wing Leader, Denys Gillam, then outlined the operations plan for the Duxford Wing to reinforce to West Malling and from there, 'sweep' behind Dieppe at 10,000 feet to provide fighter cover over a sea-borne attack on the harbour and coastal defences. There was no hesitation at all – the Wing would go to Dieppe! Grandy was clearly delighted and the rest of the day was a whirl of preparation and repolishing of windscreens, running engines, checking guns and going over the briefing. The Wing was in fact at the end of a drawn-out and frustrating introductory period with its new Typhoons, and was more than ready to have a go.

Flight Lieutenant Roland Beamont, 609 Squadron

*

In the main, briefings were quite detailed, especially for the Boston and Blenheim crews whose first tasks would be to bomb and lay smoke in support of the troop landings. The Hurricane pilots too had detailed instructions. To help them, many prints of aerial photographs taken from a few days to a few hours before were studied in depth. Gun emplacements, machine-gun nests, strong points and gun batteries were pin-pointed – those that could be seen and identified – and their locations committed to memory. Other positions, it was hoped, would be spotted during the attacks. Timing had to be perfect. Height, speed and precise landfall must be closely watched. Return fire from the defences was expected to be heavy at first until – hopefully – the opposition was knocked out and then over-run by the Canadians.

Above the battle the Spitfires must protect and maintain a complete air umbrella over the town and the ships. Each squadron would be expected to patrol for at least thirty minutes in either squadron or wing strength, each group overlapping in order to retain complete mastery of the air. Failure to keep complete dominance in the air could cost the raiding force dearly.

Losses in this expected air-battle were fully anticipated. In the planning and in the thinking, up to 100 RAF fighters was one figure given as an expected loss. Yet in this air battle, the battle in which Leigh-Mallory hoped his pilots would finally be able to give a hammer blow to the Luftwaffe; he hoped that at least the same number of enemy aircraft would be destroyed.

For the fighter pilots on the evening of the 18th, it was a time of high excitement. For months they had been trying to bring the Luftwaffe to battle by flying Sweeps, Circuses and Ramrod operations over France but quite often the Luftwaffe simply chose to stay on the ground. On this evening, however, everyone knew that the Luftwaffe could not possibly ignore this major confrontation.

We were very conscious of the fact that the enemy would surely react with every fighter aircraft within call ... We were very tensed up at the reception in store for us, especially the numerical balance of forces in the air at that particular moment.

Wing Commander Michael Pedley, OC 131 Squadron

*

Opposing Leigh-Mallory's large fighter force on the morning of 19 August the Luftwaffe had two *Jagdgruppen* in France, JG2 Richthofen and JG26 Schlageter. These two units could muster a total of 190 serviceable Focke Wulf FW190 and 16 Messerschmitt Me109 fighters, JG2 having 115, according to German strength returns. Luftwaffe bomber units which could be made available to attack both the landed troops and the convoy of ships, had a total of 107 aircraft in a serviceable state. Of these, Kampfgeschwader 2 (KG2) had 45, KG40 30 while KG77 reported 13 operational machines. Kustenfliegergruppe 106 logged 19 aircraft ready for action. Of these totals, 59 were twin-engined Dornier Do217s, the rest mostly Junkers Ju88s or Heinkel He111s.

The scene was now set. Dieppe – Operation Jubilee – received the final go-ahead. On the night of the 18/19th, 237 little ships sailed from the southern ports of Portsmouth, Southampton, Newhaven and Shoreham, and steamed out into the Channel towards the French coast. Eight of these were destroyers, the Hunt class HMS *Calpe* being the headquarters ship from which Major-General H. F. Roberts MC, a Canadian, commanded the Military Force and Captain J. Hughes-Hallett RN commanded the Naval Force. Also on *Calpe* was a First World War Australian veteran airman, Air Commodore Adrian Trevor Cole CBE MC DFC RAAF who controlled the air operation from this forward vantage point. Cole, who was 47, had flown in the Great War in the Middle East and in 1918 had commanded an Australian fighter squadron on the Western Front. His main job on 19 August was to co-ordinate the squadrons flying above the raid.

There were several important RAF personnel aboard the control ship and on another destroyer HMS *Berkeley*, which was designated first rescue ship. On *Calpe* Acting Flight Lieutenant Gerald Le Blount Kidd RAFVR was the air controller for the close support squadrons, while on *Berkeley*, Acting Squadron Leader James

Humphrey Sprott RAFVR was the controller of the low fighter cover squadrons. They were ably assisted by:

Calpe	Corporal Turner (W.E.M.) from the Combined Signal School.
	Corporal Scoffins (W.O.P.)
	LAC Irwin (W.O.P.) both from Air Co-operation Command.
Berkeley	Corporal Clark (W.E.M.) from 11 Group, Fighter Command.
	Corporal J. Boulding, 26 Sqn (W.O.P.)
	LAC Billings, 26 Sqn (W.O.P.) both from Army Co-operation Command.

HMS *Calpe* left Portsmouth at 8 pm on the evening of 18 August. At 9.30 the convoy of ships sailed past *Calpe* who checked them before she steamed ahead again towards mid-Channel. At 1.15 a.m *Calpe* went through the gap in the German minefield that had been swept clear by minesweepers, the passage having been marked with marker buoys. Once through, *Calpe* turned to port, stopped and checked the ships again as they passed through the gap.

Three am on the morning of 19 August 1942 was the deadline. If the operation was going to be cancelled the order to do so would have to be issued by this time, for out across the Channel the landing craft were being prepared for lowering onto the grey/black sea. No cancellation order was made and the first landing craft were lowered at five minutes past three o'clock. Operation Jubilee was on!

Immediately orders began to be issued by Fighter Command Headquarters. At three minutes past 3 am, the first order was sent which required Bostons to attack and blind the 'Hitler' and 'Göring'[1] gun batteries at 4.45 am, the time the troops would be approaching the beaches. Bostons of 107, 605 and 418 Squadrons received this first order.

At 3.06 am came order number two; Bostons to attack 'Rommel' at 5.09 am. 88 Squadron was given this job. And so it continued.

---

[1] All strong points, gun batteries etc: were code-named by the Allied planners (see map).

3.29 am – Hurricanes to attack beaches and 'Hindenburg' at 5.15
    am – 3, 32, 43, 245 and 253 Squadrons selected.

3.30 am – orders sent to Gatwick for tactical reconnaissance by
    Mustangs.

3.31 am – Spitfires required for escort patrol – 65 and 111 Squad-
    rons.

3.35 am – Hurricanes to attack Hitler and Göring and the Ger-
    man Divisional Headquarters at Arques at 5.15 am.
    174 Squadron got Hitler, one flight each from 175
    Squadron were given the other targets.

3.47 am – Twelve fighter squadrons to be called to immediate
    readiness:
        310, 312, 350 and 309th (US) Squadrons,
        611, 402, and 111 Squadrons,
        303, 306, 317, 308 and 302 Squadrons.

3.57 am – Two Spitfires to attack Hess observation post in the
    Pointe D'Ailly lighthouse – 129 Squadron was given
    this task.

4.29 am – 91 Squadrons to reconnoitre the Channel continuously
    each hour.

etc, etc,

At 3.48 am a star-shell burned into the dark sky to the east of
Dieppe. It was fired by a small convoy of coastal motor boats,
escorted by three German submarine-chasers. Unknown to the
attacking force this small convoy was approaching Dieppe harbour
and had run into the 23 landing craft carrying No 3 Commando in
towards the Yellow Beaches at Berneval and Belleville. There followed a brisk exchange of gunfire which lit up the night, caused
considerable casualties amongst the Commando force and at least
one of the German vessels was set on fire. Although the German
sailors could see that it was a considerable force of British boats, to
any watchers on the shore this action could just be yet another
motor torpedo or motor gun boat attack on one of their coastal
convoys. Surprise was still on the side of the attackers but only just.

However, nothing could stop Jubilee now. For the Canadians the
Dieppe Raid was on. For the Royal Air Force their greatest air
battle was about to begin.

CHAPTER TWO

Dawn
3 am to 6 am

It was still dark when either gently or noisily the pilots of Fighter Command and the Boston and Blenheim crews at Ford and Thruxton were awoken. Whether in officers' or sergeants' messes, in Nissen or prefabricated huts, in airmen's barrack blocks or even in tents, all greeted the new day wearily or excitedly, cursing or stoically, boisterously or quietly. They washed, they shaved (most of them), dressed in their usual uniformed attire of battledress or old best blues, pullovers or roll-neck sweaters, silk scarves or collarless shirts, then in the gloom of the blackout stumbled to their various dining places for breakfast. At West Malling, 610 Squadron sat down to egg and chips, 'in the wee sma' hours'. Other squadron pilots too had a special treat of a real egg, with fried bread, toast and preserves, thick chunks of bread and margarine and of course mugs of tea.

With breakfast over they made their way either by cars, in trucks, on bicycles or if not too far they even walked, to their crew rooms and flight huts to don flying gear. Soft leather flying helmets, gloves, goggles, Mae West life preservers, flying boots or leg guards. Hands fumbled to see if their lucky charm was in a pocket, or their favourite scarf tied securely. Some looked neat and tidy, others scruffy with oil stained, creaseless and well worn trousers stuffed into socks and flying boots. An occasional knife was stuffed into a boot or leg garter. Whatever was the norm, whatever was comfortable, functional, the participants prepared for action.

Then to the dispersal areas. It was still dark. Mechanics and ground crews fussed about the aeroplanes which stood ready in the gloom. It was cold. In some places, at Lympne and Tangmere among others on the south coast, there was a thick ground haze. Further inland it was clear. At Redhill 611 Squadron recorded that the stars were still shining.

At Friston 253 Squadron were at readiness by 3 am, 610 at West Malling too were ready by 3 o'clock. 222 Squadron at Biggin Hill reported a readiness state by 3.15 am. At Tangmere the pilots were called at 3 am, breakfast was at 3.15 and everyone was at readiness by 4 o'clock. 175 at Warmwell were up at 3 am and at readiness by their Hurricanes by 4. The North Weald squadrons too reported readiness by 4 am.

On the morning of the Dieppe Raid we were all up before dawn and having had breakfast were at dispersal by first light.

Wing Commander Michael Pedley, OC 131 Squadron.

A very early start up, well before dawn.

Pilot Officer Frank Mitchell, 87 Squadron

Eighty-one Squadron at Fairlop were at readiness by 4.20 and took off twenty-two minutes later, in the dark.

However, it was to be the Bostons and Blenheims which would open the RAF's battle on this day. At Thruxton and at Ford engines were running by 4.15 am. Their smoke screens must shield the landing craft from enemy guns as they approached the beaches of Dieppe. The crews clambered aboard their light bombers, checked instruments, wireless, guns etc and made ready.

Six Blenheim pilots of 13 Squadron, led by Flight Lieutenant E. L. Beverley, opened up their throttles and took off from Thruxton at 4.15 am, each aircraft carrying 100 pound phosphorous bombs. At 4.17 ten Bostons from 226 Squadron began to leave the ground, all being airborne by 4.56, led by Wing Commander Wilfred Edward Surplice DFC. In the air these ten were joined by two Bostons from 88 Squadron and two from 107 Squadron from Ford. Wing Commander Surplice was a pre-war pilot who had previously served in India. He had won his DFC during operations in Wazuristan in 1938 with 5 Squadron and later he commanded 20 Squadron. Dieppe was to be his 13th operation with 226 Squadron which he now commanded. Leigh-Mallory had put Squadron Leader Peter J. B. Reynolds RAFVR of 11 Group HQ in charge of all smoke-screening sorties for Dieppe. He had drawn up precise plans and briefed the crews whose job it would be to lay the smoke. Naturally he wanted to be sure his plans would work out so he flew as a passenger in the Wing Commander's Boston on this first sortie. The crews on this first operation were:

13 Squadron:	FL E. L. Beverley	Z6089	OO–F
	PO D. L. Rogan	Z5811	OO–P
	PO C. L. Woodland	V5380	
	FL J. H. M. Shaw	Z5882	
	PO C. A. H. Black	Z6558	
	PO A. Jickling	N3545	
226 Squadron:	WC W. E. Surplice	Z2281	MQ–B
	FO R. A. Marks	AL736	MQ–P
	PO B. R. Miles	Z2234	MQ–X
	Sgt M. A. H. Dermot	AL688	MQ–Y
	PO R. J. Corrigan	AL710	MQ–Z
	PO J. P. L. O'Malley	L743	MQ–K
	Sgt R. Parsons	Z2264	MQ–F
	SL G. R. Magill	Z2295	MQ–A
	FO D. T. Smith	Z2258	MQ–H
	FL R. A. Yates-Earl	L704	MQ–W
88 Squadron:	Sgt Savage	AL736	RH–P
	FS Attenborough	Z2217	RH–G
107 Squadron:	Sgt R. C. Grant	L708	OM–M
	Sgt G. E. Nicholls		OM–J

At 4.25 am, four Blenheim IVs of 614 Squadron from Thruxton began to lift off led by Wing Commander H. C. Sutton, but aircraft R3758 piloted by Pilot Officer P. H. C. Hanbury hit a car on the runway and failed to get airborne. Sutton (in V5534), Flight Lieutenant P. G. Roberts (V6002) and Flight Lieutenant J. E. Scott (V5626) nosed up into the darkness.

Five minutes later 88 Squadron sent off six more Bostons led by its CO Wing Commander J. E. Pelly-Fry, their task to bomb the Rommel gun positions situated behind Blue Beach at Puys. Each Boston carried three 500 lb bombs plus ninety-six 40 lb bombs. The pilots were:

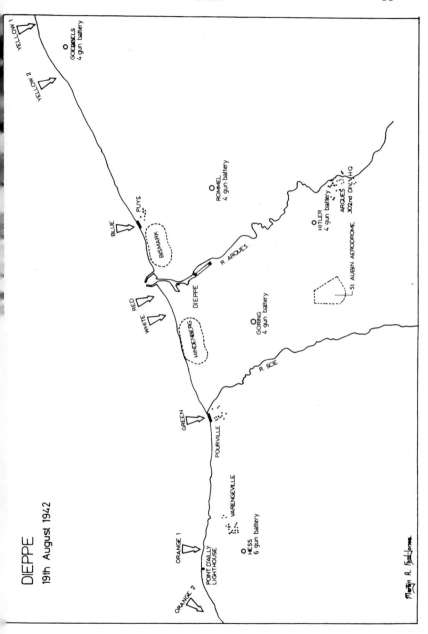

DIEPPE
19th August 1942

YELLOW 1
YELLOW 2
GOEBBELS
4 gun battery
ROMMEL
4 gun battery
PUYS
BLUE
BISMARK
RED
WHITE
DIEPPE
HINDENBERG
R. ARQUES
GORING
4 gun battery
HITLER
4 gun battery
ARQUES
302nd DIV HQ
St AUBIN AERODROME
R. SCIE
GREEN
POURVILLE
VARENGEVILLE
HESS
6 gun battery
ORANGE 1
POINT D'AILLY
LIGHTHOUSE
ORANGE 2

Martin R. Foot Jones.

WC J. E. Pelly-Fry	W8297	RH–A
PO Grundy		RH–D
FS New		RH–C
PO Campbell		RH–K
SL R. G. England		RH–B
PO Abbott		RH–E

Also at Ford two Boston Intruders of 605 Squadron took-off led by New Zealander Squadron Leader K. R. Sutton DFC, the second aircraft piloted by Flight Lieutenant M. G. Olley. In the air they were joined by one Boston from 418 Squadron piloted by a Canadian, Sergeant W. L. Buchanan. Their task was to bomb gun positions at dawn.

Thus by five o'clock 32 twin-engined light bombers of 2 Group, Air Cooperation Command and Fighter Command were on their way in the morning gloom.

Two fighter squadrons were tasked to give air cover to these first bomber attacks. 65 Squadron from Eastchurch, led by Squadron Leader D. A. P. McMullen DFC and two bars (AB902 YT–N), left the ground at 4.20 am, and 111 Squadron from Kenley took off at 4.15 led by Squadron Leader P. R. W. Wickham DFC (EP166 JU–N). McMullen had fought in the Battle of Britain and Pete Wickham, a former Cranwell cadet, had seen considerable action in the Middle East and Greece before returning to England. 111 Squadron recorded that the stars were shining but that it was hazy and there was no horizon. They flew out across the Channel arriving over Dieppe at 4.40, 65 arriving five minutes later. Not far behind them came the bombers. On that August morning pre-dawn twilight began at 4.28 to 5.14 am. Sunrise was expected at 5.50.

On the still dark water below the boats were making for the shore. At exactly 5.10 the destroyers *Slazak* and *Albrighton* led the other destroyers in to open the Naval bombardment of the beaches, to add their fire power to the bombs of the Bostons that were fast approaching.

We took off at 4.15 am. I was leading the first vic of three, consisting of Dave Rogan, an American, and Pilot Officer Woodland, and the best man at my wedding in March of that year,

1

2

3

1. Bristol Blenheims of 13 Squadron in 1942. *(E. Beverley)*

2. Flight Lieutenants Eric Beverley and John Shaw, 13 Squadron. Beverley was the first pilot to take off for Dieppe on 19 August. *(E. Beverley)*

3. Squadron Leader le Roy Du Vivier, the Belgian CO of 43 Squadron. He was the first Hurricane pilot over Dieppe. *(R. C. Bowyer)*

John Shaw, led the second vic. The take-off was in the dark, but the dawn began to break as we were over the sea. We flew low to avoid the radar cover and my recollection is that our route took us just to the north of the ships of the attacking force. The white cliffs to the north east of Dieppe stood out clearly in the morning light and we pulled up to our aiming point – a small bay well to the south-west along the line of the cliff face where the gun emplacements were and went into line astern to lay our smoke as low as we could fly. There was little or no AA fire until we had finished our smoke laying but then we were over the port itself and there we encountered a considerable amount of flak. We then turned seaward and had to pass low over the attacking fleet. They were understandably somewhat trigger happy and the silhouette of a Blenheim being not noticeably different from a Ju 88 they let us have all they had got just in case.

Either as a result of the anti-aircraft fire from Dieppe or from the Royal Navy I suffered damage to my port engine and flying controls and lost all my hydraulics. This meant that the turret in which my rear gunner was could no longer be swivelled. Despite this Sergeant Hooker kept a very sharp lookout for any rear attack from German fighters on the way home. By this time the six aircraft had got separated and as planned we made our own way home. We all made it safely except Woodland. I recall that because I could not operate my flaps or wheels I had to make a belly landing. Flying Officer Shaw was later to be killed in North Africa.

Flight Lieutenant Eric Beverley, 13 Squadron.

Thirteen Squadron's Blenheim IVs had been given the task of blinding two well positioned anti-aircraft batteries commanding the cliffs on the left side of Dieppe – the east headland, code-named 'Bismarck' by the Allied planners. The pilots had had difficulty in forming up in the dark and so the Blenheim pilots made individual approaches, all made successful drops to landward, the resulting smoke effectively screening the two hostile batteries. Five of the Blenheims flew back from the attack but Pilot Officer Woodland's machine was presumed hit by anti-aircraft fire for it failed to return. 24 year old Cecil Woodland, from Hampshire with his crew, Sergeants Henry Neville RAAF (25) from Australia and Austin Boyd

(32) from Belfast were posted as missing. The RAF's first casualties of Operation Jubilee had occurred.[1]

Wing Commander L. A. Lynn DFC (Z2286) and Flight Lieutenant R. Maclachlan (AL266) of 107 Squadron joined up with the three machines of 605 and 418 Squadrons over the Channel. Squadron Leader Sutton and Flight Lieutenant Olley of 605 formated without difficulty but the Boston of 418 Squadron was having some trouble. It continued to fly on for some time but Sergeant Buchanan was unable to raise the aeroplane's undercarriage. He and his crew, Pilot Officer P. C. McGillicuddy and fellow Canadian Sergeant C. G. Scott deduced that the undercarriage locking pins had not been removed by the ground crew at Ford (their own ground crews were, of course, at Bradwell Bay). With his wheels hanging down Buchanan had little alternative than to abort the mission. Reluctantly he dropped out of formation and turned back for England.

The others carried on and 107's two Bostons dropped two 500 lb and sixteen 40 lb bombs on both Hitler and Göring batteries at one minute to 5 am. However, the light was still poor and the results of their effort could not be seen. Sutton and Olley of 605 also bombed these two positions, located behind the town, and observed a number of large explosions after the bombs had hit.

At nine minutes past 5 am the first of 226 Squadron's Bostons reached their target, the Bismarck strongpoint on the Eastern cliffs. Over the following 35 minutes their ten aircraft plus the two each from 107 and 88 Squadrons, dropped 156 hundred pound phosphorous smoke bombs. Return fire from the ground was heavy, and nine of the Bostons received hits. Below a wheatfield was also set on fire which added to the smoke screen which gradually drifted four to five miles out to sea.

Squadron Leader G. R. (Digger) Magill's Boston was one of those hit and his smoke bombs ignited, forcing him to jettison them a quarter of a mile east of Dieppe.

The equipment we had for screen laying was a bit Heath Robinson but effective enough. It did not, however, allow one to take evasive action while smoke was being discharged; if one did the

---

[1] Woodland, Neville and Boyd were all buried at Dieppe.

aircraft itself filled with the thick choking stuff. This was quite a consideration when flying at point blank range right across the harbour defences. The so-called smoke bombs we carried as an alternative load were not too popular either. They were simple enough being largish 'biscuit tins' filled with a phosphorous compound which simply ignited and made masses of smoke when exposed to the air. A handy load to have in the bomb bay when there was a lot of flak about. I know, for the Navy put a few 20mm rounds into my aircraft as I approached the cliffs to the east of Dieppe on the first sortie of the morning. We found ourselves with a fine old fire going on underneath until we dumped the load as near as we could to the battery, our target, just over the cliff top.

Magill got back safely although his machine was damaged. Not for the first time did the crest on his Boston get them home. His usual crew was Pilot Officer Donald Walch, from Tasmania, as navigator, and 'Taffy' Gubbins, air gunner. (Gubbins was away on 19 August, his place being taken by Sergeant S. Praeger). The crest consisted of a kangaroo, a kiwi and a Welsh dragon on a boomerang, ensuring a return ticket, they hoped![1]

The Bostons flown by Sergeants Parsons and Dermot were also among those hit, Parsons flying to West Malling where he made a crash-landing (Category B damage), Dermot limping back to the same base on one engine and carrying a wounded gunner, Sergeant G. Bates. A couple of early Focke Wulf 190s appeared as 226 began to clear the coast, one attacking Wing Commander Surplice's machine. His gunner, Pilot Officer L. J. Longhurst got in a telling burst and the FW was last seen turning away with smoke pouring from its engine. Leonard Longhurst received the DFC for his part in the action, Surplice received the DSO while his navigator, a 33-year-old New Zealander, Pilot Officer Renton Rutherford, also received the DFC.

No 88 Squadron had a similar experience to 13 Squadron, being unable to form up properly in the darkness. The six Bostons flew

---

[1] Don Walch, by 1944, was on Mosquito intruders and was taken prisoner when he and Wing Commander Bob Braham were shot down over Denmark shortly after D–Day.

over the target individually at 5,500 feet but their results were poor. Nothing was seen on or around the target and some of the bombs failed to release. At de-briefing only three of the six crews actually claimed to have bombed the gun positions.

'The general plan was that the bombers would attack at first light (gun positions, radar posts, fuel dumps etc) what time the innumerable small landing craft were chugging away to Dieppe. Squadron Leader Dickie England – a superlative figure – and I were first away; it was a take off in darkness, the idea being that we would arrive on our respective targets (of which mine was a gun battery position just east of the town) just as dawn was breaking.

'No such luck. The met. men had miscalculated that cloud would be over Dieppe, the result being that we became – or tried to become – night bombers. Normally not our scene, as they say now; one result was that I was pretty quickly picked up by a radar-operated searchlight with a very bright blue light. A bit off-putting, as the Master Searchlight gave the rest an easy target. However, my crew and I, Pilot Officer Jock Cairns navigator and Sergeant "Buster" Evans, gunner, got out of that spider's web and got on with our attack. I'm told we hit it.'

Wing Commander James Pelly-Fry, OC 88 Squadron

'The main point from my view was, that it was meant to be a dawn attack on the target, which would have enabled the crews to identify the target immediately and eliminate any fears of collision with any other aircraft attacking; as it was, when we arrived in the target area it was dark – very dark! Most of the crews had only been used to daylight missions – I, possibly being the only exception – having previously done a tour of night bombing operations!

'The aircraft on this sortie approached the target too close together under the visibility conditions then existing – at least I thought so! – as they were all at the same, or approximately the same, altitude for bombing. My skipper asked me if I could see the target, and I affirmed that I was pretty sure I could, and gave him an alteration to port to bring me on to the bombing run for the battery which was my target. At that precise moment of starting the run, the battery 'opened up'. This of course made it easier to see the target, which was now showing itself against the darkness. Also, at this point, I heard over the R/T, someone from one of the other attacking aircraft, yell – "Let's get to hell out of here, it's bloody dangerous!" (Too many aircraft in the same small area, at the same time which meant near misses.)

'On our bombing run, searchlights came into operation, at the same time as the batteries opened fire, and when we were about ten seconds from dropping point, we were picked up by what would be we assumed, was the master searchlight – possibly radar controlled – as it just came straight up at us and held us without any searching, and then we were coned by several others – most uncomfortable!, I can assure you.

'Pelly-Fry uttered a few well known expletives and held the course until I'd dropped the bombs on estimated time elapse in seconds – as I was then being dazzled, but was heading straight for the target and experiencing no drift – a matter of about ten seconds.

'I asked 'Buster' if he saw the bombs hit, and he said that they straddled the target area as far as he could see, and in fact several searchlights were extinguished as well. At about this time Buster reported enemy fighters and if I remember rightly the skipper put the nose down and we dived away but I'm afraid you'll have to refer to those two for that action – that was their show.'

Flight Lieutenant Jock Cairns, 88 Squadron

Jock Cairns was Pelly-Fry's bomb-aimer/navigator; C. A. (Buster) Evans, another multi-tour man, who like Cairns ended the war with both the DFC and DFM, was Pelly-Fry's wireless operator/ air gunner.

Another feature . . . was seeing the tracer bullets, coming from the Dieppe coastline, literally bouncing on the sea; and all in that very first light when I was returning back to Ford and flying low past the landing craft going in for the assault. (A 'one-way' traffic system was laid on for the bombers; we flew in, as I remember, with the boats on our left and returned on the other side of the Armada). The up-turned faces of our troops reminded me for some reason of a *Daily Express* Giles cartoon – 'little' men with snub noses and round faces, I was thankful to be an airman.

Wing Commander James Pelly-Fry, OC 88 Squadron

The two 107 Squadron Bostons flying with 226 Squadron, each carrying twelve 100 lb bombs, made their runs at 5.16 am from a height of 50 feet. They flew in at medium speed, across the cliffs east of Dieppe to blind the Rommel battery. They too met intense and accurate return fire from light flak guns and small arms fire. Sergeant R. C. Grant led them in and the second machine piloted by Sergeant G. E. Nicholls was hit and holed in many places; Sergeant R. J. Hathaway, the observer, received slight facial injuries from broken and flying perspex.

No 614 Squadron led by Wing Commander H. C. Sutton, became separated in the dark as well. Being unable to lead a co-ordinated attack Sutton returned to base. Flight Lieutenant P. G. Roberts flew to Dieppe and successfully dropped his phosphorous bombs on target. Flight Lieutenant J. E. Scott took his Blenheim in, meeting heavy ground fire on the approach. His machine was hit in several places, Scott being wounded in both arms, and his left leg, and had his jaw lacerated – the gunfire appearing to come mainly from an armed ship. The aircraft's radio was knocked out and as he was leading the two-man attack, he carried on to the target with Roberts following. However, the damage to his machine also affected the bomb release gear, so despite his efforts he was unable to release his bombs.

Returning across the Channel he made for Friston as his star-board engine began to lose power. As he prepared to land he found that his hydraulics had been shot out, making his undercarriage and flaps useless. Scott made a belly landing, but the bombs ignited sending the Blenheim up in flames as they exploded. In addition to his wounds, Scott was badly burned but struggling free of the wreck he pulled his unconscious observer, Sergeant W. Johnson, clear. He then escaped by rolling down the Blenheim's burning wing. His air gunner, Flight Sergeant G. R. Gifkins died in the crash and Sergeant Johnson succumbed to his injuries 36 hours later. Scott was taken to the Queen Victoria Hospital at East Grinstead where he recovered, and he received the DFC in September.

The first bombing attack on the German gun positions, combined with the first smoke screen attack ended, and the Bostons returned to England.

On the way back, enough light to see all those flat-bottomed landing craft making their way. Time, about 5 am or just after. Fascinating, (and I might say a bit unnerving in case we were mistaken for an enemy aircraft) to see all the faces peering up at us under those well-known flat tin hats. Poor chaps, they had no idea just how tough their reception was going to be.

Wing Commander James Pelly-Fry, OC 88 Squadron

This first attack had cost two Blenheims and a crew, plus at least nine Bostons damaged. Already the next offensive action was well under way. As the Bostons and Blenheims returned (one 418 Squadron Boston still struggling home with its undercarriage fixed down), the Hurricanes were coming out.

At 0430 things started to happen and by 0530 hours there was a constant drone of aircraft and before long explosions were heard from the direction of the French Coast.

87 Squadron's Form 540

The Hawker Hurricanes of 43 Squadron at RAF Tangmere began to taxi away from their dispersal areas shortly after 4.15 am. Led by the Belgian Commanding Officer Squadron Leader D. A. R. G. LeRoy Du Vivier DFC, the pilots opened their throttles and were off the ground at 4.25, flying east.

At Shoreham 3 and 245 Squadrons were also taking to the air. In the pre-dawn one 3 Squadron machine piloted by Sergeant Armstong, taxied into a 245 machine piloted by Flight Sergeant C. G. Cummings and both had to stay behind. 43 Squadron arrived overhead, circling as 3 and 245 became airborne, then all three squadrons turned south. Du Vivier had been a pilot in the Belgian Air Force in 1940 but escaped to England and flew in the Battle of Britain with 43 and 229 Squadrons. He returned to 43 in 1941 as a flight commander, staying to take command in July 1942. 3 Squadron was led by Squadron Leader Alex Berry DFC who had been with the squadron since September 1940 starting out as a junior officer. 245 was led and commanded by Squadron Leader Henry Mould who had previously been with 87 Squadron.

Roy Du Vivier led them all out over the still dark waters of the Channel, 34 powerful, vibrating Hurricanes each having four 20mm cannons with which to attack the light gun-positions of the

Germans situated on the beaches west of the harbour – the main landing beaches Red and White – onto which the Canadians were about to land.

Flying low they arrived off Dieppe just as it was beginning to get light. Flying in the leading Hurricane (BN230 FT–A) Du Vivier was the first fighter pilot over Dieppe that day. He led his pilots in twice, flying in line abreast and turning to port after each attack. All 43's pilots reported cannon hits on gun-posts, buildings and wireless masts etc, but seven Hurricanes were hit by return ground fire. The enemy had been thoroughly alerted after the bombers had done their work and were ready for them. Du Vivier got a cannon shell through his starboard wing but it failed to damage anything vital. Flight Sergeant H. (Hank) Wik, from Canada, failed to come out of his attack being seen to crash into a field beyond the town. Pilot Officer A. E. Snell was hit and radioed to the others that he was baling out. This he did safely, having hauled his shattered machine up to 2,000 feet and he was later rescued by a tank landing craft (LCT), spending the rest of the day manning a machine gun.

Flying Officer Paddy Turkington and Pilot Officer E. Trenchard-Smith both flew back with damaged Hurricanes to make creditable landings. Turkington's machine had both elevators badly damaged and partly missing, while Trenchard-Smith had the top of his rudder and tailplane missing. Afterwards, Trenchard-Smith an Australian, became known as 'Tail-less-Ted' for with most of his tail gone, the remnants of the rudder only hung to the rudder post by the bottom hinge and the control cable.

Top prize for getting his Hurricane back and down went to Flight Lieutenant F. W. Lister. Freddie Lister's Hurricane had its port wing shattered by ground fire, a four foot hole being blasted right through it. This also removed most of the aileron as well as blowing away the panels above the cannons. The outermost cannon was wrenched askew, damaging the front spar and buckling the wing's leading edge.

Lister had to experiment with the best way to fly the Hurricane on the way home, finding that 190 mph indicated airspeed was the minimum speed at which he could maintain level flight. By looking at his shattered wing he felt it would not be prudent to attempt to lower his flaps. Arriving back over Tangmere Lister made several high speed attempts to get down, those on the ground watching

anxiously. Finally he hit the ground, his airspeed indicator register-
ing 210 mph! The Hurricane careered across the airfield throwing
up lumps of earth, shedding its radiator and air intake and shearing
off the propeller blades. Freddie Lister climbed down from the
cockpit totally unharmed although a trifle dazed. For this effort and
because he went on to fly a further three missions that day, he was
awarded the DFC.

Like 43 Squadron, Berry led his 3 Squadron in twice at the beaches,
encountering heavy flak. Sergeant S. D. Banks, a Canadian, was hit
and seen to be in difficulties, trying desperately to ditch on the sea.
He failed to return and was in fact lost. Flight Lieutenant H. E.
Tappin's machine had its starboard wing fuel tank shot through as
well as other damage but he brought the Hurricane back to make a
good landing. The squadron's pilots found it too dark and too
smokey to be able to pick out individual machine-gun positions so
made general strafing attacks against the beach and headland.
They approached in vic formation, then sections went in in line
astern to make their runs. They were able to take advantage of the
smoke screen after each attack by flying out low, using the smoke as
a defensive curtain behind them.

Dicky Mould, leading 245 Squadron (BN233), went in against
the same beach targets, then strafed the hotels along the promenade. On the second run the pilots had to fly in individually
through dense smoke and intense anti-aircraft fire. Pilot Officer
James Barton, from New Zealand, failed to come out of the first
attack and was killed. Flight Lieutenant Geoffrey Bennette, aged 26
also failed to come out of the attack. Pilot Officer Alfred Scott, from
Nottingham, was also hit and crashed, later being reported dead
from wounds received.

Dicky Mould's Hurricane was badly shot-up and as he struggled
back across the Channel he gave out a May-Day call, but reached
the coast. With his engine about to quit he made a wheels-up
landing on the beach at Littlehampton, ploughing through the
shore defences and a minefield. Pilot Officer Chris L. Gotch force-
landed at Friston shot through both legs. Pilot Officer I. L. Behel
also flopped down at Friston to refuel, as his main tank had been
holed. He flew back to Shoreham on the refuelled gravity tank.
After 245's first sortie only one Hurricane (Flight Lieutenant D. H.

H. Gathercole's BE497) remained serviceable and unhit.

Squadron Leader E. R. Thorn DFM and bar led 32 Squadron out from Friston at 4.45 am (in Z3581) and added their 48 cannons to the Hurricanes' attacks. Edward Thorn had flown over Dunkirk and during the Battle of Britain as a Defiant pilot, later operating at night. With more than a dozen victories he was the top-scoring Defiant man of the war. His men fared better on their attacks; all twelve Hurricanes got back although several machines sported bullet holes.

Also from Friston came 253 Squadron, with 12 Hurricanes led by Squadron Leader D. S. Yapp DFC (HL570), also briefed to attack ground defences and gun emplacements on Dieppe's west headland. Take-off came five minutes after 32 Squadron, 4.50, and they were over the target area at 5.15. Yapp was another 1940 veteran, joining 245 and then 253 as a junior officer. He later scored the only confirmed success by a Turbanlite Hurricane pilot, the operation at night when a Douglas Havoc would light up an enemy raider while a Hurricane pilot flying nearby would attempt to shoot down the German while in the Havoc's searchlight beam. He led his pilots in against houses along the front of Dieppe which attracted moderate return fire, but intense flak came up from the defences further westward. Flying officer H. D. Seal's machine was hit on the way out and was seen to hit the sea and sink immediately. However, Harry Seal survived, and his capture by the Germans was confirmed a few weeks later. Flight Sergeant J. C. Tate, an American flying with the RAF, had his aircraft shot up but he got it home, making a crash-landing as his starboard flap had been shot away. Tate sustained superficial injuries. Another 253 Squadron Hurricane returned with its propeller shot through and several others had varying degrees of damage.

We were airborne from Friston airfield before dawn with instructions to attack gun positions and any German troop movements. We were the third Hurricane squadron to cross the coast and witnessed a spectacular barrage of flak in the faint light. Flying Officer Seal, leading the third section of four, was hit and burst into flames. We were delighted to hear subsequently that he was a POW. This was a fairly inconclusive sortie – we fired all our ammunition at the flak batteries which were not the most desirable targets, and it was very difficult to observe results in the poor light of dawn. The abundant coloured varieties of tracer were a positive reminder to fly at tree-top height.

Flight Lieutenant John Ellacombe, 253 Squadron

The two bomb-carrying Hurricane squadrons, 174 and 175, took off from RAF Ford and RAF Warmwell at 4.40 am. 174 was led by their new commanding officer Squadron Leader Emile Fayolle DFC, Free French, who had only been with his new command since 1 August. After his escape from France he had flown during the Battle of Britain. 175 was led and commanded by Squadron Leader John R. Pennington-Legh, a former torpedo pilot. He led eight Hurricanes out.

Fayolle, flying his first mission as 'boss' of 174, led his pilots away but because of the bad light they had to fly out in sections. Red 4 lost his section and returned to base. The others flew across the Channel, six crossing the French coast at Camps de Cesar, five at Mesnil-en-Caux. They made straight for their assigned target, the Hitler battery which, as the light improved, they could plainly see as a large white patch on a hilltop. Amid heavy flak they dive-bombed from 1,000/1,500 feet between 5.15 and 5.20 am. John Brooks remembers distinctly the apparent newness of the concrete which was very light in colour, and that the nearby trees had been cut down and cleared.

The pilots made individual attacks on the position dropping four 250 lb and eighteen 500 lb bombs. Staying low the Hurribomber pilots sped away and made, as planned, a quick strafing run against the nearby German airfield at St Aubin. After making his attack, Fayolle was seen to head out towards England, his Number 2, Pilot Officer Harry Davies, being unable to keep up with him.

Most of Pennington-Legh's pilots dived down from 3,000 feet to 800 feet against the Göring gun position, dropped their bombs but due to heavy smoke the results could not be observed. Flight Sergeant D. W. Westcott (BP705) dropped his two bombs on three buildings nearby but again did not see them hit. Sergeant R. McGarva (BE404) could not locate Göring in the smoke so let go his bombs – two 500 pounders, on a railway siding. Flight Lieutenant B. D. Murchie's target was the German Headquarters building at Arques. Leading his section in his Hurricane (BE489) Murchie, a Canadian, failed to locate it so flew back and let his bombs go at a gun position on the coast, ten miles north-east of Dieppe. Flight Lieutenant D. G. Andrews, an Australian, (in BP295) dropped his bombs on Göring, seeing Pennington-Legh's bombs and his own explode on some huts or small houses by the guns. Flight Sergeant R. Clunie (BE687) and Sergeant T. E. Johnson (BE503) also bombed the guns while Pilot Officer A. C. N. Stewart (BE668) also detailed to bomb Arques, found the target but failed to see any results from his bombings. More fortuitously, however, all of 175 Squadron got home.

At 4.47 am, as planned, two Spitfire Vbs of 129 Squadron left Thorney Island and flew out towards Pointe D'Ailly. They were piloted by Flying Officer H. G. Jones and Sergeant R. L. Reeves, their specific target being the lighthouse situated at Pointe D'Ailly, just west of Varengeville. Below them Lieutenant-Colonel the Lord Lovat DSO MC was leading his 4th Commando towards shore at Orange Beach to attack the Hess battery – six 150mm guns. The lighthouse was known to be used as an observation post for this battery, and was protected by a flak tower.

Jones and Reeves made their landfall four miles west of the target, being greeted by alerted gunners who put up an intensive barrage of light flak. Harry Gwyn Jones, 27, from Llanelly, Carmarthen, was hit and his Spitfire crashed into the sea in flames. His was the first Spitfire loss of 19 August.

Sergeant Reeves carried on, strafed the gun position and lighthouse, his cannon shells producing flashes on the lighthouse glass, which shattered, causing gun flashes on the lantern. His objective complete, Sergeant Reeves turned for home.

While these Hurricane and Spitfire attacks were taking place, Sergeant W. L. Buchanan was still flying his 418 Squadron Boston back to England with his wheels hanging down due, as will be remembered, to the locking pins not having been removed. Enemy air activity had been virtually non-existent in these early opening rounds of the Dieppe operation but some time after 5 am at least two Focke Wulf 190 fighters had been sent out to investigate the activity over the Channel. Shortly before 5.45 these two FW190s found Buchanan's Boston some three miles off Shoreham.

The leading Focke Wulf attacked, its first burst raking the Boston's fuselage from end to end, shot the gunner's seat away from under him, set one engine on fire and the observer, Pilot Officer P. C. McGillicuddy, was hit and seriously wounded. The Boston, one engine blazing, dipped towards the sea, Buchanan struggling to keep control but to no avail. With one final effort he got the nose up and then tried to pancake on the sea but with his wheels down it was practically impossible. The Boston hit the sea and broke in half. Sergeant Clarence G. Scott, the Canadian gunner, was thrown free as the bomber broke up. As he broke to the surface he saw the front part of the Boston rolling over and over before sinking in a sheet of spray. Buchanan and the wounded observer floated to the surface dazed and helpless.

Scott swam to the pilot, inflated his life jacket and dinghy, then got the almost unconscious pilot into it. Scott then pulled McGillicuddy to the dinghy, also disentangling the observer's parachute shrouds from around his neck and got him too into the dinghy. Scott remained in the water clutching hold of the side of the dinghy for the next fifty minutes until an Air Sea Rescue launch, *HSL 442* from Littlehampton, picked them up. For his courage and presence of mind, Sergeant Scott received an immediate Distinguished Flying Medal.

The sight of the Boston going down was seen by observers on the coast. Already two Spitfires of 131 Squadron had been scrambled to patrol base when presumed enemy aircraft had been picked up on the radar screens. Two more were scrambled at 6 o'clock to escort a Walrus of 277 Squadron on the Air Sea Rescue mission to pick up the crew of the downed Boston.

It was as the Boston crashed that Sergeant Reeves of 129 Squadron, returning from the attack on Pointe D'Ailly lighthouse, saw the two Focke Wulfs, above the sea. Reeves immediately attacked the enemy fighters but one turned at him, its fire hitting Reeves' cockpit. Reeves was injured by broken glass and perspex but managed a head-on burst at one 190 and saw it fall away from 1,000 feet with thick black smoke pouring from it. The other 190 flew off.

With his Spitfire damaged by flak from Pointe D'Ailly and now from the 190s he turned for home; but radioed that enemy fighters were off Shoreham, which resulted in Wing Commander Pedley, CO of 131 Squadron being scrambled with five of his pilots to patrol off Brighton, but by the time he arrived, (flying BM420 NX–A) the enemy machines had departed.

No 277 Squadron sent out a Walrus (X9526) with Flight Sergeant T. Fletcher (pilot) and Sergeant L. R. Healey. As well as the downed Boston they were also looking for the enemy fighter's pilot which was reported probably down in the sea following a collision with either a Spitfire or a Hurricane. Whether this was in fact the scrap between Reeves and his two 190s as seen from the English coast is not certain. There is also the mystery of Squadron Leader Fayolle, CO of 174 Squadron, last seen heading towards Brighton. It is highly possible that he too had become involved in the fight of Shoreham or may have been engaged by other marauding Focke Wulfs. Green 4 of his Squadron, Flight Sergeant W. H. Wetere (BP672), a Maori, saw a Hurricane and two Spitfires engaged off Worthing with a FW190 but later saw the same Hurricane over Littlehampton. In any event 25-year-old Fayolle failed to return and was listed as missing. After the war a street just off the front at Dieppe was named after him.

The Walrus crew, Fletcher and Healey, found the dinghy in which Buchanan and McGillicuddy were huddled while Scott was still clinging to the side in the water. They directed an ASR launch to the spot and the three men were picked up. Buchanan and Scott were both taken to the Royal West Sussex Hospital while McGillicuddy went to Littlehampton Cottage Hospital where he succumbed to his injuries at 7.15 am the following morning. Buchanan recovered but was later killed in action. Clarence Scott who had received a large cut over his right eye in the crash plus a badly sprained ankle recovered to receive his DFM.

The surviving Hurricanes had all returned by between 6 and 6.20 am. This first low strafing and bombing attack had cost the Hurricane squadrons eight aircraft plus nearly a further twenty damaged, four seriously. However, the first troops were now ashore although heavily engaged, many being pinned down on the beaches. Due to the heavy cross-fire from both the town and from the two headlands, the planned rush up the beach and into the town did not happen. Eventually, just after 7 am, the Casino was taken and later still a few groups made it into the town but in the main the raiders on Red and White beaches remained on these beaches.

CHAPTER THREE

The Air Umbrella is Opened
5 am to 6 am

Sixty-five and 111 Squadrons also returned to their bases at around 6 am. They had been but the first Spitfire squadrons above the raid, yet already other Spitfires were in the air now that it was getting light. The promised air umbrella was about to be opened and put above the armada of small ships off Dieppe.

Also, now that the light was improving, Army Co-operation Mustangs were flying out to reconnoitre the areas behind Dieppe to watch for, and to report on, any troop movements towards the harbour town.

Nos 26 and 239 Mustang Squadrons at Gatwick were the first to send out reconnaissance machines at 4.35 am. 26 sent out Flight Lieutenant G. N. Dawson (AG418) and Pilot Officer J. F. Kelly (AG462), while 239's Commanding Officer, Wing Commander P. L. Donkin and his number two, Pilot Officer G. C. D. Green (AG558 and AM141) flew off at the same time. Donkin and Green flew their low tactical reconnaissance mission (Tac/R) over the roads between Le Tréport, Evernay and Blangy. Green's Mustang was hit by a single bullet without causing any damage although both machines became separated and returned independently. They got back at 6 am, the two 26 Squadron aircraft landing back at 6.10.

> My only memory apart from seeing no enemy movement was seeing in the semi-darkness what turned out to be a Boston. It was flying towards Dieppe from inland and very nearly became a casualty as it was not easy to recognise it in that light and it seemed to be going in the wrong direction for an RAF aircraft.
> *Wing Commander Peter Donkin, OC 239 Squadron*

Meanwhile, 414 Canadian Squadron sent out a pair of Mustangs at 4.45 am, the Tac/R leader being Flight Lieutenant F. E. Clarke, his 'Weaver' (Number Two) being Flying Officer H. H. Hills. All Tac/R sorties were usually flown in pairs, the leader concentrating on studying the ground while the Weaver kept a watch on the sky while flying a short distance away and above, his task to cover and protect his leader from surprise attack. Clarke and Hills covered the area St Valery-Doudeville-Bacqueville, landing back at Gatwick at 6.20 am.

By this time other Mustangs were out. 26 Squadron sent out Flight Lieutenant Donald N. Kennedy (AG536) and Sergeant G. D. M. Cliff (AG584) at 5.15 but neither pilot was destined to return. Kennedy was killed and the 21-year-old Geoffrey Denys Maynard Cliff, from Essex, also lost his life. 239 sent out Flight Lieutenant E. K. Barnes (AG614) with Pilot Officer J. R. Cruickshank (AG537) 35 minutes later to check on the roads west of Dieppe and onwards to St Valery. Barnes landed back at base at 6.15 having been attacked by four FW190s as he recrossed the French coast but he managed to get away. James Cruickshank was not so lucky. As he reached the French coast he was heard over the radio to comment briefly on the flak and failed to return. Whether hit by flak or attacked by the Focke Wulfs is not certain but he was later reported killed.

No 414 Squadron sent out a second pair of their Canadians at 5 pm, Flight Lieutenant J. A. Amos and Flying Officer R. C. Mac-Quoid (AM160 and AG582), watching the roads in the area Blangy–Neufchatel–St Victor–Longueville. Both returned safely at 6.30. Fellow Canadians in 400 Squadron flew the first of their pilots out at 6 o'clock, Flying Officer W. H. Gordon being the Leader, Flying Officer F. Grant his Weaver. A second pair, Flying Officer Clarke and Pilot Officer J. A. Morton, left a few minutes later.

With the Mustangs risking much down low, the Spitfires were now over the ships off Dieppe. 71 and 124 Squadrons from Gravesend took off at 4.50 and 4.45 respectively led by Wing Commander R. M. B. D. Duke-Woolley DFC and bar (EP179). 71 Eagle Squadron was commanded and led by Squadron Leader C. G. Peterson DFC, 124 by Squadron Leader T. Balmforth DFC (BR987). Peterson was one of the foremost Eagle pilots, American volunteers who flew with the RAF before America came into the war. They flew to Beachy Head where they joined the Spitfires of the Hornchurch

Wing, 81, 122, 154 and 340 Squadrons. Hornchurch Wing was led by Wing Commander P. H. Hugo DFC and bar, in his personal Spitfire coded P–H. A very experienced fighter pilot, Hugo, a South African, had joined the pre-war RAF and in 1940 had flown in both France and the Battle of Britain. In early 1942 he commanded the Tangmere Wing prior to taking over Hornchurch. He had more than a dozen victories and was to end the war at least 22. He led his men off at 4.40 while it was still dark.

No. 81 Squadron was led by Squadron Leader R. Berry DFC, an equally experienced pilot and Battle of Britain veteran. 122 Squadron was led by New Zealander Squadron Leader J. R. C. Kilian (BL812), who had gained valuable experience when flying with 485 NZ Squadron in 1941. Fellow New Zealander, Squadron Leader D. C. Carlson was at the head of 154 Squadron (BM476) while 340 Free French Squadron was commanded by Commandante Bernard Duperior, who had escaped from France in 1940 and later flown with 242 and 615 Squadrons. His was the first French fighter squadron operational with the RAF.

'We were routed all day via Beachy Head, and turning SSE for Dieppe immediately had the benefit of the lighter sky to the east as a reference. On this first sortie, and we were the first day fighters on the scene, the sea was a dark grey below and the invasion fleet not easy to detect. However, we swept up to the front at Dieppe and set up a patrol with the squadrons staggered upwards and to seaward, the leading squadron at around 2,500 feet with the Wing Leader peering owl-like around to see what, if anything, there was to see. Broadly speaking that was just about nothing. We patrolled and hoped that we were good for the morale of those below.

'It may help those who have seen war films, but have not flown piston-engined fighters (especially) to emphasize that the single-seater Spitfire pilot is a lonely man. Lift the flap of your flying helmet and the noise is a compound of air rushing past at triple-severe-gale-force-ten and open exhausts delivering twice the power of a Formula One Grand Prix racing car. So if you're wise you do not raise the flap of your flying helmet but snug it close to your ear so as to hear what your radio has to offer. Your mouth and nose are enclosed in a tight-fitting mask containing your microphone transmitter – and pulled tight to exclude the noise which you have just been advised not to listen to. Your shoulders brush the sides of the cockpit as you turn your body; the nose of the aircraft, like a vast bonnet, limits your forward vision, and your restless eyes are your only contact with the world outside. No noise of the battle below can penetrate, and if guns are firing you may see soundless puffs appear on the ground. If they appear in the air, it is you who are being shot at probably and if you see some red in the puff it is close and you are being shot at certainly. Since there is very little that you can do about that you do your best to ignore the prospect of an explosive brick coinciding with you in space and measuring 3½ inches across. One is quite enough to make a considerable mess of your aircraft, but then you personally occupy only a very small part of the sky. So you console yourself and think of other things.

'The main "other thing" to scare the pants off me happened about five minutes after we arrived. Nobody had let me know about the new LCR (landing craft, rocket) which was used at Dieppe for, I believe, the first time on a combined operation. This craft carried, reputedly, 960 mortar type missiles fired in sequence electrically and the whole salvo was discharged in less than a minute. I discovered that at least one such device was in use when the first fifty or so rockets passed through the squadron which I was leading. When I say through I do mean that some went over the top of my head and some passed under my personal tail, and the LCR miraculously did not score one Spitfire squadron – but only by virtue of one of these coincidental miracles that makes one sweat slightly in retrospect. All the rockets continued to their apogee and duly plunged to earth somewhere off to port and a quick check showed that we remained not merely intact but untouched. I managed some feeble jest about Mr Brock evidently having been enlisted in response to a (decorative) question from my Number Two enquiring about this phenomenon. "Who needs enemies when we've friends like that?" was another question which expressed our collective thoughts.'

Wing Commander Myles Duke-Woolley, Leader Debden Wing

No 71 Eagle Squadron headed out towards Dieppe, Peterson leading, with Flight Lieutenant Gus Daymond (BM510) leading the second section, and Flying Officer T. J. 'Andy' Andrews the third. Andrews' number 3 was Pilot Officer Harold H. Strickland, who had celebrated his 39th birthday at the beginning of the month!

I became separated from the squadron of the first sortie because well after take off and climb into the darkness I noticed that my No 2 (Pilot Officer W B Morgan, from Honolulu) was not keeping up as well as usual, so I throttled back and could then see that his landing gear had not retracted fully. We had been briefed to maintain radio silence but I warned him with a two-word transmission, then accelerated in an effort to overtake 71 which by then had turned off their small blue navigation lights and disappeared. I flew at high speed towards Dieppe but could not find 71. I encountered four FW190s somewhere west of Dieppe in the half-light just before dawn. With my high speed I had a shot at a straggler then pulled into a steep, high climb, came down in a dive, but all the FW190s had disappeared.

Pilot Officer Harold Strickland, 71 Eagle Squadron.

'Strick' recorded in his personal diary:

I saw the flashes of heavy gunfire to my left, which was towards the sun, which was still below the horizon. In all other directions it was very dark. About 8/10ths cloud covered the sky at 7,000 feet. As I proceeded towards the enemy I could see the outline of four aircraft patrolling about E – W, line astern, I closed toward them from out of the darkness and identified them as four FW190s. I attacked the No 4 with cannon and m.g. with about 45° deflection and saw my explosive shells strike the fuselage. He dived. The other three turned into me. I turned right, pulled into steep climbing turn and entered the cloud. Was counter-attacked three times upon leaving the cloud cover. Landed at Gravesend shortly after dawn.

Brewster Morgan also carried on alone to Dieppe and was attacked. His Spitfire developed a glycol leak but he got back to the English coast where he crash-landed at Friston. He came down near a Blenheim which was on fire with bombs exploding – this was Scott's Blenheim of 614 Squadron.

*

Meanwhile, the six squadrons, having reached their patrol area five miles off Dieppe at 5.23 am, relieved 65 and 111 Squadrons. Below and to the south the pilots could just make out the troops streaming ashore in the gloom. Guns flashed and shells exploded on the shoreline and smoke was everywhere. 124 Squadron could see assault and tank landing craft still arriving at Orange Beach while a ship of around 700 tons was on fire about five miles north-east of the harbour. (Probably the German ship encountered by the Commandos on their approach to Yellow Beach.) 124 also saw a Junkers 88 shot down into the sea by AA fire from a destroyer after dropping its bombs. There is little evidence that any enemy bombers were over the ships at this early time and from 9–10,000 feet, 124 Squadron had, in fact, seen Pilot Officer Woodland's Blenheim going into the sea. (It has been assumed that this Blenheim went down to flak but if 124 saw the action correctly one wonders if in fact the Navy's anti-aircraft fire hit the Blenheim. There were several reports of RAF aircraft being fired on by the ships during the day – an attitude of 'shoot first and ask questions later!') Meantime, fire from German shore batteries was seen to be straddling the ships, whilst light flak was seen coming up from Camp de César and heavy flak from the town itself.

Right below the Spitfires the pilots could see lines of tracer bursts passing to and from the darkened beaches. It was fascinating to watch and difficult to concentrate on keeping a careful lookout for enemy aircraft. However, 2 Group bomber's smoke soon began to blot out the colourful yet deadly tracer fire. In the gloom higher up it was difficult to make out the aeroplanes. Capitaine René Mouchotte of 340 Squadron was twice attacked by sections of Spitfires and then a FW190 passed quite close by him without the pilot taking the slightest bit of notice of him, if he saw the Spitfire at all.

The six Spitfire squadrons split up over the ships to give the maximum spread of cover, so that when eight FW190s suddenly appeared not all the squadrons saw or engaged them. 81 saw them but did not engage. They chased two FWs five miles inland but lost them. Berry's pilots also saw the Bostons laying smoke which appeared to obscure most of the town. A large explosion occurred and several buildings were seen to be on fire.

No 122 Squadron saw nothing while 124 saw only three 190s but the Germans kept well out of range. Flight Lieutenant A. F. (Shag) Eckford DFC, Sergeant E. Hansen (Norwegian) and Warrant

Officer J. G. Buiron (Free French) of 154 Squadron fired at these
190s but no hits were claimed. Sous-Lieutenant Michael Boudier of
340 Squadron (BL262 GW–K) did claim hits, however, on one
FW; Sous-Lieutenant Kerlan was hit and had to ditch his Spitfire
(W3457 GW–K) in the sea but he was picked up safely.

After 30 minutes patrol time the Spitfires turned for home. As 81
turned for home at 5.50, they could still see the shore batteries
firing.

The Spitfires began to land back at their bases at between 6.15
and 6.30.

The whole of this first sortie was, in practical terms, a waste of
time but a necessary show of force nonetheless. It must have
heartened the Canadians below to see 48 friendly aircraft moving
up and down but from my point of view we did nothing but
provide some small cheer of that order. It was too dark below to
decipher what was happening in any detail. We could not have
attacked any ground targets in support of the landing even if we
could have seen, because air to ground support techniques simply did not then exist as they came to be developed by 1944. We
carried no bombs, and if we had we could not have dropped
them accurately with no previous training. So we patrolled and
waited and patrolled and the day gradually lightened from the
east. More and more craft became visible on and near the beach,
moving so slowly and of course silently and towing white strips of
disturbed water behind each one. No enemy aircraft were
reported by radar and we sighted none ourselves. I think we
must have been over the area for about forty minutes when the
relieving Wing approached, led by Brian Kingcome, and we
exchanged pleasantries. Wing Leaders in those days usually
used their own Christian or nick-names and on establishing contact I recall Brian's question, 'Duke, what on *earth* are you doing
up so early?' It seemed very appropriate at the time and after
assuring him that we were 'savaged, dear boy, by friend if not by
foe', we returned to Beachy Head, base and breakfast.
          Wing Commander Myles Duke-Woolley, Leader Debden Wing

Already the relieving Spitfires were over the ships. The Polish
fighter pilots from Northolt and Heston, 302, 306, 308 and 317

Squadrons, had all been airborne shortly before 5 am. Again the units split up over the cover area. 302 Squadron led by Flight Lieutenant Stanislaw Lapka (EN865) patrolled for their allotted 30 minutes but saw nothing. Squadron Leader Walerian Zak, holder of the Polish Virtuti Militari, leading 308 Squadron arrived over Dieppe at five minutes to five o'clock, patrolling at between 8,000 and 9,000 feet but only saw one enemy aircraft in the distance.

Squadron Leader Stanislaw Skalski DFC VM, veteran pilot from the first air battles over his native Poland in September 1939, was by this date an extremely effective fighter pilot and air leader. He led his 317 Squadron from Northolt but made no contact with the enemy but the enemy made contact with them. A single FW190 came screaming down on 317 Squadron, the pilot selecting the Spitfire flown by Flying Officer M. Cholewka. The German scored a telling burst on the Spitfire which broke away from the squadron and went down. Cholewka was himself hit and badly wounded, his right arm being smashed and also his right leg was shot through. However, in spite of this he regained control of his machine and made a landing at Manston in between bouts of unconsciousness. He was immediately admitted to hospital and when his Spitfire was cleaned up, pieces of bone were found in the cockpit.

No 306 Squadron was led by Squadron Leader Tadeusz Czerwinski and included Group Captain Stefan Pawlikowski among its twelve pilots. Pawlikowski was without doubt the oldest flyer at Dieppe, having flown in France in 1918, and later with the Polish Air Force in the mid-war years. In 1939 he commanded the Polish Pursuit Brigade. 306 patrolled over Dieppe for its half hour but without incident.

On the return flight Sergeant S. Czachla got into difficulties. He began to run short of fuel even though his fuel gauge showed a 20-gallon reading. It became obvious that he would not make Northolt so as his engine began to die he tried to force-land on a roadway but the road ended suddenly and houses appeared at the end of it. Czachla pulled up his flaps and banked steeply to the left but didn't make it. His starboard wing hit the roof and upper wall of No 205 Malvern Avenue, South Harrow. The Spitfire lost a wheel and ricocheted across the road. One of its wings ripped along the front bedroom windows of 244, 246, 248, 250 and 252 Malvern Avenue, before he crash-landed in the front garden of No. 252.

Czachla received a slight injury to the left side of his head plus some bruises which kept him in hospital until the 22nd, but was otherwise unhurt. A lady occupant of one of the houses was also slightly injured.

Meanwhile, 402, 602 and 611 Squadrons had left to patrol over the ships, 402 and 611 taking off at around 5.15, 602 taking off from Biggin Hill at 5.50.

The Canadians of 402 led by Squadron Leader N. H. Bretz (BS200) made rendezvous over Beachy Head, arriving over Dieppe at 5.50 at a height of 10,000 feet. 602 joined 611, the latter only numbering 11 aircraft. 602 at high cover was led by Squadron Leader P. M. Brothers DFC (EN904), 611 by Squadron Leader D. H. Watkins, DFC (BR631), both Battle of Britain pilots. As they flew out over Beachy Head the sun was just appearing over France although it was still quite dark. Below them they could see a long line of barges (sic) stretching back twenty miles from Dieppe. On the enemy held coast, bursting shells and red fire glows lit up the beaches and coastline. The squadron patrolled in loose fours from between 1,500 to 5,000 feet, two to four miles off Dieppe. Heavy and light flak was lacing the air low down between the shore and the landing craft. As the squadron diarist later wrote of this deadly yet colourful scene, ' . . . which might be described as beautiful.'

Some FW190s were still buzzing about, although as yet still not in any force. Like the Poles, 602 and 611 had brief skirmishes with them. Blue Section of 611 Squadron were bounced by a small gaggle of 190s who sent the Spitfire of Flight Sergeant André Paul François Vilboux, aged 21 from Rennes, (Free French)[1] spinning towards the sea. Another 190 curved in behind Squadron Leader Watkins' Number Two, but Watkins saw the danger and quickly turned into the German fighter, firing a burst into it. The 190 dived away to crash-land west of Dieppe. As the brief scrap continued Flight Lieutenant W. V. Crawford-Compton DFC, a New Zealand pilot, destined to become one of the RAF's top scorers, and Flight Lieutenant Manak both damaged other Focke Wulfs before the German fighters broke off and dived away. 602's CO, Peter Brothers (EN904) also claimed a 190 damaged, Pilot Officer R. W. F. Sampson hitting another which was seen to go down smoking.

[1] Vilboux escaped to England in June 1940. Dieppe was his 32nd operational sortie. He was awarded a posthumous Croix de Guere.

We were airborne at first light to patrol over the landing area. This we did at low level and watched with considerable interest the troops landing. A small number of enemy aircraft appeared on the scene but sheered off when they saw us and it seemed obvious that they were very disorganised and had been taken by surprise. After an hour and a half we were replaced and withdrew to refuel.

Squadron Leader Peter Brothers, OC 602 Squadron

During their patrol, 602 observed a large ship blow up whilst 611 saw a gun battery blow up. Ten minutes later they were relieved.

Shortly after 602 and 611 turned for home a lone Spitfire squadron was heading towards Dieppe, fast and low. 129 Squadron led by Squadron Leader Rhys Henry Thomas DFC was racing in to strafe the Hess gun battery. This attack would be the prelude to the assault by Lord Lovat's 4th Commando who had landed at Vastérival (Orange Beach) and made their way to the gun positions soon after dawn. The Commandos were already sniping at the German gunners waiting for 129 to strike. The Spitfire pilots approached Varengeville-sur-Mer where the guns were situated, and where ninety minutes earlier their brother pilots Jones and Reeves had attacked the lighthouse. Thomas made landfall close to the same lighthouse, found the target through dense smoke from what appeared to be burning buildings and went in. Actually the initial battle between the Commandos and the Germans had started and a 2-inch mortar shell had ignited a stack of cordite behind the No 1 gun which caused a big fire. Then the Commandos fired a smoke bomb into the battery position.

Rhys Thomas led his men in at 6.20 am; the twelve Spitfires raked the target thoroughly and silenced several guns sending up defensive fire. Twelve FW190s appeared from the south as the Spitfire pulled away and a brief dog-fight ensued. Pilot Officer J. B. Shillitoe got in a quick burst at one and claimed he had damaged it. The fight ended and 129 went home with two of their aircraft carrying flak damage. Shillitoe believed his machine too had been hit and gingerly flew his Spitfire back across the Channel, concerned in case the damage forced him to ditch. In the event he reached Thorney Island safely and with some relief came into land.

However, he quite forgot to lower his undercarriage, but got away with his involuntary belly-landing without injury to himself. As for the Commandos, they completed their task, completely destroyed the Hess battery and with only light casualties got safely away again. Theirs was one of the few completely successful events of the Dieppe Raid.

At 4.45 the phone range from Ops and instructions were given that we were to take off with the rest of the Wing at 6 and go over to Dieppe and stay over the town for half an hour to protect our boats from dive-bombing, etc. The names went up on the board and I was not down so I sat back and relaxed.

Pilot Officer John Godfrey, 412 Squadron – from a letter home dated
20 August 1942.

Spitfires of the Tangmere Wing, 41 and 412 Squadrons, took off at fifteen minutes to six. Twelve of 41 and 12 Canadians of 412 were led by Tangmere's Wing Leader, P. R. (Johnnie) Walker DFC, with 41 flying as top cover. They flew out over Selsey Bill, arriving off Dieppe at 6.05. They patrolled over the ships at between 4,000 and 8,000 feet for 30 minutes. Their main task being to provide cover for a further bomb raid by 107 Squadron's Bostons, ordered out to attack the Hitler battery.

No 107 took off at 6.15, led by Wing Commander Lynn (again in Z2286) but by the time they reached Dieppe at 6.47, the Tangmere Wing had turned for home. The Spitfires had experienced heavy flak but it proved very inaccurate. Squadron Leader Geoffrey Hyde (BL777) and the others of his 41 Squadron saw some enemy fighters some way off but made no contact. Squadron Leader C. J. (Nobby) Fee DFC and his Canadians had a brief brush with six FWs although neither side inflicted any damage on the other. It had been almost impossible for the Canadians to keep together, the squadron splitting up into twos. As John Godfrey later described it from reports from his comrades, 'It was evidently the worst shambles since the Battle of Britain.'

When the Bostons appeared, they made their bombing run from 7,000 feet, from west to east but due to ground haze, smoke and the early sunlight they let their bombs (24 x 500 lb and 120 x 40 lb) go too late and mostly they overshot. The bombs fell on some camouflaged houses beyond the battery. Heavy flak came up and fortunately no enemy fighters were about. They landed back at Ford at 7.25 am.

No 222 Squadron and the American 307th Fighter Squadron, both from Biggin Hill took over from the Tangmere Wing. 222 was led by Squadron Leader R. W. (Bobbie) Oxspring DFC (BL267), former Battle of Britain pilot who had only taken over command of the squadron one week before. His unit made no contact with the enemy. The Americans on the other hand got into a fight with a bunch of Focke Wulfs, losing Lieutenant Ed Tovrea, who was taken prisoner, but they did claim one 190 as a probable. Tovrea, from Arizona where his father was a big name in the meat industry, found himself in Stalag Luft III POW camp after his capture. He later helped to dig the escape tunnel which was used in the Great Escape in March 1944.

Probably the most senior officer to fly this day was Group Captain Harry Broadhurst DSO DFC AFC. Until May 1942, 'Broadie' had been Station Commander of RAF Hornchurch and at 36 years of age was one of Fighter Command's most energetic fighters. Often leading the Hornchurch Wing during 1941–42 he had personally destroyed nearly a dozen enemy fighters before going to 11 Group Headquarters. He had been in on the planning of Dieppe and had some strong views on how the air battle should be fought.

I flew a Spit 9 on four sorties, having borrowed the aeroplane from my old station Hornchurch, – I was at that time Deputy SASO at 11 Group. There was a specific reason for me going on these patrols. During the planning I had strongly disagreed with the proposal to patrol the beach-head with stepped-up wings, emphasising that they would be too unmanoeuvrable against the sort of opposition the Germans would put up, ie: fighter bombers and small formations of escorted bombers. I was firmly in the doghouse for my outspoken opposition, and so I arranged to go on the first patrol to see for myself. In the event, whilst at 20,000 feet, I spotted small formations of FW190s coming in from the sun and diving straight down through the beehive and attacking the ships, and then going off back into France at low level.

Group Captain Harry Broadhurst, 11 Group HQ

In the borrowed Spitfire (BR370) Broadhurst took off from RAF Northolt at 6 o'clock and climbed steadily in the direction of Dieppe arriving at approximately 6.30 at 25,000 feet. The weather was clear and he could see the shipping anchorage just north of Dieppe taking shape and the Spitfire patrols above it. Dropping down to 20,000 feet, Broadhurst took in the whole panorama of the scene of action spread out below him. He could see FW190s coming out from France, mainly in pairs or in sections of four from the general direction of Le Tréport at 15,000 feet. When they had gained a position up sun of the British patrols they would dive straight down towards the ships and beaches, some dropping bombs, some clashing with the Spitfires while others attempted to strafe the ships.

He watched for some time before reducing height to 15,000 feet towards Le Tréport and found a pair of Focke Wulfs approaching. He picked on the number two 190 and shot it down into the sea. He then broke away and headed back to England and landed at Biggin Hill.

The Mustangs were still busy, 239 Squadron sending out Flying Officer P. A. L. Gompertz (AM134) and Flying Officer W. T. McKeown (AM533) just after six o'clock. They were tasked to reconnoitre the roads from Fécamp to four miles east of Le Havre but saw nothing. Then McKeown radioed that he had been hit by anti-aircraft fire and failed to return.

Meanwhile, three Spitfires led by Pilot Officer R. M. Batten from 91 Squadron, the RAF's famous 'Jim Crow' Squadron commanded at this time Squadron Leader Jean Demozay DFC (Free French), went out low on a shipping reconnaissance, covering the area Ostend-Somme-Le Havre, looking for any signs of hostile shipping that might interfere with the landings, but the sea remained empty.

The sea may have been empty of German ships but soon the sky over Dieppe was to be full of their fighters.

CHAPTER FOUR

The Luftwaffe Reacts
6 am to 9 am

A few minutes after six o'clock the engines of 36 Spitfires roared into life at RAF Manston, in Kent. Wing Commander F. D. S. Scott-Malden DFC led his three squadrons, 242, 331 and 332, away from their temporary base at between 6.10 and 6.20 am. No 242 Squadron was led by Squadron Leader T. C. Parker (BM539) while the two Norwegian squadrons were led and commanded by Major Helge Mehre DFC (BL681 FN–E) and Major Wilhelm Mohr DFC (EN901). David Scott-Malden was flying his usual Spitfire (AB202) coded with his personal initials S–M, his prerogative as a wing leader. He led his North Weald Wing out over the sea with 332 flying top cover, 331 below them and 242 underneath at 3,000 feet.

Since shortly before dawn several small groups of FW190s had been in evidence and several skirmishes had taken place. Now, as the North Weald Wing swung over the ships off Dieppe, the first really big enemy fighter reaction came. The Spitfires arrived over Dieppe at 6.55 am and shortly afterwards 331 and 332 were attacked by 20 FW190s and Me109s. These were the fighters Group Captain Broadhurst had seen coming out from Le Tréport. British radar stations on the south coast of England began to pick up enemy aircraft plots at 7.05 am; two EA coming from the direction of Abbeville. These were followed by what appeared on the screens as a constant stream of EA flying in the general battle area from St Omer, Poix and Abbeville.

A terrific dog-fight began: 332 shot down three FW190s – Captain From, Sergeant Marius Erikson and Sergeant Janeigil Lofsgaard. From and Erikson also damaged two more. However, Sergeant Per Bergsland and Sergeant Johnny Staubo failed to return, both pilots being taken prisoner.

Bergsland was flying as Scott-Malden's Number Two, but the battle was fought in and out of cloud and the Wing Leader was not surprised that eventually the young Norwegian lost him. Yet it was not until he returned to base that he knew for certain that his wingman had been shot down. Bergsland was taken into captivity and eventually wound up at Stalag Luft III at Sagan. He was one of the escapers in the Great Escape and one of the only three who succeeded in returning to England, in his case via Sweden. Johnny Staubo, six feet tall, extremely good looking and a former Davis Cup Player, also found himself at Sagan where he helped dig the tunnel, of Tom, Dick and Harry.

Major Mohr's machine was hit and he had to break away. Sergeant B Raeder's Spitfire was also hit and he was obliged to force-land near Lewes.

No 331 Squadron also got their share of the claims in the mêlée, Major Mehre claiming two 190s, one destroyed and one probable.

I remember that the first clash with the Luftwaffe in the morning was with rather more FW190s than Me109s, or perhaps we just had more respect for the FW190, being a newer aircraft and better. During the dog-fight my No 2 was hit by a FW190, two of which came down on us, but they had too high speed from their dive and they overshot. My number two had to bale out, while I managed to turn in behind the 190s and closed on the rear one. I put a good 4–5 second burst into him. He emitted black smoke, the pilot jumped out of his aircraft, which then turned over into a vertical dive.

Major Helge Mehre, OC 331 Norwegian Squadron

Captain Kaj (pronounced Ky) Birksted, a Danish pilot flying with the Norwegians, destroyed another and shared a probable with Sergeant Fredrik S Fearnley. Another 190 was claimed as a probable, shared by Lieutenant Einer Sem-Olsen and Sergeant Guy P Owren, and one was damaged by Lieutenant Rolf A. Berg and Sergeant Helmer Grundt-Spang. Major Mehre's number two, was Second Lieutenant Johannes Greiner. After he was hit by the diving FW190 he was then hit by flak. He spun down with shell splinters in his right leg but he regained control, climbed to 4,000 feet where he baled out. He was later picked up by a motor launch.

No 242 Squadron down low were not engaged. They had seen a large tanker on fire in the harbour which exploded. Squadron Leader Parker radioed to the control ship to direct fire on gun positions north-east of the town which were firing at the beach and landing craft. Flight Lieutenant D. I. Benham saw two FW190s dive down and strafe the harbour area and although he attacked one of them he saw no strikes. Pilot Officer D. Fowler (BL992) was hit in the shoulder by either a piece of AA shell splinter or cannon shell, which hit the armour plate behind him. He also had part of his tailplane shot away. However, he brought the machine back but landing with no air pressure he was forced to turn sharply to avoid some aerodrome huts and his port oleo leg collapsed.

The Canadians of 403 Squadron got in on the tail end of the battle, having started their patrol from Manston at 6.45. Led by Squadron Leader L. S. Ford DFC (BM344) the twelve Spitfires reached Dieppe half an hour later and almost immediately became embroiled with Focke Wulfs and Messerschmitts above the ships.

Flight Lieutenant George Hill and Sergeant M. K. Fletcher attacked and shot down a 190 while Pilot Officer H. J. Murphy went after an ME109F. Murphy squeezed off three long bursts at the German fighter and it fell to pieces and dived away in flames, turning onto its back as it went. It was last seen a few feet above the ground completely out of control south-east of Dieppe. This was claimed as destroyed making it two for the Canadians, but three of them failed to extricate themselves from the battle, Pilot Officers J. E. Gardiner, L. A. Walker and N. Monchier.

Fellow Canadians of 416 Squadron, led by Squadron Leader Lloyd Chadburn (EP110) together with Squadron Leader H. L. I. Brown's 616 Squadron patrolled Dieppe at 7.20 flying at 12,000 feet. They saw a few 190s but did not engage. 416 had been briefed to patrol above Red, White and Blue beaches, 7,000 feet below 616. 416 were only 11 strong for Pilot Officer P. G. Blades (EP581) had struck an uneven patch of ground at Hawkinge when about to take off. One of the undercarriage wheel fairings had torn loose as he became airborne. In the air he could not retract his wheels so had to land again, the damaged undercarriage collapsing altogether. His Spitfire had Category B damage.

While the fight raged above, HMS *Calpe* sailed close inshore to observe the progress on Green and Orange beaches. Red and White beaches were experiencing heavy fire from shore positions while the landings on Yellow and Blue beaches were reported to have failed. The first doubts by the commanders were beginning to creep in.

Landing back at Manston, David Scott-Malden and Wilhelm Mohr clambered into a car and drove around to each dispersal to talk to the pilots and to ascertain the losses in order to assess aircraft availability for the next sortie. Having done this they agreed on the flying formations and section leaders etc. Scott-Malden voiced his assumption that Mohr would be leading his squadron, but Mohr said no. He thought that perhaps his senior flight commander should lead the next show. When the Wing Leader showed some surprise, the Norwegian, with the typical understatement so characteristic of his race, said, 'I am sorry but I am afraid I haf a bullet in my body!'

Scott-Malden was aghast, then Mohr indicated a bullet hole in the back of his flying boot. During the dog-fight when his Spitfire had been hit, a bullet had drilled into his right leg, yet he had made no mention of it until this moment. Scott-Malden soon had him sent off to hospital. Mohr kept as a souvenir the map which he had stuck in his flying boot, bloodstained and with a neat hole through it.

Meanwhile, Helge Mehre was seeing to his squadron personnel.

We had about three hours before the next mission, so I made a quick trip round the squadron to tell the ground crew what we had seen and what we did, but most of them were too busy servicing their aircraft.

Major Helge Mehre, OC 331 Norwegian Squadron

The 308th Fighter Squadron from RAF Kenley, led by the CO of 111 Squadron, Squadron Leader P. R. W. Wickham DFC (EP798) took off at 7.15. Their top cover was provided by the Belgians of 350 Squadron from Redhill. They reached Dieppe just before 8 o'clock, the Americans seeing 20 to 30 enemy fighters at 11,000 feet. These attacked the top squadron and some dived through to make a pass at the Americans. One 308th Spitfire was lost, Lieutenant Robert D. (Buck) Ingrams, from Idaho, taking to his parachute.

Meantime, the Belgian pilots dog-fought the 190s, Flight

Lieutenant I. G. du Monceau (EN794) claiming one destroyed. Pilot Officer H. A. Picard (BM297) and Pilot Officer E. J. Plas (AB912) hit another which they saw crash into a field.[1] Sergeant Flohimont knocked pieces off a third but Pilot Officer H. E. Marchal went down; he was later rescued and reported safe.

Two further squadrons patrolled Dieppe at this time, 133 Eagle Squadron and 165 Squadron. 133 was led by Flight Lieutenant Don Blakeslee DFC (EN951 MD–V), his pilots orbiting Dieppe at 7,000 feet. FW190s were eagerly engaged by the Eagles, Blakeslee and Pilot Officer W. H. Baker each claiming one destroyed, Flight Sergeant R. L. Alexander probably destroying another.

No 165 Squadron had ten machines over Dieppe as bottom cover squadron. Led by Squadron Leader H. J. L. (Darkie) Hallowes DFC DFM, a veteran fighter with 19 victories and who had only joined 165 from 222 squadron on 13 August, they made no contact, but looking down from his Spitfire (BL664 SK–A) Hallowes could clearly see Royal Navy destroyers laying smoke and also spotted two Mustangs leaving the French coast, clearly recognised by their markings.

Further Tac/R sorties had been carried out by the Mustangs during the last hour. 239 Squadron had sent out Flying Officer D. A. Lloyd (AG564) and Pilot Officer P. O'Brien (AG146) to cover the roads between Fécamp-Yvetot-Tôtes. They encountered their share of flak but saw little of interest. 414 Squadron sent out Pilot Officer F. J. Chapman (AG470) and Pilot Officer D. A. Bernhardt (AG376) who spied out the area Longroy to Haute Forêt, while Flying Officer F. H. Chesters (AG375) and Pilot Officer G. W. Burroughs toured St Leger-Gauville-Amiens, the same area being covered by Flying Officer C. L. Horncastle (AG459) and Pilot Officer C. H. (Smokey) Stover (AG601) shortly afterwards.

Horncastle, as if there was not enough dangers for the Mustang pilots, hit a seagull at high speed which tore a hole in the leading edge of his starboard wing, but he returned safely. His Weaver, Smokey Stover, was jumped by a FW190 at low altitude. Taking understandably violent evasive action he hit a telephone pole, los-

---

[1] Henri Picard was shot down and taken prisoner on 2 September 1942. He was one of the 50 escapers from Stalag Luft III who were murdered by the Gestapo in March 1944.

ing three feet from his starboard wing and half the aileron. However, he too got back and made a successful belly-landing.

Twenty-six Squadron sent out Flight Lieutenant A. G. Baring (AG574) with Sergeant P. P. Bannerman (AM110) between 6.20 and 7.55 am, to be followed by Pilot Officers J. E. A. Hartill (AG462) and R. J. C. W. Giles (AG535) while Pilot Officer J. A. Manson (AM215) patrolled between 6.40 – 8.15 am.

Back at Ford, all the usual high-pressure activity associated with the need to carry out almost continuous operations during the day, conditioned of course, by the requirements. This was a normal affair once D-Day had arrived and the Tactical Air Forces virtually set up a 'Cab-Rank' system. But for Dieppe, it was a bit hectic and exhausting for the organisers. Thus, in my case, I found that I was more useful as a team manager than team leader.

Wing Commander James Pelly-Fry, OC 88 Squadron

No 88 Squadron's Bostons made their second appearance above Dieppe when the battle with the Focke Wulfs was in full swing above them. An order had been sent to the squadron at 6.45 to attack Rommel as soon as possible with one flight. Six machines led by Squadron Leader Desmond Griffiths (Z2211 RH–L) were detailed to make this attack; Rommel was the battery situated behind Puys. The Bostons went in from 5,000 feet, carrying out the attack at 7.35 am: Griffiths, Warrant Officer Gallant 'Q', Sergeant Simpkins 'V', Flight Lieutenant Adams 'N', Pilot Officer Hughes 'O' and Warrant Officer Beach 'S'. Some twenty FW190s attacked the formation but most were held at bay by the Spitfires.

After the bombs had gone down, all the Bostons were taken down to sea level by the pilots but five of them were hit. One Focke Wulf which attacked Griffiths' Boston was hit by his gunner and the German fighter broke off with smoke pouring from it and with its propeller stopped. The gunner was Pilot Officer Harold Stuart Jack Archer, aged 22 from Moulscombe near Brighton, who in addition to hitting the 190, then kept up a running commentary on the progress of the fighters and directed the return fire. He was awarded the DFC for these actions. For 'Griffs' navigator, Pilot Officer Alan Baxter, from New Zealand, 19 August was his 31st

4

4. Douglas Boston heading towards Dieppe with bomb doors open. Below, the Navy spreads a smoke-screen in front of the harbour. *(IWM)*

5. Squadron Leader Emile Fayolle, Free French, CO of 174 Squadron. He failed to return from his squadron's first attack.

6. Squadron Leader Desmond Griffiths and Wing Commander James Pelly-Fry of 88 Squadron on 19 August. *(IWM)*

birthday. He had already completed more than 60 operations and he too received the DFC for the two missions he completed on this his special day. Later in the war he added a bar to this decoration and after the war became an MP.

I did in fact lead two raids in support of the Commando Operation by the Canadians. The first was shortly after the operation started when I led six Bostons for an attack on gun emplacements. We were due to be met over the sea by a fighter escort, but this did not turn up. In view of the important attached to the destruction of the shore batteries at our briefing, I decided to go in without the escort. As far as I can remember we were intercepted at about the time we were lined up to drop our bombs, by (according to the entry in my log book) about 25 FW190s, who attacked us continually for about five minutes until we were able to get down to sea level, where the high speed of the Boston combined with the tight formation and combined firepower of the rear guns, enabled us to get away. My log book records that we lost one aircraft and all the others were damaged, much of it caused by heavy light flak over the target area. My airgunner Pilot Officer Archer claimed one FW destroyed and I believe this was later confirmed from other sources.

Squadron Leader Desmond Griffiths, 88 Squadron

Squadron Leader Griffiths also received the DFC for his part in the Dieppe Operation.

Warrant Officer C. A. Beach's Boston was severely damaged and he was forced to ditch fifteen miles from the French coast. Both gunners aboard, Sergeants L. Senour and P. S. Woolston baled out and were rescued, Senour being picked up by a tank landing craft. Beach and his observer, Sergeant D. F. J. Hindle died in the Boston. Carl Adrian Beach, RCAF left a wife in Vermont, USA.

Almost at the same time as this action occurred, another Hurricane strike was being made. 87 Squadron led by Squadron Leader D. G. Smallwood (BE500 LK–A) comprised 12 Hurricanes which attacked the east headland in sections of four in lines abreast. They strafed houses, machine-gun posts as well as setting fire to a round tower on the cliffs. They met deadly return fire, Flying Officer Antoni Waltos, a Pole, being shot down and killed, Pilot Officer J.

Baker's machine was also hit but he struggled up to a safer height before baling out; he was rescued by the Navy. Baker in fact was spotted as he floated down, by a Naval vessel and they manoeuvred under him in order to be close by when he finally landed in the sea. They judged it perfectly, so perfectly that he actually landed on the boat's foredeck!

Flight Lieutenant Alec Thom, OC B Flight, and who had risen from sergeant to flight commander with 87 and was soon destined to command it, was also hit but managed to coax his Hurricane back to England to crash land near Eastbourne. He got back in time to fly on 87's third sortie, and he too received the DFC after the raid.

Also at 7.35 am, three Blenheims of 614 Squadron were ordered up to lay further smoke over Bismarck on the east headland. Squadron Leader P. de Le Cheminet (V6002) led Pilot Officer C. H. Georges (V5534) and Pilot Officer R. L. W. Baely (T2288). Two Spitfire Squadrons from the Ibsley Wing, 118 led by Squadron Leader E. W. (Bertie) Wootten DFC (AR447) and 501 led by Squadron Leader J. W. (Pancho) Villa DFC, both Battle of Britain pilots, flew out to provide cover but after fifteen minutes the raid was cancelled by radio. The Blenheims returned to Thruxton having covered twenty-five miles out from Selsey Bill. 118 Squadron spotted what appeared to be an empty bomber's dinghy (possibly from the 418 Squadron Boston), orbited it and gave a radio fix. They also saw a Mustang coming out of France. Its pilot saw the Spitfires and immediately took violent evasive action. 118 at first thought it must be a 190 but at 800 yards they identified it and let it pass by. Both squadrons returned without further incident, although Flight Sergeant S. A. Watson had burst a tyre on take off and been left behind, (EN964).

As this abortive mission was getting underway, Wing Commander Pat Jameson's 12 Group Wing from West Malling, comprising three Spitfire squadrons, were flying out low towards Dieppe. Jameson was leading 485 New Zealand Squadron, commanded by Squadron Leader R. J. C. Grant DFM, 411 Canadian Squadron as the middle squadron and commanded by Squadron Leader R. B. Newton, plus 610 Squadron led by Squadron Leader J. E. Johnson DFC as top cover. Up above all was Squadron Leader Raz Berry's

81 Squadron from Fairlop. They would all meet the Focke Wulfs.

The Wing raced above the wavetops at zero feet then nearing the hostile smoke covered shore began to climb. Bob Grant (BM147) had taken his New Zealanders up to between 3,000 and 4,000 feet when they arrived over the ships at 8.15 am. Above them they could see many enemy fighters. Robert Newton (BL385) too saw enemy fighters above, noticing that the Wing was greatly outnumbered by 190s. Johnny Johnson (EP254 DW–B) led his pilots up to 7,000 feet (they had orders to fly top cover at 10,000 feet) but before they could get higher they were engaged by an estimated 50 FW190s and ME109s.

Johnson, flying as Red 1, shot down one Focke Wulf into the sea, then shared a Messerschmitt with Pilot Officer L. A. Smith and Flight Sergeant S. C. Creagh. South Creagh (EP198 DW–H) was then hit by fire from a 190 and had to bale out. He was later pulled out of the water by Motor Gun Boat (MGB) No 317, six miles north-east of Dieppe.

Johnson then saw more enemy fighters arriving from inland and radioed this information to Pat Jameson. Having done this he then waded into them, his fire causing glycol to stream from one German fighter which was then attacked by Sergeant Smith, before it fell away. Flight Lieutenant Denis Crowley-Milling DFC (EP361 DW–X), an experienced air fighter who had flown in France and later in Douglas Bader's squadron in 1940, was leading B Flight. Following the German fighters with his Number 2, Flying Officer Reg Pearson, he looked back to see a Messerschmitt closing up behind his Number 4, Warrant Officer Maurice Goddard (Free French). 'Crow' winged over and yelling a warning to the Frenchman, attacked the 109, his first burst hitting the target. The 109 went over onto its back streaming a cloud of glycol but then Crow was engaged by another enemy fighter and lost sight of his victim for a moment. Then, having shaken off his immediate antagonist, he looked down to see a pilot jump out of a Messerschmitt;[1] Johnnie Johnson in his book[2] wrote this of 610's first air battle of that morning.

'A heavy pall of black smoke hung over Dieppe. We listened

[1] Goddard was killed in a beat-up of 610's base a month later.
[2] Wing Leader, op cit.

intently to some wing leader who instructed his pilots: "Fight your way out. Get out. Watch those 190s above at six o'clock. All Elfin aircraft – get out!"

'Ahead of us Spitfires, Messerschmitts and Focke Wulfs milled about the sky. It was too early to search for an opening, since the 190s had the height on us and my task was to keep the squadron together as long as possible and guard the two squadrons below. Crow called a break and we swing round together to find the 190s at our own level in pairs and fours and seemingly baffled by our move. A 190 pulled up in front of my own section and I gave him a long burst from the maximum range. Surprisingly it began to smoke, the wheels dropped and it fell away to sea, and Crow said, "Good shooting, Johnnie."

'The Messerschmitts and Focke Wulfs came down on us from astern and the flanks. They were full of fight and for the present we thought of nothing but evasion and staying alive. During a steep turn I caught a glimpse of a strong formation of enemy fighters heading towards Dieppe from inland and I called the wing leader: "Jamie, strong enemy reinforcements coming in. About fifty plus. Over."

'Jamie was hard at it but he found time to call 11 Group and ask for assistance. During a lull in the attacks my own section, which had been reduced to three aircraft, fastened on to a solitary Messerschmitt and sent it spinning down. Then they came at us again and we later estimated that we saw well over a hundred enemy fighters. Three of my Spitfires were shot down and I saw my own wingman, the Australian South Creagh, planing down streaming white glycol from his engine. It was impossible to protect him, for if we took our eyes off the enemy fighters they would give us the same treatment. They're bound to finish him off as he nurses his crippled Spitfire, I thought, I still had another Spitfire alongside, but I lost him when we broke in opposite directions. Then I was alone in the hostile sky.

'Ranging from ground-level to 20,000 feet and having a diameter of twenty-five miles, the air battle drifted and eddied over the coast and inland. The wing had lost its cohesion, but thirty-six Spitfires, or what was left of them, still carried out their task by fighting in pairs and fours and so achieved some concentration in the target area.

'I spotted a solitary aircraft over the town. I eased towards him and recognised the enemy fighter as a Focke Wulf 190. For once, I was not harried and I yawed my Spitfire to cover the blind spot behind me. But these movements attracted the attention of the enemy pilot and he snaked towards me, almost head-on, and then we both turned hard to the left and whirled around on opposite sides of what seemed to be an ever-decreasing circle.

'With wide-open throttle I held the Spitfire in the tightest of shuddering vertical turns. I was greying out and where was this Italian[1], who should, according to my reckoning, be filling my gunsights? I couldn't see him and little wonder, for the brute was gaining on me and in another couple of turns he would have me in his sights. I asked the Spitfire for all she'd got in the turn, but the 190 hung behind like a leech and it could only be a question of time, and not much of that!

'Stick over and well forward and I plunged into a near-vertical dive – a dangerous manoeuvre, for the 190 was more stable and faster than my Spitfire in such a descent, but I had decided on a possible method of escape. At ground-level I pulled into another steep turn, and as I gauged the height and watched the rooftops I caught a glimpse of the promenade, of stationary tanks, of the white casino and a deserted beach. The 190 was still behind and for a few seconds we dodged round the spires and columns of smoke. Then I made my bid to throw him off.

'A short distance off-shore I could see a destroyer surrounded by a clutter of smaller ships. We had been carefully briefed not to fly below 4,000 feet over the shipping, otherwise they would open fire. I rammed the throttle into the emergency position, broke off my turn and at sea-level headed straight at the destroyer. Flak and tracer came straight at me from the destroyer, and more, slower tracer from the 190 passed over the top of the cockpit. At the last moment I pulled over the destroyer, then slammed the nose down and eased out a few feet above the sea. I broke hard to the left and searched for the 190, but he was no longer with me. Either the flak had put him off or, better still, had nailed him. I made off at high speed to West Malling.'

Squadron Leader Johnnie Johnson, OC 610 Squadron

---

[1] Johnson clearly saw Italian markings on this FW190, just below the cockpit.

Johnson also related: ' ... our Spitfire 5s were completely outclassed by the FW190s and on (this) occasion I was certainly lucky to get back.'

Pilot Officer L. E. (Hokey) Hokem (EP238 DW–D) fired at a 190, blasting pieces off its tailplane but with so many fighters in the air it was only a second later that his own machine was hit by enemy fire and severely damaged. Hokem disengaged and brought his Spitfire home although he left most of his tail at Dieppe.

When finally the other Spitfires broke away as the battle died away, two other Spitfires were missing, flown by Flight Lieutenant Peter Poole (DW–F) and Sergeant John Leach (DW–S). At the height of the battle one Spitfire was seen heading towards Dieppe streaming glycol. Peter Poole, A Flight commander, had only arrived on 610 Squadron on 12 August, posted in from AFDU at Duxford.

Immediately below 610's battle, Newton's Canadians too were hotly engaged by enemy fighters. Pilot Officer Reid's machine was hit by cannon and machine-gun fire but he (Red 4) returned safely. Red 3, Pilot Officer P. R. Eakins was seen to be hit by cannon fire which blew off his Spitfire's radiator. He failed to return. Pilot Officer D. Linton Red 2, was last seen going after a German fighter and he too failed to get back to West Malling. Red Leader, Squadron Leader Newton, got in a telling burst at a 190 which was claimed as destroyed. Flight Lieutenant R. W. McNair also saw strikes on a 190 which he claimed as probably destroyed. Blue 4, Sergeant S. A. Mills was hit and wounded in the head by shrapnel but got his machine home (AD263).

Pat Jameson, Grant, and the other New Zealand pilots of 485 Squadron fought the Focke Wulfs at 3,500 feet. The 190s attacked repeatedly all three squadrons in pairs and fours, diving out of the morning sun. Jameson (BM232) attacked one 190 and saw it nose down in flames, confirmed by Red 3 and Red 4. Red 4, Pilot Officer C. Chrystell (BM205) fired at another 190 whose pilot subsequently took to his parachute. Flying Officer Lindsey S. Black snapped a burst at yet another Focke Wulf but although he saw no results of his fire, Jameson saw this 190 begin to leave a trail of smoke.

No 81 Squadron too engaged 190s high up. They had reached Dieppe at 8.24 and the action started almost immediately. Flight

Lieutenant J. W. Walker, a Canadian (BM315) fired at a 190 then saw a Ju88 about six miles east of Dieppe but lost sight of it. Two 190s dived down from the sun trying to head off Squadron Leader Berry but they broke away when Flight Lieutenant L. G. Bedford, leading Blue section, (BM369) fired at them.

At 8.56, when turning for home, two 190s dived to the attack. Flight Lieutenant Bedford fired but without result. Pilot Officer P. J. Anson, Blue 3, (BM158 FL–Y) fired at the second 190 and saw strikes behind its engine cowling and a piece of panelling blow off. Berry saw this 190 fluttering down apparently out of control and was claimed as a probable.

When Jameson and his wing landed at West Malling and held an informal debriefing, he and his squadron commanders all agreed that they had never before experienced such an intensive battle with so many German fighters. The battle had cost the wing five Spitfires, four pilots missing, another wounded plus three Spitfires damaged.

The CO of 400 Canadian Squadron, Squadron Leader Robert Waddell, and Pilot Officer M. B. Pepper, took off from Gatwick at 7.30 am. During their Tac/R sortie they strafed a water tower which housed a flak gun on its top (at 8.49) and later they observed and reported troops on bicycles moving north to Yvetot.

Three Spitfires of 91 Squadron took off at 7.40 on a 'Jim Crow' sortie between Ostend and the Somme Estuary. One machine had to return with engine trouble. No sooner had those Spitfires gone out when four more were 'scrambled' to patrol their own base at Hawkinge but nothing happened.

It was quite evident from the fire which was sweeping the beaches that the attacks made upon the machine-gun positions at Dieppe had not inflicted any lasting damage and so, following an urgent request via HMS *Calpe*, a further strike against the Dieppe water-front was organised. Squadron Leader Thorn's 32 Squadron, code-named 'Ecrum Squadron', took off from Friston at 7.35, Thorn leading (Z3581). Arriving off Dieppe, Thorn made radio contact with *Calpe* and was ordered to attack the many machine-gun emplacements located in the caves on the Bismarck cliff face. The fire from these strategically placed positions was pinning down the Canadians behind the promenade's sea wall and it was almost certain death to try to move forward from this wall.

Thorn led his 12 Hurricanes into the attack, experiencing heavy return fire but their 20mm cannons pounded the cliff face. As the Hurricanes roared away from Dieppe, two FW190s dived through the Spitfire screen but failed to hit any of the Hurricanes.

Then, shortly before half-past seven, a report was received that a force of German E-boats was out in the Channel making for the shipping off Dieppe. Quickly 3 and 43 Squadrons, already rearmed, refuelled and ready following their earlier attack were alerted. Squadron Leaders Berry and Du Vivier led their units out from Shoreham and Tangmere at 7.50, Du Vivier in a fresh machine (Z3081 FT–C). The two squadrons made rendezvous at five minutes past eight being joined by their escort, two Czech Spitfire Squadron, 310 led by Battle of Britain pilot Squadron Leader F. (Dolly) Dolezal, and 312 commanded by Squadron Leader J. Cermak. Among Cermak's pilots flew Wing Commander K. Mrazek DFC who had flown with 43 and 46 Squadrons in 1940. The force headed out towards Boulogne from where the E-boats were reported to have set off but no sign of them was seen. Five miles south-west of Boulogne both moderate and later heavy flak came up from the shore but neither the Hurricanes, flying at 100 feet, or the higher escorting Spitfires were hit. Four fishing-boats and one 500 ton merchant vessel were found, however, which might have been earlier mistaken for the E-boat force and some of the Hurricanes attacked. Flight Sergeant J. Pipa (EP432) of 312 Squadron, peeled off and made a strafing run, leaving one boat damaged and smoking.

At 8 o'clock 26 Squadron sent out two Mustangs on a Tac/R sortie, Pilot Officer E. E. O'Farrell (AG463) and Pilot Officer A. G. Christenson (AL977) being the pilots, the latter having only arrived on the squadron from 41 OTU on 13 August. Neither pilot returned. Arnold Christenson, a New Zealander of Danish parents who had emigrated, was taken prisoner. He was among the escapers from Stalag Luft III in March 1944 and one of the fifty murdered by the Gestapo.

Squadron Leader Harry Philip McClean (AG557) with Pilot Officer G. C. D. Green (AG560) of 239 Squadron flew out from

Gatwick at 8.10 am for a Tac/R on the roads from Le Tréport but they became separated. Both pilots completed their mission although McClean was hit by flak which damaged his oil tank as he recrossed the coast between Dieppe and Le Tréport. However, he made it back across the Channel but had to force down at Friston with no oil.

At 8 am Group Captain Broadhurst lowered his wheels and came into land at RAF Biggin Hill having returned from his first 'look-see' over Dieppe. As the mechanics rearmed and refuelled his Spitfire IX, Broadhurst met the Station Commander, Group Captain J. R. Hallings-Pott DFC AFC, and then visited all the squadrons at their dispersal areas. From his talks with the pilots of 222 Squadron, the Americans of the 307th 'Pursuit' and 602 Squadron all of whom had already flown over Dieppe, he was able to confirm what he had himself seen from the air. Broadhurst immediately telephoned 11 Group Operations Room, and gave the Commander in Chief an outline of the situation as he had seen it, asking him to suggest to the AOC that patrols of Spitfire IXs in pairs be put up with the hope that these would be able to counter the FW190s as they approached the battle area. As it happened, the main Spitfire IX units available had been assigned as escort for a raid against Abbeville by the American 8th Air Force.

As Pat Jameson's Wing was battling with the Focke Wulfs, 130 and 131 Spitfire Squadrons, plus Spitfires of the 309th US Fighter Squadron, were flying out to relieve them as air cover. These three squadrons arrived over the ships at 8.50, 131 and the 309th below, 130 flying as top cover squadron. The Focke Wulfs were still very much in evidence, the relieving Spitfires being continually engaged by an estimated 25 Focke Wulf fighters during their whole patrol. Indeed, enemy fighters were reacting vigorously. British radar picked up several plots on their screens between 8.29 and 9.14 am; 50 German aircraft from or near St Omer and the Desvres area, twelve or more up from Lille plus another dozen from around Dunkirk. It was estimated that during this period there was a total of over fifty German fighters constantly in the battle area. What was also evident was that so far there were no German reinforcements from Le Havre or the south-west, indicating that so far only JG26 pilots were engaged.

7

8

9

7. Wing Commander Minden Blake's Spitfire (W3561) in which he was shot down off Dieppe by a FW190. *(M. V. Blake)*

8. Sergeant Per Bergsland, 332 Norwegian Squadron. Taken prisoner at Dieppe he later escaped and returned to England. *(P. Bergsland)*

9. Wing Commander M. V. Blake DSO, DFC, the most senior RAF officer taken prisoner at Dieppe. *(M. V. Blake)*

Wing Commander M. G. F. Pedley was leading 131 Squadron at this time and one of his flight commanders, Flight Lieutenant Ray Harries, another air fighter destined for a high personal score, claimed one FW190 destroyed, flying his Spitfire BL600.

The general scene over the beaches was pretty chaotic. The shipping off shore was wreathed in smoke as it bombarded targets behind the town. Water spouts were everywhere as shore batteries returned their fire and the sky was covered in the black smudges of bursting anti-aircraft shells. Most of the time at least one aircraft could be seen spinning or diving down somewhere in a trail of smoke or flame. Johnnie Walker allowed me to take over from him as wing leader as I had recently been promoted on seniority, much to my disgust, for I had no wish to be relieved of my squadron.

On that occasion when over the beach-head my Number 2 called to me to 'break' as I was apparently at risk of being shot down by one of our own Spitfires as it looped its way towards the sea firing its guns each time the dead pilot fell against the control column.

Wing Commander Michael Pedley, OC 131 Squadron[1]

The whole wing formed a defensive circle and the enemy fighters climbed away but in the subsequent dog-fight which started, everyone was split up, 130 Squadron dividing into sections.

Wing Commander Minden Vaughan Blake DSO DFC flying with 130 Squadron should not really have been flying at all on this particular day. He had just been notified of a posting to Operations with a promotion to group captain in the offing. However, Blake, apart from being an experienced fighter pilot and wing leader, was also something of an engineer and had been, in his spare time, developing his ideas for the design of a gyro gun-sight for single-seater fighters. He had virtually perfected his idea and had rigged up a sight in his personal Spitfire and was keen to try it out in combat. Dieppe would provide the chance he felt sure.

Flying as Number Two to the CO of 130 Squadron, Squadron

[1] Pedley was posted to command 323 Wing for Operation Torch shortly after Dieppe. He was the first RAF pilot to land in Algiers.

Leader Peter Simpson DFC, another Battle of Britain pilot, Blake saw some FW190s over the ships and dived down after one of them. 130 had been split up and he was alone but he continued after his 190 and with some satisfaction shot it into the sea. However, three of the German's companions took on the New Zealander. For some minutes the four fighters waltzed round and round, losing height all the time. Then one Focke Wulf came in head-on, Blake seeing the 190's big engine cowling 'as large as a house' right in front of him – then his Spitfire was hit. His cockpit canopy burst, the perspex on the left side being blown in and Blake felt the blast through his flying helmet. His goggles were not over his eyes but pushed up on his head, therefore, his unprotected eyes were suddenly full of perspex splinters and dust, temporarily blinding him. Having regularly practised the procedure for a 'blind' bale-out in just this circumstance, he undid the straps and leads, got rid of the shattered cockpit hood and being low, simply kicked forward on the stick and shot out of the Spitfire's cockpit like the cork from a bottle. His parachute just opened before he splashed down into the water.

Clambering into his dinghy his eyes cleared slightly but his sight was still badly impaired. He found that he was quite near another dinghy in which sat Lieutenant Buck Ingrams of the 308th American Squadron who had been shot down an hour earlier. When they had introduced themselves, Ingrams asked what they should do. They were only a few miles off shore, just north of the ships and the tide and wind was rapidly taking them towards the French beach. The previous year, Blake had had to ditch a Spitfire off Cherbourg yet he had successfully rowed back to England to be rescued. He now told the young American that he proposed to repeat the performance.

Together in their respective dinghies which they tied together, they started to row, trying initially to just keep from drifting inshore, hoping that the wind would change. One thing Blake remembers was the terrific noise of the battle which was being fought just a few miles away.

The two fighter pilots struggled for the rest of the day and into the night. Blake was well clothed but Ingrams had only flown out in shirtsleeves and slacks and soon became affected by the wet and cold. Finally he had to give up and saying his farewell, allowed his dinghy to drift ashore where he was taken prisoner. The wind did finally change and Blake began to make headway. For a while it looked as if he would indeed make it back again but then late on the afternoon of the 20th while opposite Cap Gris Nez, and when only about five miles from the cliffs of Dover he was picked up by the Germans to become a prisoner.

He was taken to Paris where a German doctor, who had been busy with German casualties from the battle around Stalingrad on the Russian Front, operated on his eyes. With most of the splinters removed, he was taken to Frankfurt and questioned daily about the undamaged FW190 fighter which a German pilot had landed at RAF Pembrey in South Wales back in June, the German thinking the Bristol Channel to have been the English Channel. The Germans thought it had been Blake who had test flown the Focke Wulf. Over the radio the Germans had heard a wing commander give a Mayday call at about the time Blake had hit the sea. From the call-sign, the wing commander had been identified and they knew that he had test-flown the 190. As Blake's watch had stopped at this precise moment the Germans thought this was indeed their man. They continued their questioning for six weeks until they finally gave up and sent him to a POW camp. On the train journey he smashed a toilet window and dropped from the speeding train although he damaged his left arm and his head. Because of the speed of the train, the German guard thought him only to be on the roof of the train. In spite of his injuries he evaded for several days until finally recaptured and sent to Stalag Luft III where he met Ingrams again, and remained for the rest of the war.

Flight Sergeant Alfred William Utting, Blue 4, (BL356 PJ–Q) of 130 Squadron was also shot down and killed in the fight. Yellow 4, Flight Sergeant Cane's machine was badly shot up, Cane being wounded but he managed to get back to land at Ford. Meanwhile, Sergeant Snell fired into a 190 and claimed a probable.

Squadron Leader Peter Simpson wrote in his log book after this sortie, 'What a show, W/C M. Blake and Sgt. Utting missing – the RN could brush up on their aircraft recognition.'

The Americans of the 309th Squadron under Major Harrison Thyng were in the thick of the battle and had three pilots shot down into the sea. One of them was Lieutenant Sam Junkin Jr from Natchez, Mississippi, who moments before had sent a FW190 down to crash, this being the first confirmed victory by an 8th Air Force pilot in WW2. Junkin was slightly wounded before he baled out but was rescued and later received the American DFC. Lieutenant Collins was not so lucky and was lost. Thyng scored a probable. So again the FW190s won the moment. Five Spitfires shot down and a sixth British pilot wounded for the possible loss of two or three German fighters plus others damaged.

The remaining Spitfire pilots disengaged at around 9.20 am and began to land back at their bases at just after 10 am, their place above the ships having been taken over by 19 and 121 Squadrons from Southend with a low patrol provided by 111 Squadron from Kenley. Michael Pedley however, remained out for several anxious minutes.

At the termination of our patrol we were about to turn for home when the Guard Ship called up on the R/T with the urgent request to stay overhead as the relief wing had not yet reached the battle area. Calling up my pilots I sent back all who were very low on fuel and then stayed on patrol with only six aircraft for some of the most nervous fifteen minutes of my life! Happily the enemy remained away for all that period. Relieved at last we made for the nearest airfield, Shoreham, and all got down safely although for my part I ran out of petrol taxying in to dispersal.

Wing Commander Michael Pedley, OC 131 Squadron

Meantime, with the number of pilots that had failed to get back during the last hour or more, the Air Sea Rescue services were hard pressed. Therefore, 41 Squadron were asked to help. They sent out four Spitfires to scour the Channel while two became airborne to patrol base during an alert.

No. 26 Squadron provided two Mustangs at 8.30 for a Tac/R mission, the unit's Commanding Officer, Squadron Leader Michael Goodale, a pre-war pilot, taking off (AM148 RM–G) in company with Pilot Officer C. B. McGhee (AG531). They successfully completed their task but Goodale's machine was hit by a bullet which damaged his hydraulics. On his return to Gatwick his brakes failed causing him to overshoot the runway and hit an obstruction. The Mustang was damaged but Goodale was not hurt. It was AM148's one and only combat sortie. Flight Lieutenant Graham Dawson

DFC, also of 26 Squadron, took off alone at 8.45, again flying AG418, for his second sortie of the day but on this occasion he failed to return. He was 21 years old and came from Bromley in Kent.

No. 400 Squadron had sent out two further teams, Flight Lieutenant William Blakeney Woods (who later commanded 400 Squadron) and Pilot Officer Carlson at 8 am, then Flight Lieutenant Herbert P. Peters with Flying Officer S. M. Knight at 8.25. The latter pair encountered light flak and saw a FW190 over Le Tréport but happily they left each other alone. However, this attitude did not prevail above the ships. There the activity was about to increase in deadly fashion.

Meanwhile, Per Bergsland of 332 Squadron, was in the water, and soon to be taken into captivity.

I was Scott-Malden's No. 2 over the Dieppe raid, but after a while we lost each other. I saw a Focke Wulf 190 and immediately tried to attack the aircraft which disappeared behind a cloud. I followed the 190 a few times around the cloud, but decided then to turn around 180° and then meet the German head-on. Exactly that happened and when we saw each other we both fired. Everything went very quickly and we passed each other with a distance of probably 6 feet. Shortly afterwards oil floated over my windscreen and I could not see out at all. It did not take many seconds before I came to the conclusion that my only chance to survive was to bale out. I turned my Spitfire upside down and fell quietly out of the aircraft. The weather was good and it was a pleasure to descend in a parachute and end up in warm water. The dinghy functioned perfectly and I spent several hours watching aircraft combat overhead. It was like sitting in a theatre front row. Unfortunately a German warship discovered me instead of a ship from my own side.

Sergeant Per Bergsland, 332 Squadron

CHAPTER FIVE

The Dorniers Arrive
9 am to 11 am

Squadron Leader Patrick Davies led his 19 Squadron away from Southend at 8.41 am in company with 121 (Eagle) Squadron. They flew across Kent and Sussex to cross the English coast at Beachy Head at 3,000 feet, gradually gaining height over the Channel. By the time Dieppe was below them they had reached 10,000 feet. The American Eagle pilots, usually commanded by Squadron Leader Hugh Kennard DFC, were led on the 19th by fellow British RAF pilot, Squadron Leader W. D. (Bill) Williams DFC, another former Battle of Britain pilot, as Kennard had been away sick since 2 August. The Americans stayed at a lower altitude, 5,000 feet. These two squadrons arrived at Dieppe at 9.20 am.

At 9 o'clock 111 Squadron had left Kenley. Its CO, Squadron Leader Pete Wickham, who had led 111 on a dawn mission had been given other flying duties and so the squadron on this mission was led by Flight Lieutenant F. Vancl, a Czech pilot (AD252) ordered to patrol Dieppe at 3,000 feet.

The Focke Wulfs were still very much in evidence. An almost continual stream of 190s and a few Me109s had patrolled over Dieppe, meeting an equal number of RAF Spitfires. These same RAF pilots were also expecting German bombers and had been since dawn. On this patrol they would not be disappointed.

Davies, Williams and Vancl could see the mass of small ships even now filling the sea off Dieppe and plying to and fro, some still taking troops towards the shore, others firing into the harbour defences. Soon after 19 Squadron turned over Dieppe they saw eight 190s west of the town at 12,000 feet. At first they made no attempt to engage the Spitfires but as soon as the Spitfires passed over the harbour the 190s came down to attack.

Pilot Officer Jack Henderson, Blue 3, (BL380) fired at two of the 190s which immediately dived away steeply. Henderson tried to follow but as he did so his engine cut out. Levelling out, his engine coughed back into life, and then he spotted two more Focke Wulfs weaving south-west of Dieppe at 10,000 feet. Both 190s began to dive but Henderson closed with them and fired. White smoke emitted from both sides of one of the 190's fuselage and it dived vertically. Henderson watched as it dived away before he lost it when it was about 6,000 feet. He claimed it as damaged. Henderson was then attacked by two more 190s their fire hitting his port mainplane and port machine-gun ammunition bay. He escaped further damage by taking violent evasive action, extracting himself from the battle and flew safely back to base. He received the DFC after Dieppe.

Meanwhile, Squadron Leader Davies (AR364) and Sergeant I. M. Munday, a Rhodesian, (AR422) as Red 1 and Red 2, both made astern attacks on a 190 from 500 yards and it dived away towards the land, last seen in a steep dive. Flight Lieutenant C. F. Bradley, Blue 1, attacked a Focke Wulf which dived down to 2,000 feet above the sea. He then saw a Dornier 217 bomber at 7,000 feet, attacked it but saw no results of his fire. Pilot Officer R. Royer (Free French) Red 3, (BM526) attacked two 190s but without visible results. Then two 190s came down on his wingman, Sergeant E. R. Davies (BM542) and his Spitfire began to trail smoke. He had to bale out and was later picked up safely but with a bullet wound on his forehead. Blue 4, Sergeant E. A. Blore failed to return.

The Eagle Squadron pilots also became embroiled with the Focke Wulfs, were split up and lost two pilots, Pilot Officer J. B. Mahon and Pilot Officer J. T. Taylor. The next day the squadron was notified that Barry Mahon had been awarded the DFC. He was later reported a prisoner of war, but Taylor had been killed.

Pilot Officer G. B. Fetrow's machine was hit and he baled out but was picked up by the convoy. In return Flight Lieutenant S. R. Edner (EN918) claimed one 190 destroyed while Pilot Officer Gilbert O. Halsey (BM590 AV–R) and Sergeant Leon M. Blanding (EN822) both claimed probables and Pilot Officer F. D. Smith (AR423) damaged a fourth. Selden Edner's machine was hit in the fight by cannon fire, returning with a holed tailplane. He was awarded the DFC after Dieppe.

The twelve Spitfires of 111 Squadron down at 3,000 feet also saw the first of the bombers. They saw some Ju88s and Do217s escorted by 190s trying to get through to the ships. Flight Lieutenant Vancl and his Number 2, Sergeant B. A. C. Spranger attacked one Dornier and objects were seen to fall from it. Sergeant F. H. Tyrrell was hit by flak during the action and had to bale out. He spent five hours in his dinghy before being rescued by an ASR launch. This launch was strafed by German fighters on its return trip and some of the crew were wounded but Tyrrell was landed safely at Dover. Again it was a Focke Wulf victory. In the last clashes, five Spitfires were shot down (plus one lost to flak) and two others damaged for only one certain victory plus others probably destroyed or damaged.

So, at approximately 9.30 am, nearly five hours after the first shots of the Dieppe Raid had been fired, Luftwaffe bombers had finally been met over the ships. The Spitfire pilots quickly reported the fact but on board HMS *Calpe* they were only too aware that above them the long awaited bombers were coming in.

Radar stations on the English south coast began to record increased German air activity shortly after 9.30. At 9.41 20+ EA came on the radar screens from the direction of Abbeville followed by a further 20+ from the same area five minutes later. Between 9.40 and 9.45 three small plots of three to five aircraft appeared coming up from Lille and Merville. Also at 9.45 came the first confirmed reaction from Le Havre area. JG2 were on their way. Three minutes later, at 9.48 am, the Germans began to interfere with British radar signals which lasted on and off until 10.12 am.

As 19, 121 and 111 Squadrons broke off the actions at ten minutes to ten o'clock, three further units were arriving, already warned that German bombers were in the area.

Wing Commander Dutch Hugo, lead the Hornchurch Wing's three squadrons, 122, 154 and 340, away from their base at 9.15, arriving over Dieppe 35 minutes later. For all three squadrons this was their second mission of the morning. Over Dieppe, Kilian's 122 Squadron broke up into sections at the beginning of their patrol. Flight Lieutenant L. P. Griffiths saw six Dornier 217s approaching at 4,000 feet and he and Pilot Officer B. J. Bland slid in behind the last one and opened fire. Strikes were observed on the bomber which they claimed as damaged. Squadron Leader Kilian and Sergeant W. W. Peet, Pilot Officer L. C. Collingnon and Sergeant

A. Williams attacked another Dornier. Its port engine caught fire and the cockpit canopy blew off. It was last seen diving with both engines stopped. They initially claimed only a damaged but this was later raised to one destroyed.

Don Carlson and his 154 Squadron boys went off after two Dorniers they saw approaching the ships and drove them off. Even so, some bombers did get through. *Calpe* was narrowly missed by one large bomb which exploded less than fifty yards from her, two smaller bombs churning up the water a little further away.

Not unnaturally the Navy gunners were firing at everying that appeared to them to be hostile. On *Calpe* Flight Lieutenant Gerald Kidd saw one Spitfire in trouble, making its shortest way home, being shot at all the way over the convoy and it appeared to go into the sea to the north. This occurred several times during the day and waggling of wings by friendly aircraft was not enough to stop the ships from firing if the aeroplane was below the minimum permitted height, whether they were in trouble or not.

No 340 Free French Squadron under Commandant Duperior were down to 11 men as Capitaine René Mouchotte had developed an undercarriage problem after take off. Patrolling just west of the harbour they found several Dorniers trying to get through to the ships. Capitaine Francois de Labouchère DFC, Yellow 1, (EN908 GW-Y) and Sous Lieutenant Pierre Laureys (EN889 GW–Z), his Number 4, each shot down a Dornier while other Frenchmen damaged four more. Adjutant René Gerard Darbins, aged 21[1], (GW–U) was shot down into the sea off Dieppe and did not get back. (Whether this was the Spitfire seen by Kidd to have been shot down by the ships is not certain but it appears to be the only Spitfire lost at the approximate time of Kidd's sighting – 10 am).

The Polish pilots of 303 and 317 Squadrons arrived in the battle area shortly after 10 o'clock having made rendezvous with each other over the English coast. This was 303's first mission of the day, having been at readiness since 4.20 am. Skalski's 317 Squadron was on its second op. With the Polish Wing were two experienced fighter pilots, Wing Commander Stefan Janus, Northolt's Wing Leader and Squadron Leader Teofil Nowierski DFC, the latter currently with HQ Fighter Command but who had gone to Northolt so as not to miss the action over Dieppe.

[1] Darbins was flying his 28th operational sortie.

As the Poles met the Germans, Janus warned the others of the 190s above and then he and Nowierski dived down and waded into the Dorniers head-on. Both pilots fired as they came within range, which effectively broke up the formation forcing some of the bombers to jettison their bombs.

No 303, possibly one of the most famous of the Polish Squadrons to fly with the RAF, was led by Squadron Leader Jan Zumbach (EN594 RF–H), holder of the Polish Virtuti Militari and British DFC. His twelve aircraft reached Dieppe flying at 8,000 feet, being met by heavy flak from the shore. Almost at once the squadron was attacked by German fighters who came down in twos and fours from all directions. The ever aggressive Poles took on the strong challenge and a hefty dogfight began. Flight Lieutenant Jan Marciniak probably destroyed one 190, while Pilot Officer Antoni Glowacki claimed one destroyed.

Zumbach then saw several Dorniers heading in from the east at 8,000 feet, then spotted three Junkers 88s. He immediately ordered his port and starboard sections to attack the 88s. Pilot Officer T. Kelecki went, as ordered, down after the Junkers, following one down to 3,000 feet, then seeing it continue down, hit the sea and explode. Pilot Officer S. Socha, orbiting the ships, saw two FW190s heading for the French coast. Coming in behind one, he shot it down in flames. He then went after a Ju88, fired both cannon and machine-guns into it and Zumbach saw it fall away and crash into the sea.

Zumbach himself saw two 190s on his port side and fired into one from 450 yards, whereupon it began to smoke and dive steeply. He then attacked another 190 he saw below him, firing three bursts from 100-150 yards. The 190 shed some pieces, broke away sharply, caught fire and dived vertically. In addition, Flight Sergeant W. Giermer and Sergeant J. Karczmarz each claimed a 190 as probably destroyed.

No 317 got in amongst the Dorniers after Janus' attack had split them up. Flight Lieutenant Kazimierz Rutkowski shot down one Dornier into the sea while Pilot Officer Mike (Michal) Maciejowski DFM (AD295) who had flown with the RAF in 1940-41, shot down a Ju88 which fell into the sea in flames, then attacking a 190 he sent this too into the water. Sergeant W. Powlowski's Spitfire was hit and damaged by a 190 but he in turn damaged a Focke Wulf. The two squadrons then broke away as briefed, having suffered no serious casualties to themselves.

Further Mustangs were winging their way to the rear of Dieppe at this time, 239 sending out Flight Lieutenant E. K. Barnes (AG614). This was Barnes's second sortie of the morning, having lost his Weaver to flak on the unit's second operation. Barnes was lucky to escape that sortie but went out alone at 9.25 to scour the roads from Yerville to Rouen to Yvetot. Barnes was intercepted by German fighters near Envermeu after crossing into France at Ault, but he managed to shake them off. Carrying on with his task he was later found again by hostile fighters, four FW190s attacking him over the Forêt D'Arques. He fired two bursts at one, seeing pieces fall away from one 190's tail unit. A Spitfire then came down and finished off the German enabling Barnes to successfully evade the others and get away.

No 414 Squadron sent out Pilot Officer W. T. Blakeney (AG612) and Pilot Officer J. C. Davidson (AG582) at 9.30 to locate gun positions firing on the convoy off Dieppe. 400 Squadron provided Flying Officers Jones and E. I. Hall at 9.30 who wisely stayed well clear of a big dog-fight they saw over Dieppe. On their way back they saw three pilots in dinghies.

No 91 Squadron carried out a Jim Crow patrol to Ostend at 9.40 to look for any shipping activity. Pilot Officer A. M. Le Maire (DL–S) a Belgian pilot, was attacked by two FW190s but he escaped unharmed although his machine was slightly damaged on landing.

As a result of 414 Squadron's report on the gun battery firing on the ships and also the beaches, the Hurribombers of 175 Squadron were ordered to fly against the Rommel position behind Blue beach. 87 Squadron was alerted to follow up 175's attack with a cannon attack. They began to leave Tangmere at 10.15 am. Nobby Fee's 412 Canadian Squadron and Geoff Hyde's 41 Squadron were detailed to escort the Hurricanes, taking off from Tangmere at 9.45, Fee leading (BL632). The Hurricanes of 175 left Warmwell at 10.05, led this time by Pilot Officer R. A. Peters DFM, a New Zealander (BP705). 253 Squadron was also ordered off in support, and led by Flight Lieutenant Gerald Fisher (BV172) began taking off from Friston at 10 am.

Nos 175 and 253 met up with the Spitfires over the Channel, flying towards Dieppe at zero feet. As the hostile coast came into view the Spitfire pilots opened their throttles so as to cross the coast at maximum speed. Fee ordered 41 Squadron to orbit off Dieppe to cover 412's and the Hurricanes withdrawal, 41 climbing to 2,000 feet. Meanwhile the Hurricanes rose to a sufficient height to lob their bombs into the Rommel site. They each let go two 250 lb bombs.

Sergeant E. O'Bart (BE417) aimed his Hurricane at the gun position but another Hurricane dived wildly between him and his section leader, forcing him out of formation. Pilot Officer Peters let go his two bombs as he swept over Rommel and as he pulled up he saw flames flare up from the position. The Hurricanes became surrounded by heavy and intense flak. Sergeant D. S. Conroy (BE404) dropped his bombs but was hit in three places on his main planes.

Flight Sergeant J. E. Meredith (BE394) approached the target but as he came roaring in saw a German Heinkel 111 bomber slanting down towards the offshore shipping. Meredith curved towards it, fired and it belched smoke and flame. He last saw the Heinkel going down trailing smoke, at 1,200 feet and claimed a probable. Meredith then turned back to his main task and bombed the gun position. Meanwhile, Peters too had found an enemy aircraft. Pulling away from his dive-bombing attack he came upon the ever present Focke Wulfs, hitting one seriously enough to be credited with a probable and then he damaged another.

Flight Lieutenant D. G. Andrews (BP295) an Australian, dived through the flak, placing his bombs right on target, which was confirmed by 87 Squadron who were now making their approach. The following 175 Squadron pilots also bombed successfully: Pilot Officer R. J. Emberg and Sergeants H. W. Read (BE687), R. Kelsick (BE492), and G. Cockbone (BE668). Considering the amount of anti-aircraft fire being thrown up, 175 were lucky to get away without losing a single pilot.

Eighty-seven Squadron came in against the Eastern headland led by Squadron Leader 'Splinters' Smallwood, meeting heavy flak but they strafed the gun positions and got away without loss.

Beautiful sunny day. Remember looking down on our family

holiday centre at St Helens (nr Bembridge) IoW. Flew low over a calm sea. Expected to be given instructions as we approached Dieppe by Radio Control Ship, but no contact made, so our CO, made up his own mind to attack the East Cliffs, hoping we would thereby help the Commandos. The overall picture was striking – my first sight of action in the war. A beautiful day, sea alive with landing craft, air above us full of action, much smoke from the town centre, and as we came in an aircraft spinning down in flames with a smoke trail as the back-cloth to the action. Twelve of us in close formation at cliff-top height – more concerned with keeping formation than in observing our surroundings. One run in over the cliffs, a quick burst of fire – wide turn to port and away out and home.

Pilot Officer Frank Mitchell, 87 Squadron

No 253 Squadron hit Dieppe at 10.40, strafing gun positions, railway sidings etc., behind the town and other targets all of which were hit with success. They remained over the target area for 15 minutes and observed several Churchill tanks in the town. Several FW190s were also seen above but none attacked. All got away and landed safely, even Flying Officer D. W. Shaw (BP707) who had his machine's rudder controls shot away by flak.

Pancho Villa's Squadron, 501, came out with 87 Squadron. They found a thick pall of yellow evil smelling smoke over Dieppe. They watched 87 go in from 2,000 feet, seeing them apparently inflict considerable damage. The Spitfires were fired on by flak from east of the town, hitting the machine flown by Flight Sergeant A. R. MacDonald (SD–D), a Canadian, damaging his tail wheel. As 501 looked down they saw a ship on fire and as they flew over it, it blew up, leaving only a flicker of burning oil on the surface. Four FWs approached the Spitfires but did not attack. The pilots became split up and Villa (EP300 SD–Z) led his section in close to some Hurricanes and led them home.

Meanwhile, 412 Squadron, had flown in with the first wave of Hurricanes.

'About five miles off the French coast we gradually opened up so that we hit the coast going flat out to the right of the town. Here, there is quite a high hill which slopes down to the water. Up over the hill we went, right down on the deck. We were to the right of the Hurri-bombers, but the other squadron didn't come in but waited a mile or so offshore for us to come out. We went inland about three miles, weaving amongst the trees and I don't think I was ever more than five feet from the deck. The lower you are, the safer, because they can't see you coming and you are over their heads and behind the trees before they get a shot at you.

'After about three miles, we swung to the left. I was following J – [Pilot Officer John Brookhouse (EN831)] slightly to the right and about 75 yards behind. All this time we were passing over Jerries who were trying to take pot shots at us. After we had made our turn to the left we were in a bit of a gully with trees on either side and no trees ahead. The ground started to rise and there, at the top of the rise, was a big flak position. We were going so fast that we were on it before we realised it. All hell breaking loose. There were heavy ack-ack guns and I don't know how many machine-guns, etc, blazing away at us from point-blank-range. We had come right to a funnel completely exposed. The next thing I saw was the tail of J's kite just blow away and the fuselage break in two right behind the cockpit. His kite seemed to go slowly over on its nose. I didn't see it hit the ground as I was past, but one of the other lads saw it and it really spread itself all over the ground. I don't suppose poor John even knew he was hit before it was all over.

'I weaved wildly to the left and the next thing I knew, I was in the midst of the Hurries. We swing again to the left and headed for the sea. There was a ridge between us and the sea where all the Jerry batteries and ack-ack were that had held up the landing. The ground was cleared for about a mile before we got over the ridge and all hell broke loose again. Over the ridge we went, absolutely flat out, praying that our engines would hold out. As we hit the sea, we fully appreciated the reception we were getting. There was literally a shower of splashes all around us from ack-ack, which followed us about three miles out to sea. Why I wasn't hit, I don't know. Maybe luck was in. I was following up in the rear of the Hurries but soon passed them and then swung around looking for Jerries that might bounce us as soon as we got out of the flak. The squadron that stayed outside were looking after them however, so I remained on one side, weaving like mad and expecting to be jumped by a 190 at any time.

'About 15 miles off the English coast, I suddenly heard the CO yell, "Red 4, you are pouring glycol out of your rad. Climb like h–." Then a few seconds later, "Bail out, Red 4." Then, "Nice going Red 4." The CO and a couple of other pilots managed to direct a launch to where the pilot was and he was picked up just 40 minutes later. His 'chute had evidently just opened before he hit the water.'

Pilot Officer John Godfrey, 412 Squadron,
from a letter home dated 20 August 1942.

The pilot who baled out was Flight Sergeant W. F. Aldcorn and he was picked up safely.

Forty-one Squadron, who had orbited off Dieppe to cover the withdrawal, had four FW190s attempt to bounce them. Sergeant A. Imbert (Free French) (AR392) went into a skidding turn and one Focke Wulf overshot him. Imbert opened fire as the 190 went over him and white smoke poured out from the cockpit area. Flight Lieutenant M. L. Stepp (BM573) went after another 190, his attack producing black smoke from the German fighter but it flew off inland. All 41 Squadron's aircraft returned safely although several carried bullet holes in them.

The Belgian pilots of 350 Squadron had arrived in the battle area at 5,000 feet, having left Redhill at 10 o'clock. The sky was still very full of activity and almost immediately Ju88s, escorted by FW190s were met. The 190s took on the challenge and 350 Squadron were hotly engaged. Pilot Officer F. A. Venesoen (AD475) selected one of eight 190s, seeing his fire rake the German machine which disintegrated in the air. Flight Lieutenant A. L. Boussa (EN769) battled with two 190s and although his Spitfire was damaged and himself slightly wounded in the leg, he succeeded in hammering one 190, whose pilot took to his parachute. He then damaged another. Sergeant R. A. Alexandre claimed a probable and a damaged while other 190s were claimed as damaged by Flight Lieutenant Count Yvan Du Monceau de Bergandael, who had flown with the Belgian Air Force in 1940 before escaping to England, Pilot Officer G. M. Seydel and Sergeant F. E. Boute.

Flying in company with 350 were Squadron Leader Dolezal's 310 Czech Squadron and the American 307th Fighter Squadron. The Americans saw 14 FW190s but were unable to engage. However, the Czechs, reaching Dieppe at 10.50 am, at 6,000 feet, saw several dog-fights in progress and joined in. At 11.05, Dolezal attacked a Dornier which was approaching the harbour and was able to claim a probable. He then attacked a Focke Wulf which was attacking a Spitfire seeing his bullets score hits on its starboard wing and its fuselage. Flight Lieutenant E. A. Foit attacked a Dornier and it fell away into some clouds. He then went after another Dornier, blasting some pieces from its wings before he opened up on a third bomber, damaging its starboard wing.

Flight Lieutenant V. Chocholin also damaged a Dornier, while Flying Officer J. Hartman attacked a black camouflaged Dornier (obviously a machine used for night operations but pressed into service for this operation), hit it and blew pieces off it. Hartman saw it go down but then lost it. He attacked another Dornier sending it down with smoke pouring from one engine. Pilot Officer J. Doucha got in amongst the bombers, hammered one the half rolled to attack a second from astern with cannon and machine-gun fire, seeing strikes on its port wing. Warrant Officer A. Fornusek closed with a Dornier but was intercepted by two 190s. He shook them off and attacked yet another bomber seeing it lose height over the land with black smoke pouring from its fuselage. Other Czechs to make claims were Sergeant V. Popelka, one probable and one damaged Dorniers, Sergeant J. Stivar a 217 damaged, Sergeant K. Pernica a 217 probable and another damaged while Sergeant A. Skach damaged a Focke Wulf before losing it in cloud.

The air battle, now five hours old, was really hotting up, while on the ground things were becoming desperate.

CHAPTER SIX

Abbeville
10.30 am

The famous German fighter base at Abbeville/Drucat was only
about thirty miles north-east of Dieppe, or only minutes' flying time
away. It was part of the overall Jubilee plan to attack this important air base in order to deny its use to the Luftwaffe for most of the
day. This attack had been planned to coincide with the main withdrawal of the raiding troops from Dieppe, for it was anticipated
that this local aerodrome would be highly active at that crucial
time. The attacking force came from the newly operational American 8th Air Force.

The bombers of the United States Army Air Force in Europe had
flown their first war mission only two day prior to Dieppe, on 17
August. On that memorable occasion 12 Boeing B17E Flying Fortresses from the 97th Bombardment Group had attacked the
Rouen-Sotteville marshalling yards. On 19 August it was again the
97th Group that provided the aircraft which were to take part in the
Dieppe operation. The Americans would take 30 tons of general
purpose high explosive bombs and five tons of incendiary bombs to
the airfield target. The aerodrome of Abbeville/Drucat was situated
2½ miles north east of Abbeville and one half mile west of Drucat.

Twenty-four B17s from the Group's four squadrons, the 340th,
341st, from their base at Polebrook and the 342nd and 414th from
Grafton Underwood took to the air between 8.32 and 8.45 am and
headed south towards the Sussex coast. Twenty of the bombers
carried the high explosive and four the incendiary bombs. Four
British fighter squadrons were detailed as escort, 64, 611, and 401
and 402 Canadian Squadrons, all equipped with the latest Spitfire
IXs. Officially the operation was mounted as Circus No 205.

For 64 Squadron, commanded by Squadron Leader W. G. G.
Duncan-Smith DFC and bar, from Hornchurch, this was their first
mission of the day. Douglas Watkins' 611 Squadron was on its

second. 401, commanded by Squadron Leader K. L. B. Hodson from Lympne were also on their premier mission but for Norman Bretz' Squadron, 402 from Kenley, this was also their second operation of the day.

Duncan-Smith (BR851) led his men off at 9.35, 611 led by Watkins taking the air at exactly the same time. 401 and 402 also took off at 9.35, 401 led by Hodson (BS172), 402 by Bretz.

In the air too, was Group Captain Broadhurst. Taking off from Biggin Hill in his Spitfire IX (BR370) he intended to rendezvous over Beachy Head with the bombing force and accompany them to Abbeville. However, another issue forced him to change his plan.

The Spitfires made their rendezvous with the Fortresses over Beachy Head at approximately 10.05 am. The Americans, according to 611 Squadron's report, were nine minutes late but the formation set out from Beachy Head at 10.14 am. The B17s flew at 23,000 feet, 64 and 401 two thousand feet above, 402 at 27,000 feet with 611 as top cover one thousand feet above them.

The French coast was reached and crossed at Cayeux, at twelve minutes past ten. Medium and heavy flak reached up for them as they crossed into France, and this followed them for the next six minutes which was the total time it took the 24 bombers to reach Abbeville. 23 B17s made their bomb runs at between 10.32 and 10.40 am, one failing to bomb due to a mechanical failure; its crew later jettisoned their bombs over the Channel. At 10.35 the tail gunner of one Fortress saw an Me109 closing and he fired a quick burst in its direction. The 109 swerved away and was chased firmly away by a Spitfire. Exactly ten minutes later a B17's top gunner fired at an unidentified fighter which broke away and disappeared.

The bombs rained down, many bursts seen on the north-west dispersal area, others exploding on two of the three runways, those running east to west and north to east. Fires were also started in the woods adjoining the dispersals. A flak site near the northern dispersal was thought to have been hit and some bombs fell on the village of Drucat.

Eight or nine aeroplanes were seen at the northern dispersal, five or six more on the eastern area. It was also possible that other machines were on the flying field itself. During the raid 10 or 12 German fighters were seen to take off into the smoke over the aerodrome but failed to emerge, or be seen to emerge. A dozen or so other fighters were later seen taxiing on the field.

Over the target the B17s watched by 611 Squadron who later recorded: ' ... watched some superb bombing of Abbeville.' 401 saw ' ... many direct hits ... on admin: area, and also on southern runway.' 64 Squadron reported that the Americans ' ... successfully bombed from 23,000 feet.'

Some moderate flak had been experienced during the bomb run but as the Fortresses turned back towards the coast this intensified. Heavy flak came up from Crécy Forest and three B17s caught flak splinters but no crewmen were hurt. The Luftwaffe made no further attempts to interfere with the bombers although some FW190s were later seen but they made no move to come near. Obviously the German fighter pilots were far too occupied at a lower altitude over Dieppe.

The American formation flew out north of the Somme Estuary and began to land back at their bases, having recrossed the Sussex coast over Bexhill at between 11.25 and 12 o'clock mid-day.

As the Fortresses headed away from Abbeville, 64 Squadron went back to England with them but off the French coast the other three Spitfire units were released and given the freedom to fly a sweep over Dieppe. They split up and flew independently, 611 and 402 making no contact with enemy aircraft, but Ken Hodson's Canadians did.

Hodson led his boys towards Dieppe, gradually reducing height from 25,000 to 10,000 feet. As they came into the general battle area, enemy fighters were found. Hodson saw a Focke Wulf, closed with it from the starboard quarter and then astern slightly below, and gave it a three second burst from 200 yards but saw no result. Flight Sergeant B. M. Zobell, his Number 2, (BS120) also attacked this 190 and claimed to have damaged it. Hodson then saw friendly bombers below but then realised that they were in fact Dorniers. He attacked one of them, seeing his fire splatter on its tail and fuselage. Zobell also opened fire twice at another Dornier, seeing strikes on its fuselage and wings but the Canadian was then hit, having his rudder shot through while other bullets holed his wings, perspex canopy, smashed his gun-sight and sent a splinter of glass into his left eye. He broke away and returned safely to base, his machine having Category B damage.

Flight Sergeant S. Coburn also damaged a Dornier while Flight Sergeant R. D. Reeser battled with several 190s at 11,000 feet. Pilot Officer D. R. Morrison DFM (BS119) attacked a 190 seeing his fire hit its tail and fuselage. The Focke Wulf went to pieces and spewed out black smoke. However, Morrison's machine had been damaged and it later caught fire, forcing him to bale out. Flight Sergeant Reeser saw Morrison jump and radioed a Mayday call from 500 feet, then saw rescue boats approaching. Reeser was also able to confirm that Morrison's 190 was destroyed. Later Don Morrison wrote the following account[1] of his action and subsequent rescue.

' . . . I saw a single FW190 just ahead and about 1,500 feet below me. I did a slipping barrel roll, losing height and levelled out about 150 yards behind and slightly to the starboard and above the enemy aircraft. I opened fire with a 2-second burst closing to 25 yards. I saw strikes all along the starboard side of the fuselage and several pieces which seemed about a foot square flew off from around the cowling. Just as both the enemy aircraft and myself ran into cloud, he exploded with a terrific flash of flame and black smoke. I was quite unaware that my own aircraft had been damaged (probably by flying debris) and we were flying at about 1,000 feet. Suddenly my engine started to cough and the aircraft shuddered violently. My engine cut out completely but I had managed to reach 2,000 feet. I took off my helmet, and undid my straps and opened the hood. I crouched on the seat and then shoved the stick forward. My parachute became caught somehow and I figured I was about 200-250 feet above the water when I got clear. The aircraft plunged into the water below me as my parachute opened.

'Almost immediately I pressed the quick release, just as I hit the water. I inflated my dinghy without any trouble and then climbed in. I had only been in the water for about fifteen minutes [before a rescue boat arrived]. The captain of the boat estimated my position as 17 miles off Dieppe. I was picked up about 1110 hours and immediately got into dry clothes. Unfortunately I was told that I would have to stay on the boat until it returned to port at night, so that I would miss the rest of the day's fun. During the afternoon we went on several other crash calls without success, often operating within sight of the French coast. We saw the attack by the bombers

[1] Quoted in *The RCAF Overseas: The First Four Years*

on the convoy beaten off by heavy ack-ack fire. We saw the explosion and pall of smoke caused by two Spitfires colliding head-on. We saw gun-fire from the shore and from the boats and aircraft laying smoke screens. Later on in the afternoon two FW190s passed over us about 5,000 feet. Shortly afterwards, I saw them attack and set on fire another ASR boat. Knowing that we could not do much with our light armament, we raced back towards England to get the help of a Navy boat which we had previously noticed.'

Group Captain Broadhurst, instead of making his intended rendezvous with the bombing force, had turned towards Dieppe following a call from the Hornchurch controller, informing him that German dive-bombing was being reported from the battle area. Reaching Dieppe he saw Dornier 217s and Junkers 88s escorted by an estimated 30/50 FW190s. The bombers were at 11,000 feet, the 190s stepped up to 15,000 feet.

Broadhurst attacked one FW190; his cannon failed to fire but he did damage it with his machine-guns, before breaking away and flying towards Abbeville. He reached Abbeville just as the Fortresses were making their bombing run and he watched the bombs bursting on the aerodrome before flying home with the B17s. Over the south coast he left them and landed at Hornchurch to rearm and refuel.

At Hornchurch he chatted to Wing Commander Dutch Hugo and with him went to dispersal to talk to the pilots. They discussed the Germans' tactics and the general situation at Dieppe. Again he put a call through to Group Operations, spoke with the AOC, describing the attack on Abbeville and suggesting an alteration to the patrol height of the RAF's fighters to combat the enemy bombers now appearing over Dieppe. The AOC did alter the height and diverted some of the Kenley Wing's Spitfires. They had immediately had success which is why Broadhurst later flew to Kenley following his third sortie.

At Dieppe itself the position ashore was obscure. As few radio messages had been received, and some of those had been wrongly interpreted, the raid commanders were having difficulty in establishing just what was happening. In addition it was believed that other messages were false reports being sent by the Germans.

One firm report received by HMS *Calpe* was that Lord Lovat's 4th Commando had succeeded in its task of knocking out the Hess battery and re-embarked safely. The failure of the Yellow Beach landing to deal with Goebbels was also known. Yet firm news from Blue beach at Puys was not forthcoming. And at Dieppe itself the position was totally obscure. What could be established was that enemy defensive fire was increasing making it extremely dangerous to approach the shoreline.

At 8.30 am the Royal Marine Commandos were sent in to White beach to help support and consolidate what was thought to be an advantage gained ashore. This advantage was a false report and the Marines met a withering fire and had to turn away, their CO, Lieutenant Colonel J. Picton-Phillips being mortally wounded. Clearly none of the raid's main objectives was going to be taken. On the main beaches the troops, those that were still alive, were pinned down behind the sea wall. The withdrawal time must be brought forward.

CHAPTER SEVEN

Withdraw
11 am to 12 noon

The hurriedly revised time for the withdrawal of the land forces from Dieppe was 11 am. Following the decision at around nine o'clock that withdrawal was necessary, the RAF had to be given time to prepare smoke-laying missions, bombing and cannon attacks etc. At the appointed hour of eleven, the RAF would unleash a massive assault on the defensive positions and the landing craft, equally supported by the destroyers and other smaller Naval craft, would go in and pick up those who survived. Meanwhile, above, in the still blue sky, the air umbrella would continue the battle with the ever present Luftwaffe.

In the air the German bombers, escorted by fighters were continually trying to penetrate the Spitfire screen in order to get at the ships. In the main the Spitfires were succeeding and inflicting damage on the attackers but the Luftwaffe's continuing offensive actions only added to the decision to recall the raiding forces earlier. It was quite obvious that all heavy equipment, the tanks etc., would have to be abandoned – the evacuation of the Canadian troops must be paramount.

At 10.15 am four Spitfire squadrons took off to take their place above the anchorage, knowing full well that they would be involved with the German bombers. 65 and 165 left Eastchurch, led by Flight Lieutenant Colin R. Hewlett (EP165), who would win the DFC for his part in the day's operations. 165 was led by Squadron Leader Darkie Hallowes (BL664). 222 Squadron led by Squadron Leader Bobby Oxspring took off from Biggin Hill while the American 308th Fighter Squadron, again led by Pete Wickham (EP166), CO of 111 Squadron, flew out from Kenley. These squadrons arrived over Dieppe at ten minutes to eleven o'clock.

Sixty-five flew as top cover at 10,000 feet, and saw two Dornier

217s three thousand feet below and attacked. Sergeant T. D. Tinsey (AD309), Yellow 3, shot down one in flames, and Sergeant K. A. Biggs (BL435) in company with Sergeant R. Brown (AB786 YT–W), Red 2 and 4, sent the other down, both bombers crashing into the sea.

No 165 found Dorniers, Hallowes claiming one of them and damaging another, while four pilots ganged up on another and destroyed this also. Flight Lieutenant E. W. Colquhoun (BL530 SK–H), Pilot Officer H. L. Pederson (AR272 SK–L), Pilot Officer B. Warren (BM367 SK–F), and Pilot Officer D. Warren (AR403 SK–M). Pilot Officers L. R. Disney and H. C. Richardson also damaged a Ju88.

No. 222 Squadron failed to engage and the 308th Squadron only had a brief tangle with some FW190s.

These squadrons were supported above the ships by 133 and 602 Squadrons from Lympne and Biggin Hill. Don Blakeslee led 133's Eagles as top cover (in EN951) flying at 12,000 feet and many combats began immediately Dieppe was reached. The Americans shot down one Ju88, two FW190s and damaged four other Focke Wulfs and three Dorniers. The scorers were: Blakeslee, Flight Lieutenant E. G. Brettell RAF[1], Pilot Officers R. N. Beatty, D. S. Gentile[2], G. G. Wright, W. H. Baker and D. D. Gudmundson, and Flying Officer E. Doorly. Gil Wright, flying Dixie Alexander's Spitfire, was shot up but reached base safely.

No 602 led by Pete Brothers waded into a mass of Dorniers, Junkers and Focke Wulfs, claiming three Dorniers destroyed, Flight Lieutenant E. P. W. Bocock DFC, Sergeant P. L. Hauser one each, Sergeants W. W. J. Loud and W. E. Caldecott sharing the third, one Dornier probably destroyed by Sergeant Caldecott and a further six Dorniers, a Junkers and two 190s damaged. They lost one pilot, Pilot Officer M. F. Goodchap, who was later reported to be a prisoner.

After a short break, we returned to the area for our second patrol at 3,000 feet. By now the activity was intense, and I attacked a

---

[1] Edward Gordon Brettell was captured in September 1942 and was murdered by the Gestapo following his escape from Stalag Luft III in March 1944.

[2] Don Gentile later became one of the top aces of the American 4th Fighter Group, 8th AF. 30 victories. KIFA 1950.

Ju88 and a Dornier 217 but had to break off when we were jumped by a number of FW190s, one of which shot down my No 2, Pilot Officer Goodchap, who crash-landed and was taken prisoner. In the mêlée of Spitfires and 190s it was difficult to conclude an attack and I fired quick bursts at several aircraft without result. Fortunately we were relieved after an hour and able to return to refuel and rearm.

Squadron Leader Peter Brothers, OC 602 Squadron

As these battles raged above, the hour for withdrawal had arrived. The Royal Air Force was ready.

As with the dawn attack, Bostons and Hawker Hurricanes had been briefed to hit the German positions with bombs, cannon and smoke. Already the Hurricanes were flying in low and fast.

Flight Lieutenant W. W. McConnell DFC (BE405) and Flight Lieutenant de Soomer (HV365) led 174 Squadron off from Ford. They made rendezvous with 32 Squadron and two Spitfire squadrons as escort, 66 led by New Zealander Squadron Leader R. D. Yule DFC (EP686) and 118 Squadron. It was 66's first operation of the day, having been up and ready since 3 am.

No 174 Squadron made contact with the control ship (code-named 'Crowfoot') who directed them to hit the east headland. This they did at exactly 11 am, shortly after the attack by 87 Squadron. They dived into the smoke above the town letting go their 500 lb bombs. During a turn made over Dieppe itself, Pilot Officer R. L. N. Van Wymeersch (Free French) was hit by flak, the starboard wing of his Hurricane crumpling. He was last seen diving into the smoke out of control.[1] Heavy smoke obscured the targets so results of the bombing could not be seen. Two other Hurricanes failed to come out of the smoke, Flight Sergeant C. B. Watson, an Australian (BE505 XP–L) who was shot down into Dieppe harbour

---

[1] Raymond Léon Narcisse Van Wymeersch, aged 21, was wounded in the leg and taken prisoner. He was among the escapers from Stalag Luft III in March 1944, was recaptured and survived Gestapo interrogation. He escaped again in May, was recaptured and finally escaped in April 1945. He received the Legion of Honour, Croix de Guerre, Medaille de la Résistance, Croix de la Valeur Militaire and Medaille des Evédes. His father was shot as a member of the Resistance. Van Wymeersch remained in the French Air Force after the war.

to become a prisoner of war, and Sergeant Charles Frederick James who was killed.

No 32 Squadron, again led by Squadron Leader Thorn (Z3581) attacked the west headland. They too met heavy return fire and the smoke was very thick. In this attack Flight Lieutenant Harry Connolly, on his third sortie of the day, collided with his Number 2, Sergeant H. Stanage and crashed in flames. Stanage lost three feet from his port wing but managed to get home. Squadron Leader Thorn was awarded the DFC for his leadership at Dieppe.

Two further Hurricane squadrons made cannon attacks at this time, 3 and 43, code-named 'Seaport' and 'Rooky'. Alex Berry led his squadron against gun positions on the west headland. Flying Officer E. J. Pullen was hit by flak and turned for home. He seriously contemplated baling out but reached the English coast and made a crash landing on Brighton Golf Course.

No 43 attacked Bismarck, making one strafing run. They reported less flak than they met on their dawn attack although some of the Hurricanes received hits. 43 were assisted by the Spitfires of 129 Squadron led by Squadron Leader Rhys Thomas. 129, with 12 aircraft, (two having been borrowed from 130 Squadron) gave cover by flying in and using their cannons to strafe the beaches thereby helping to spread the German's return fire. They suffered no losses despite heavy return fire. Later 43 thanked 129 for this excellent cover. 129 also saw a pilot waving from a dinghy and hoped that this was Flying Officer Jones lost at dawn during the attack on Pointe D'Ailly lighthouse. Sadly Jones was beyond help.

Sixty-six Squadron escorted the Hurricanes in, then patrolled above the Dieppe anchorage before picking up the surviving Hurribombers to escort them home. They saw two Dornier 217s bombing the ships, seeing one shot down, but they themselves were not engaged. They returned to Tangmere without having fired a single shot in anger which ' . . . sadly disillusioned the Squadron armourers.' 118 Squadron likewise made no contact.

It was now the turn of the light bombers of 226 Squadron to attack. Squadron Leader Joseph Shaw Kennedy DFC (AL278 MQ–W) led four Bostons in, the target for their smoke bombs being the Hindenburg battery on the west headland. They had to blot out this gun position's aim now that the landing craft and launches were making for the shore. His three companions were Flight Lieutenant A. B. Wheeler (AL680 MQ–G), Pilot Officer W. R. Gellatly (L710 MQ–Z), and Sergeant W. Lyle (L680 MQ–L). They made their run-in despite heavy AA fire, successfully laying their smoke which effectively covered an area one to one and a half miles to seaward.

Two further Bostons from 226 also took off carrying smoke, which Sergeants T. Goodman (R708 MQ–M) and L. G. Littel (L736 MQ–P) successfully trailed from fifty feet for a mile or more over the Dieppe beach. All aircraft had to fly through a curtain of flak from both the Germans, and, due to the ever increasing Luft-waffe presence, AA fire from 'friendly' ships.

The first four Bostons received the worst of the fire, Kennedy's Boston being hit forcing him to make a crash landing at Shoreham. His gunner, Flying Officer George A. Casey, a Canadian, was wounded while Flight Lieutenant O. G. E. McWilliams, who had gone along as a passenger, was hit by a cannon shell and killed. Shaw Kennedy was awarded a bar to his DFC for his leadership, while Casey received the DFC. Kennedy's observer, Flying Officer Harold Asker DFM also received the DFC.

Pilot Officer Gellatly's machine also received flak damage, his gunner, Pilot Officer L. J. Waters being killed, and his observer, Pilot Officer F. G. Starkie, was wounded. Gellatly had to belly-land his Boston at Gatwick.

Nos 302 and 308 Polish Squadrons led by Flight Lieutenant S. Lapka (EN865) and Squadron Leader Walerian Zak, holder of the Virtuti Militari, escorted the six Bostons and safely brought them home.

Thirty-six Spitfires from 81, 131 and the American 309th Squadrons flew escort to a further Boston raid mounted by 88 Squadron and led by Squadron Leader Richard Geoffrey England DFC (Z2229). He led the Bostons into an attack against gun positions on the east headland, having taken off from Ford at 11.23. Their bombs were seen to straddle the target. The Spitfires saw little enemy aircraft activity, although the 309th lost one Spitfire, the pilot taking to his parachute.

Under cover of the smoke screens the small boats ran in upon Green and Blue beaches. German gunners fired blindly into the smoke, heavy guns, mortars and machine-guns sending death and destruction in among the boats and soldiers. Many soldiers were picked up only to be thrown back into the sea as their craft were hit, sunk or turned over. However, the struggle went on, and as the smoke began to thin out and disperse other aircraft were already on their way to re-lay the precious protective cloud.

The Blenheims of 614 Squadron had left Thruxton at ten to eleven, flying out in two formations, escorted by 306 Polish Squadron from Northolt. One Boston of 226 had also left Thruxton and with another lone machine from 88 Squadron, headed for Dieppe, escorted by the Canadians of 411 Squadron. 411 had been briefed to escort the Blenheims but failed to meet up with them but seeing the two Bostons, decided to cover them instead. 13 Squadron also despatched three Blenheims but their fighter escort indicated that they were returning to base and so they too turned back.

Meanwhile, the Spitfires above were still bitterly engaged. 350 Squadron after their earlier battle, had reported that enemy fighter opposition had increased and that the bombers were still attempting to bomb the ships. With the landing craft trying to pick up troops from all the beaches, this Luftwaffe activity had indeed increased.

Thirty-six Spitfires of the Debden Wing set out at approximately ten minutes to eleven o'clock, arriving at their patrol area at 11.15. Also, three further squadrons, two from Hawkinge (416 and 616) and one from Redhill (312) were away at the same time to reinforce the battle area.

The three Debden squadrons, led by Wing Commander Duke-Woolley, formed up over Beachy Head and made their way out across the Channel at zero feet, rising to 10,000 feet ten minutes later. They found the air full of enemy aircraft and the squadrons were split up. Tommy Balmforth's 124 Squadron broke into three sections over the anchorage and saw over twenty enemy aircraft, 217s, 88s and escorting 190s. Flight Lieutenant William Gregson, Red 1, (BR587) and his Number 2, turned with Red 3 and 4 to attack. Then two 190s came screaming in from the south. Gregson attacked the leading Focke Wulf from the beam, giving it a two second burst from 200 yards. Strikes appeared on the German fighter and a small flash emanated from under its port wing-root. A panel ripped back and the port undercarriage leg flopped down. The 190 turned, dived away and was lost to view. Gregson then saw another 190 pulling out of a dive right in front of him. This 190 had yellow bars painted horizontally on its engine cowling. He climbed quickly behind it and fired both cannon and machine-guns from 200 yards. The 190's pilot obviously had no idea that Gregson was upon him and Gregson saw an explosion behind the FW's cockpit and bits fly off. Smoke and flame belched back and the 190 dived, went into a spin and crashed just off the beach east of Dieppe having practically disintegrated in the air. This was confirmed by his 2 and 3, Pilot Officers B. R. Murphy and M. P. Kilburn.

Flight Sergeant Peter Durnford DFM, White 3, (BR569) attacked a 190 from 200 yards and it caught fire and went down – he claimed a probable. He then spotted a Ju88 at 2,000 feet and closed to 300 yards. The German pilot dived down to tree top height; Durnford attacked again from 250 yards, seeing hits on its port engine. The Junkers jettisoned its bombs and then crashed into a field with its engine on fire and stopped. His camera-gun later identified the German machine as a Dornier 217.

Pilot Officer Michael Kilburn (BR579) attacked a FW which he saw climbing away following an attack on a Spitfire. He opened fire at 250 yards keeping his guns firing down to 100 yards. Many strikes sparkled over the fighter which half-rolled and dived. Kilburn attacked again and the 190 continued down in an inverted dive and went straight into the sea.

Sergeant J. B. Shanks was seen to go down and crash-land near Dieppe where he was taken prisoner.

Squadron Leader McDowell (BL806 EF–B) and his 232 Squadron led by Duke-Woolley was bounced by a FW190 who shot down two Spitfires. Flight Lieutenant Percy Strong (EF–Y) and his wingman Sergeant Kenneth George Walker (EF–M), a 20-year-old pilot from Bournemouth, were lost, Walker being seen to lose his port wing.

'My saddest recollection is when I led a squadron new to the scene on its first offensive operation. Our job was to patrol the anchorage at around 3,000 feet, and that leaves hardly any room to do anything but show the flag to those below and to distract the attention of enemy aircraft. The other squadrons of the Wing, deployed up to

11

DIEPPE N

1. BASSIN DE MI-MARÈE
2. DRY DOCK.

W. JETTY E. JETTY

ENTRANCE

OUTER HARBOUR

INNER HARBOUR

1
2.

59.49°51'30"N. 01°04'E. 40.W.5".29.C. 40.BW. 326<HEAD

10.   Flight Lieutenant Gus Daymond and Squadron Leader Chesley Peterson of 71 Eagle Squadron. Peterson was shot down off Dieppe but was rescued. Daymond flew four missions, leading 71 on the unit's last patrol. *(via R. C. Bowyer)*

11.   Aerial photo of Dieppe and its harbour from 10,000 ft.

20,000 feet or so as top cover alone had much chance of engaging on reasonable terms. All I could do was to give a new squadron a safe view of the operation, ensure that no low-fliers sneaked up on our craft below and not expose ourselves to any stray attack which eluded the top cover. I reckoned normally to spot enemy fighters a long way off – it was an essential skill, if you like, and needed a lot of practice. But on that third sortie one German fighter dived out of the sun from a great height, attacked us head-on, and I did not see him until he was maybe 600 yards away and firing. Our continued closing speed was probably around 800 mph, say 400 yards a second, and I failed to react in the second or second-and-a-half at my disposal.

'He shot down two aircraft in the squadron I was leading and both pilots were killed. We could do nothing but carry on and the squadron most commendably did not waver. The German's attack was skilful and right from the eye of a blazing sun in a cloudless sky and in those conditions quick positive identification is very difficult. But I have always felt that I should have seen him coming. To illustrate the point of lack of manoeuvre, let me digress for a moment.

'I had the Debden Wing for 7 or 8 months on offensive operations of all sorts, including low-level ground attack as well as fighter sweeps and bomber escort operations. During that time we were credited with 52 enemy aircraft destroyed (apart from probables and damaged) and we lost a total of four pilots. In that one attack over Dieppe, with a squadron attached to the Wing for the day, I lost two pilots for nothing in return. It was bad, and a sad business but part of the sort of price you incurred (I suppose) by being pegged on a leash with a small fixed area in which to "work". We were sitting ducks, really, and unfortunately were singled out by a first-class poacher.'

Wing Commander Myles Duke-Woolley, OC Debden Wing

*

The Eagle pilots of 71 Squadron, led by Squadron Leader Peterson (BM361) had a brief brush with enemy aeroplanes, Peterson damaging a Ju88.

Pilot Officer Stanley M. Anderson, from Indiana, (BL376) noted in his flying log book:

Airborne Gravesend 1045 – Beachy Head 1100 – Convoy 1120. Our job to protect shipping – town on fire – resistance was evident.

As the Eagle pilots looked down they could see two ships on fire in Dieppe harbour. As Peterson was to remark when he returned and was climbing out of his Spitfire: 'It's like a goddam 4th of July.' 'Strick' Strickland recorded in his diary:

We arrived over patrol area at Dieppe with many air combats in progress. Blue Section attacked and chased away 109s believed to be carrying bombs. Dornier 217s and Ju 88s were chased away after jettisoning their bombs. Enemy reaction was reaching its peak. We encountered terrific flak and on two occasions flew through our own flak manoeuvering for position. Many fires were burning in Dieppe. Many stores and ammunition dumps several miles from the centre of the town were ablaze. Many of our assault boats were wrecked and burned on the beach. A continuous fire was put up by the naval forces against Varengeville, Dieppe and Berneval.

We returned, refuelled and re-armed but in using my emergency boost in combats, excessive oil accumulated on my windscreen. I traded places with O'Regan [Pilot Officer W. T. O'Regan from Los Angeles] and flew formation on him. With my propeller defective my Spitfire (BL499 XR–P) was unserviceable for the third sortie which I missed.

Peterson's scrap with his Ju88 was the only combat claim. After this skirmish, Flying Officer R. S. (Bob) Sprague spotted a pilot in a dinghy and radioed a fix for the ASR boys.

Twelve aircraft of 312 Czech Squadron led by Squadron Leader J. Cermak (EN841) flew out via Beachy Head, reaching Dieppe at 11.20. During their 30-minute patrol several FW190s were encountered, Flight Sergeant T. Motycka and Flight Sergeant V. Ruprecht each claiming a probable while Pilot Officer V. Smotik damaged another. Sergeant J. Liskutin's Spitfire was damaged.

Squadron Leader Lloyd Chadburn (EP110) led his Canadians over the ships at 6,000 feet with Squadron Leader Harry Brown's 616 Squadron above as High Cover. Some 50 Focke Wulf 190s were seen by 616 Squadron and a lone Dornier. This bomber was attacked by Flight Lieutenant F. O. A. Gaze and was claimed as destroyed, while Flight Lieutenant J. S. Fifield, Flying Officer G. B. Maclachlan, Pilot Officer J. H. Smithson and Sergeant M. Cooper each damaged a 190. Sergeant N. G. Welch's Spitfire was damaged but he made a successfully belly landing at base. Sergeant N. W. J. Coldray, a Rhodesian, failed to return.

Some of the 190s dived right through the top cover squadron but did not get too close to the Canadians below, although some of the latter gave them the odd 'squirt'.

Below them, the Blenheims and Bostons were now approaching Dieppe.

No 614 Squadron were split into two formations for this mission. Wing Commander H. C. Sutton (V5534) led five Blenheims (originally six but one had to abort due to engine trouble) piloted by Squadron Leader P. D. Le Cheminet (V6002), Pilot Officers P. H. C. Hanbury (R3758), C. P. C. De Wesselow (N3536), R. L. W. Baely (V5808). The second group of three Blenheims was led by Pilot Officer D. Smyth (V6078) with Pilots Officers C. H. Georges (Z6104) and M. E. Porter (Z6173).

All laid smoke successfully; Smyth's section went in without their fighter escort due to their failure to rendezvous with 411 Squadron. Robert Newton's Canadians, however, latched onto the two Bostons from 226 and 88, who had been briefed to lay smoke over the harbour entrance. Pilot Officer Robert James Corrigan RCAF, 27 years of age (an American who enlisted in Quebec) led the two-man formation (L736 MQ–P), the 88 Squadron machine being piloted by Sergeant Savage (Z2216 RH–F). Both met heavy flak but they laid a good smoke screen over the east jetty and cliffs at 11.52 am. Moments later Corrigan's Boston was hit by the groping flak and it crashed into the sea two miles off Dieppe, Corrigan was killed and so was his gunner, Sergeant William Osselton, aged 23 from Wallsend, Northumberland. Only the observer, Sergeant S. Moth survived although he was wounded.

No 416 Squadron still above saw the Boston go in on fire and 411 too saw it crash into the sea with one engine in flames and disintegrate. 306 Squadron covered the Blenheims as they withdrew and during the return one pilot found a dinghy and radioed a fix.

While all this activity was in progress, 91 Squadron was still sending out its Jim Crow patrols. At 10.45 am Sergeant C. H. Evans (DL–A) took off to recce. the Ostend area but developed engine trouble. He baled out safely having radioed a Mayday call. Warrant Officer R. Knowlton and Flight Sergeant J. Rose of 277 Squadron scrambled from Hawkinge to search for him off Deal. They found him without too much difficulty and directed a rescue launch to the spot twenty-five miles off the English coast.

Meantime, Pilot Officer I. G. S. Matthew (DL–T) flew an Air Sea Rescue patrol off Ramsgate and found one pilot in his dinghy.

The ever watchful Mustangs were also out. 239 Squadron sent Flying Officer Philip A. L. Gompertz (AM134) out at 11 o'clock to reconnoitre the roads from Le Tréport to Envernay to Blangy. Gompertz, who had lost his Weaver on an earlier mission, went out alone. He was aged 21 and the son of Lieutenant Colonel A. C. Gompertz MC RE, of Watchfield, Berkshire; he failed to return.

No 414 Squadron had sent out Flight Lieutenant F. E. Clarke (AG375) and his Weaver Flying Officer H. H. Hills (AG470) at 10.25 am to cover the Gamaches, Neufchatel, St Victor and Quiville areas. During the mission Hills' radio packed up and he was unable to contact his leader. This deficiency became acute when three Focke Wulf 190s came into view and attacked them. Unable to warn Clarke of the immediate danger, Hollis Hills, an American volunteer from Los Angeles, serving with the RCAF, battled with the 190s even though Clarke's Mustang was hit. Later Clarke recorded this account of the scrap.

Flying Officer Hills and I took off to carry out a reconnaissance of the Dieppe area. Flying Officer Hills was flying cover for me. We crossed the French coast at St Aubin-sur-Mer and I picked up the road which was my task and had followed it in behind Dieppe. Then I was jumped by a Focke Wulfe 190 which shot my oil and glycol cooler away. I immediately turned tight left and three-quarters of the way round the turn I saw that my oil pressure was nil. My engine started to seize. I immediately straightened out, used my excess speed to gain height to about 800 feet and headed for the sea off Dieppe. Just before straightening out, on my port rear quarter I saw a FW190 with grey smoke pouring from it heading towards a wood apparently out of control. In my opinion it was impossible for the pilot to do anything but pile up in the wood. This is definitely the aircraft which Flying Officer Hills claims as destroyed.

This 190 had been on Clarke's tail when Hills shot at it, and it was the first confirmed kill by a Mustang in the war. Clarke, meantime, struggled over the coast near Dieppe, surrounded by bursting AA shells from both the Germans and the ships off shore, the Mustang looking very much like a Messerschmitt 109 from certain angles. However, he got his Mustang down to ditch successfully in the sea although he cut his forehead in the splashdown. He was fished out of the water by a destroyer, probably HMS *Calpe*. Hollis Hills landed back at Gatwick at 11.40.

Ten minutes earlier, at 11.30 am, 414 Squadron sent out its last pair of Mustangs of the Dieppe operation, Flight Lieutenant J. A. Amos (AM160) and Flying Officer R. C. MacQuoid, to cover the Trouville, Cleres, Cailly and Toray areas. MacQuoid, however, was hit by flak and forced to abandon the mission.

No 400 Squadron also sent out Flight Lieutenant L Bissky and Flying Officer Stephens at 10:35. They completed their Tac/R patrol and successfully evaded the attentions of two FW190s off Le Tréport. At 11.32, Pilot Officer G. A. Rogers and Pilot Officer Roberts flew a recce sortie and spotted three or possibly five light tanks heading towards Dieppe along the Rouen-Dieppe Road. This sighting report was quickly radioed through to 11 Group HQ, and a bomb strike was immediately set in motion. Bostons of 107 and 88 Squadrons were alerted.

*

At Duxford, Wing Commander Denys Gillam DSO DFC AFC, former Battle of Britain pilot and late CO of 615 Squadron, briefed all three of his Typhoon squadrons at 9 o'clock, referring to the 8 am news broadcast announcing the raid.

I attended a conference at Fighter Command a few days before the Dieppe Raid and at that time the Duxford Wing of Typhoons was not involved. However, I pressed the case very strongly and had a very 'wordy' battle with Group Captain Broadhurst as he did not wish to use the Typhoon squadrons but Air Marshal

Leigh-Mallory over-ruled him and we were assigned to cover the beach-head at low level during the day. This we did, refuelling at West Malling.

Wing Commander Denys Gillam, OC Duxford Wing

Gillam's three squadrons were, 56, commanded by Squadron Leader H. S. L. Dundas DFC, 266, commanded by Squadron Leader C. L. Green (a Rhodesian, commanding this Rhodesian squadron), and 609, whose 'boss' was Squadron Leader P. H. M. Richey DFC and bar. 'Cocky' Dundas, like Gillam, was a former Battle of Britain pilot while Paul Richey had won his first DFC in France during the Blitzkreig. He later wrote his well-known book *Fighter Pilot* based on his experiences in France.

The Typhoon Wing took off at 11 am led by Gillam (R7698). Their sortie was to make rendezvous with nine calibration Defiant aircraft off Clacton and fly with them to within ten miles off Ostend. It was hoped that this would look to the Germans on their radar screens like a bombing raid, which would allow the new Typhoons to have a chance of engaging any enemy aircraft enticed up to investigate them. The Typhoons picked up the Defiants off Orfordness at 11.15, 609 escorting them at 18,000 feet, led by Richey (R7752), 56 led by Dundas (R7825) while Green led 266 (R7686). As they neared Ostend the Typhoons flew ahead of the Defiants, then swept along the coast as far as Mardyck, but no hostile aircraft came up (they were far too busy over Dieppe) and they saw nothing. After the mission the Typhoon pilots flew to West Malling.

The Wing took off to sweep down the enemy coast from Dunkirk to Calais without result before landing at West Malling .... Richey taking the opportunity for some close formation practice on the way back.

Malling was hot and dusty in the August sunshine and appeared to be almost submerged in fighters as we taxied in past squadrons of Spitfires, Hurricane bombers and Beaufighters. Then, after a quick refuelling we were back in the cockpits awaiting the green Very light which would signal 'start up'.

Flight Lieutenant Roland Beamont, 609 Squadron

CHAPTER EIGHT

Dog-fights over Dieppe
12 noon to 1.30 pm

As the landing craft braved the deadly return fire from Dieppe as they took off as many of the surviving Canadians as they could, the Luftwaffe maintained a constant stream of fighters and bombers high above. The RAF's air umbrella, while it occasionally let a few droplets through, managed to keep off the main deluge from the ships below.

David Scott-Malden's two Norwegian Squadrons, 331 and 332, joined with the Canadians of 403 Squadron to cover the ships at this time, having left Manston at 11.15. They arrived on station at ten minutes to noon. Flying high above them as top cover were 485 and 610 Squadrons. Heavy smoke from Dieppe rose into the air, rising in some places to over 3,000 feet and fierce fires could be seen raging.

Major Helge Mehre's 331 Squadron was attacked by Focke Wulfs, one Spitfire being damaged but then Dorniers were encountered and the Norwegians went after them. Captain Anton C. Hagerup (BM295) and Second Lieutenant Helge Sognnes went down on one bomber which fell away in flames and hit the sea. Sergeant F. S. Fearnly claimed another probably destroyed while Lieutenants Einar Sem-Olsen and Tarold Weisteen damaged others. Scott-Malden flying with 331 (AB202) directed the battle as 332 encountered six more bombers coming in from the south-east.

Sergeant Olav Djonne (AB184) attacked one which dived away seriously damaged. He watched three of the bomber's crew bale out before the German pilot crash-landed on the beach. The pilot was later seen standing by his machine in the water looking at his broken aeroplane. Sergeant Marius Erikson (BL634) turned after two of the Dorniers, opening fire on one of them. One crewman baled out but his parachute failed to open, then the Dornier turned over onto its back and dived steeply from 2,000 feet. Black smoke

12, 13, 14. Three of the Norwegians at Dieppe. Fred Fearnley of 331 Squadron (killed in action 25 February, 1944). (13) Janeigil Lofsgaard of 322 Squadron (killed in action 11 October, 1942). (14) Einer Sem-Olsen of 331 Squadron (killed in action 29 November, 1942). *(Norwegian Forsvaramuseet)*

12

14

13

poured from it and Erikson lost sight of it but then saw a lot of oil and wreckage floating on the sea where it went down.

At about 1,500 – 2,000 feet just off the coast they (about 5 to 8) came flying outwards towards our ships and one of them I got. It was a mad chase. Can also remember a Spitfire appearing in my sights (from underneath) and I was firing my guns. After all, we had for so long been waiting a chance like this – all of us. It was the first time we had seen a 217, it had some kind of dive-brakes as far as I remember.

Sergeant Marius Erikson, 332 Norwegian Squadron

Sergeant Janeigil Lofsgaard fired twice at another Dornier. It went straight down and hit the water with a big splash but Lofsgaard's Spitfire was hit by the German's top gunner and he had to bale out. Two pilots of 331 circled as he parachuted down, one being Lieutenant Martin Gran. Lofsgaard was rescued and landed ashore safely an hour later. Meanwhile Captain Finn Thorsager (EP283) and Sergeant O. Fuglesang (W3647) saw a Dornier on fire and finished it off, the bomber crashing into the sea.

Wing Commander Scott-Malden was also credited with the destruction of a Dornier during this action. However, he is not that certain that it was all his. Several pilots were firing at several bombers. He recalls one going down ahead of him, its top gunner gallantly returning fire, but in his log-book he only recorded a possible.

By the end of their patrol, the Canadians of 403, flying at between 2,500 – 3,000 feet saw enemy aircraft approaching. 403's CO, Squadron Leader Les Ford (BM344) swung behind a 190, fired at it from close range and it fell to pieces, parts of it hitting his wingman's Spitfire – Pilot Officer R. Wozniak, but is suffered no serious damage. The 190 burst into flames and went down over the Dieppe waterfront.

Flight Lieutenant P. T. O'Leary (AD329) got in a burst at a 190 from 150 yards. Black smoke streamed back before it disappeared into a cloud. Flight Lieutenant George Hill (EN858) hit another Focke Wulf from 100 yards and this too was lost to view as it went into cloud pouring out smoke. Hill was immediately after another 190 which he hit from 250 yards. It fell away out of control swaying violently. His combat film supported his claim for this 190 being destroyed. Sergeant A. L. Haynes also fired at a 190 but saw no results.

In total the Norwegians and Canadians claimed five Dorniers (but probably only three were actually destroyed) plus three damaged, plus two FW190s destroyed with two more damaged.

Bob Grant, leading his New Zealand pilots of 485 Squadron (BM417) at 9,000 feet, saw the lower squadrons shoot down four Dorniers but at their higher level they were not engaged. Johnnie Johnson leading 619 saw four FW190s, however, and chased them inland. Denis Crowley-Milling was flying just off to one side of Johnson and as they chased after the 190s, huge black clouds towered high above the French countryside. The 190s stood out against this dark blackcloth in stark relief. Johnson opened fire from 800 yards, trying a long shot. Then Crow fired at a second Focke Wulf being rewarded by seeing a puff of black smoke blow back from his target. They were gradually closing but suddenly from the rear came a warning to break! The leading Spitfires of Johnson, Crowley-Milling and their wingmen broke away only to find it was a false alarm and the 190s disappeared into the clouds.

No 610 had also seen the Dorniers low down, or at least four of them, but they were all accounted for before they could engage. The pilots of 610 were, however, highly pleased that they, in their Spitfire Vs, had held their own with the Focke Wulfs and during that brief chase into France had actually started to close with them.

The air was now full of whirling Spitfires covering the withdrawal. As Scott-Malden's wing was ending their patrol period, sixty Spitfires from 19, 121, 122, 154 and 350 Squadrons, plus twelve Spitfire IXs of 64 Squadron, arrived over the ships at twenty minutes past mid-day.

Squadron Leader Bill Williams led 121 Squadron out from Southend (EN853) in company with 19 Squadron. The weather over Dieppe and the Channel was beginning to deteriorate; rain clouds were massing over France and gradually coming into the battle area.

No 121 were not engaged to any great degree, although Flight Lieutenant W. J. Daley DFC (AA841) had his Spitfire hit by a shell which produced a large hole in the starboard side of its tailplane.

The engine cut out and Jimmy Daley was about to bale out when it suddenly restarted.[1]

Nineteen Squadron led by Pat Davies (AR364) had crossed Beachy Head at 1,500 feet to climb slowly towards Dieppe. Flying then at 4,000 feet they spied four or five unidentified aircraft up sun at 20,000 feet. Four FW190s then climbed out of clouds at 3,000 feet but seeing the Spitfires just above, dived back in. Two Dorniers were encountered briefly and Flight Lieutenant C. F. Bradley (EN971) fired at them but saw no results.

Squadron Leader Kilian (BL812) led his 122 Squadron out at 10,000 feet, flying a wide orbit off Dieppe and saw 154 Squadron dive down after a Dornier. More Dorniers were seen, 122 having a free-for-all fight against them. Flight Lieutenant L. P. Griffiths and Pilot Officer R. van de Poel fired but made no claims. Kilian and his section chased another Dornier but were attacked by eight FWs. One 190 fired at Kilian and a single bullet hit his tailplane, travelled the length of the Spitfire's fuselage, smashed the perspex cockpit cover and finally took a chunk out of the propeller. The broken perspex blew in, slightly lacerating Kilian's forehead.

Sergeant D. Mercer chased a Dornier across the French coast and last saw it apparently trying to belly-land five miles south of St Aubin.

Don Carlson (BM476) commanding 154 Squadron, saw the Dorniers, or at least one Dornier, and came down from 18,000 feet to attack it. The Dornier was flying towards France at 6,500 feet. Nine of 154's pilots all attacked it and literally tore it to pieces. With both engines burning furiously as well as the forward nacelle area, it crash landed about ten miles inland from Cayeux. The victorious nine were, Carlson, Flight Lieutenant G. A. Harrison, Flying Officer A. S. Turnbull, Pilot Officers M. Davies, H. W. Chambers, I. T. Garrett, Warrant Officer J. G. Buiron and Sergeants J. S. Whaley and F. J. Flote.

No 350 Squadron found a lone Ju88 which was attacked by Pilot Officers H. J. Smets, A. M. Plisnier, and Sergeants F. E. Boute, and J. L. Vanterberghe. This 88 lost part of its tail and crashed into the sea. The Spitfire IXs flown by 64 Squadron also encountered Dor-

---

[1] The following month Daley became a Major in the USAAF and given command of the 335th Fighter Squadron, 8th AF.

niers. Flight Lieutenant Don Kingaby DFM and two bars, shot down one which crashed eight miles behind Dieppe – his 19th victory. Squadron Leader Duncan-Smith claimed another and shared a second with Flight Sergeant W. J. Batchelor (BR980); Flight Lieutenant Tommy Thomas DFC (BR625) damaged a Messerschmitt 109E. The squadron lost one pilot, Sergeant Eric Norman McCuaig, a married man from Sterlingshire. He was reported buried at sea.

At exactly 12-noon two more Spitfire squadrons took off to patrol over the ships and the evacuation, 242 from Manston and 340 from Hornchurch.

Meanwhile, Bostons of 88 and 107 Squadrons reached Dieppe shortly after mid-day, escorted by 81, 131 and the 309th Fighter Squadron. 107 had been briefed to attack the Hindenberg battery which was firing on both the ships and the soldiers on the beaches and sea front. 88 Squadron led by Squadron Leader Desmond Griffiths with Squadron Leader Richard England, again went for Rommel.

An hour or so after returning [from his first mission] I led a further raid on the same target, but this time I had twelve Bostons with me, and we were met by a considerable force of our own fighters over the sea who remained with us throughout the raid. They prevented any enemy aircraft from approaching us and we managed to score many direct hits on the target. All aircraft returned safely but some were damaged by the heavy flak over the target area.

Squadron Leader Desmond Griffiths, 88 Squadron

Squadron Leader A. M. Phillips (AL266 OM–T) led 107 Squadron in against Hindenburg but cloud was beginning to obscure the target area. Too late the first box of Bostons saw the German battery through the cloud. They decided to chance an attack from 3,000 feet at exactly 12.10 pm. Owing to a slight misunderstanding seven 500 lb bombs fell into the sea but 17 more were seen to hit the target area. The second box bombed through a gap in the clouds from 5,000 feet. The attack left a heavy pall of smoke over Dieppe. The pilots on these raids were:

88 Squadron: S/Ldr Griffiths, W/O Gallant, Sgt Simpkins, F/Lt Adams, P/O Peppiett, Sgt Mayne, S/Ldr England, P/O Abbott, P/O Powell, P/O Grundy, P/O Campbell, Sgt Carpenter.

107 Squadron: S/Ldr Phillips, F/Sgt Reid, Sgt Simpson, P/O Rushton, P/O Hall, P/O Turner, F/Lt Carlisle, Sgt Scott, P/Os Healey, Crump, Burley and Brewer.

Their escort fighters saw little enemy activity although the 309th lost one Spitfire, its pilot parachuting down into the Channel.

Nos 242 and 340 Squadrons arrived over the ships to find enemy air activity just as strong. Squadron Leader Parker (BM539) took his pilots over at 5,000 feet and he was attacked by a FW190. Parker sustained hits on his port wing and undercarriage wheel cover. One bullet blasted a hole in the left side of his cockpit canopy and he was lucky to escape injury. Sergeant W. C. Meachen attacked a Ju88 which was going for the ships and drove it away. Sergeant J. H. Watling also drove off a Dornier.

The Frenchmen of 340 Squadron flew above at 12,000 feet and several pilots attacked a Dornier whose crew was seen to bale out.

Flight Sergeant W. D. Waddington and Flight Sergeant R. C. Glew of 277 Squadron took off from Hawkinge. Off Dungeness they saw a Spitfire crash into the sea. They circled the spot, saw oil but no sign of its pilot.

Ten minutes after 107 Squadron had bombed, 111 Squadron led by Peter Wickham (EP166) led his pilots away from Kenley. Five minutes later, at 12.25 pm, 133 Eagle Squadron left Lympne and 402 also lifted off from Kenley, while Desmond McMullen led 65 Squadron away from Eastchurch. When these squadrons reached Dieppe they were, with the exception of 65, each engaged by enemy aircraft.

No 111 Squadron met Dorniers and Focke Wulfs. Flight Lieutenant F. H. R. Baraldi, B Flight commander, and Sergeant Y. Henrickson, a Norwegian pilot, each damaged a Dornier while Pilot Officer B. E. Gale, an Australian, damaged a 190. They lost Sergeant Edward James Hindley, from Birmingham, who was killed.

Don Blakeslee led 133 (EN951 MD–U) and they too met Dorniers. Flying Officer James Nelson probably destroyed one whilst Flight Sergeant R. L. (Dixie) Alexander claimed one destroyed.

On the third operation I shot down a Do217; he crashed in a field south-west of Dieppe. In this show, and in the following, I was flying MD–J. [MD–J] is still active in the Battle of Britain flight; it was for a time owned and flown by Max Aitken. I was privileged to see it, and sit in the cockpit, during our reunion in London.[1]

Flight Sergeant Dixie Alexander, 133 Squadron

Don Blakeslee knocked pieces off a Focke Wulf. While over Dieppe the Americans saw two small ships and a destroyer receive bomb hits.

The Canadians of 402 led by Norman Bretz, found Dorniers and Junkers bombing at 12.50 pm. They were at 15,000 feet, the Germans 5,000 feet below. Bretz led his men down and singled out an escorting FW190, fired, and saw cannon strikes blast a large chunk off the German fighter. His Number 3 saw it begin to trail smoke. Flight Lieutenant E. A. Bland damaged another 190 and Pilot Officer G. N. Keith knocked pieces off a third. These particular FW190s carried a six inch yellow stripe around their wings, about three feet from the wing root, and a narrow yellow band around their wing tips.

While these almost continuous and terrific fighter versus fighter or fighter versus bomber combats were in progress, the four Bostons from 107 and two from 88 Squadrons, ordered up in response to the sighting of tanks on the Rouen-Dieppe road were approaching the French coast, escorted by 130 Squadron.

Flight Lieutenant R. Maclachlan (AL738) of 107 led the formation, with Pilot Officers Hammond, Russell and Allen piloting the others. 88's Bostons were piloted by Pilot Officer Hughes and Sergeant Rand. However, on searching the road they could find no sign of the tanks and rather than bring their bombs back, 107 flew to the west of Dieppe and bombed the railway at Ouville, their

---

[1] AB910 now coded QJ–J, served with 222, 130, 133, 242, 402, 416 and 527 Sqdns. Later with 53 OTU at Hibaldstow, it was involved in an incident when the pilot took off with a WRAF hanging to the tailplane.

500 lb bombs being dropped from 5,000 feet at 1.29 pm. The two 88 Bostons, being unable to locate the target, jettisoned their bombs in woods near Le Tréport.

Crossing the coast, their fighter escort spotted four Ju88s below. Blue 1 and 2, Flight Lieutenant P. L. Arnott and Sergeant A. W. Braybrooke damaged one. A few 190s were also engaged shortly afterwards, Pilot Officer R. P. Leblond claiming a probable. 'I remember having a squirt at a FW190 but to no effect,' said Squadron Leader P. J. Simpson, OC of 130 Squadron.

Some quite heavy clouds began to roll in over Dieppe. At first they remained high enough not to interfere with the air operations. However, they did make it possible for some squadrons, either below or above them, to see nothing of the Luftwaffe, while others were hotly engaged with German aeroplanes.

There was a slight lull in the German air activity at around 1 o'clock. It was brief and those squadrons who patrolled at that time saw little of the enemy and when they were close by, the cloud obscured them. The two American fighter squadrons, the 307th and 308th, arrived over Dieppe just after 1 pm, had a brush with enemy fighters, losing one Spitfire. At 1.20 pm 47 Spitfires of the Polish Wing, 302, 303, 308 and 317 Squadrons, took their turn to cover the withdrawal, being joined by 71, 222 and 611 Squadrons. They had mixed fortunes.

No 302 led by Flight Lieutenant M. Chelmecki (EN861) saw nothing and Squadron Leader Zak's 308 Squadron also found an empty sky. 317 led by Flight Lieutenant Marian Trzebinski (AR424) saw a few 190s but did not engage them. This was no doubt a disappointment to at least two of the Polish pilots, Wing Commander Tadeusz Rolski and Squadron Leader Teofil Nowierski who had come from Fighter Command HQ to get a part of the action. This was Nowierski's second sortie of the day.

These three squadrons were patrolling above the clouds but 303 were below them. They found the Luftwaffe. 303 flew in at 5,000 feet and saw 20 FW190s attacking the ships and they saw a large ship explode. It was of such force that the shock wave was felt at 303's height. This explosion was also seen by 222 and 308 Squadrons.

The Poles dived down on the Focke Wulfs, and Flying Officer

Eugeniusz Horbaczewski (AR366) sent one of them into the sea; its pilot baled out. Sergeant S. Stasik (BL574) claimed another while Flight Sergeant M. Popek (BL670) shared a third.

The Biggin Hill Wing, 222 and 611 in company with 71 Eagle Squadron from Gravesend, also had mixed fortunes. 222 again led by Bobby Oxspring saw nothing. 611 led by Douglas Watkins flew at 23,000 feet and saw little activity. Flight Lieutenant Crawford-Compton, Pilot Officer A. H. Friday and Pilot Officer Prince Emanuel Galitzine (611's 'Fighting Russian') were surprised and bounced by some 190s but none of them was hit. However, the Eagles, led by Duke-Woolley (EP179) were lower and found the bombers. Squadron Leader Chesley Peterson shot down a Ju88 which Duke-Woolley saw go into the sea. However, the 88's rear gunner managed to get in a telling burst at Peterson's Spitfire. His cockpit rapidly filled with smoke and the American quickly jettisoned his hood and baled out. As he floated down he remembered his revolver which he carried in his flying boot. Realizing that he would lose this in the sea he pulled it out and fired off all the rounds to his complete satisfaction before throwing the gun into the water. Seconds later he too hit the sea, being rescued within minutes by a Naval MTB. This did not end his adventures for the boat was strafed by German fighters later and an RAF pilot, similarly rescued, was killed as he sat next to Peterson. For Peterson, this day's action was the culmination of an extensive period with the first Eagle Squadron and he was awarded the DSO for this and previous actions.

Meanwhile, Flight Lieutenant Oscar H. Coen DFC (BM293), Blue 1, and Flying Officer 'Wee' Michael McPharlin (W3767) his Number 2, damaged another Junkers sufficiently to substantiate a claim for a probable. Coen emptied his guns into the bomber's port engine which belched out black smoke in addition to pieces being blasted from both wing and engine. The 88 let go its bombs as McPharlin attacked and then the 88 dived violently to the right. As the two Americans dived after it, flames began to flicker near the port wing root, but then they saw some Focke Wulfs and they had to leave the bomber still diving at 1,500 feet five miles off the French coast.

McPharlin's Spitfire was also hit by return fire, and his compass was damaged. Flying into cloud to evade the 190s he lost his way and eventually he ran out of petrol and had to bale out but was rescued by the Royal Navy. Pilot Officer Stanley Anderson (BL376) damaged a third Ju88 which he and Pilot Officer B. D. McMinn went after; Anderson's fire hit it and apparently silenced the rear gunner.

A happier, and rather funny, recollection was of an Eagle pilot ... who was shot down about three miles off the coast. He baled out successfully and duly organised himself into the single-seat inflatable dinghy which we all carried – sitting on them as part of the parachute pack. Bobbing up and down he could intermittently see the French coast and determined to avoid capture he started to paddle north for England. He then decided that it would take some time to get home and that an energy boost would help. So he ferreted into his escape kit, which included Horlicks and Oxo tablets – and benzedrine. Seizing on the benzedrine he took the lot and, super-charged with zeal and a feeling that for hours he would become a human dynamo, he thrashed away with the hand paddles. One suspects he resembled a sort of static whirling Dervish. Happily for him he was scooped up inside twenty minutes by one of our indefatigable Air Sea Rescue launches and duly arrived back at Debden that night.

Wing Commander Myles Duke-Woolley, Leader Debden Wing

Stanley Anderson recorded in his flying book:

Plenty of FW190s, Ju88s, Do217s and Me109s – I took a crack at a Ju88 damaging it and killing the rear gunner. CO and Mike shot down but were picked up by air sea rescue. Plenty of fun and games for all.

While this activity continued above, the scene below had now changed. The Dieppe raid itself was over and the survivors were now on their way home, although as yet still within range of coastal gunfire. They still had to re-cross the English Channel.

CHAPTER NINE

Air Cover
1.30 pm to 2 pm

The evacuation was over. At 12.30 pm a signal was sent to the Beachmaster at Dieppe to withdraw. The Beachmaster had already decided to call off any further attempts to rescue survivors from some of the beaches. The tide was going out making it further for men to run to get to the boats and the deadly gunfire from the headlands as well as the town continued to pin troops down to positions which they had taken up after landing at dawn. Many made the dash for safety and made it – many tried but were cut down in the attempt. Now, finally, it was over. The boats and ships began to turn away.

With the armada of small ships now starting to head back towards England, German fire from the town and headlands had to be diverted and suppressed. The Hurricanes were on their way yet again.

At 12.50 pm the Hurribombers of 175 Squadron began to take off from Warmwell for their third and final mission of the day. Along the coast at Shoreham five minutes later 245 Squadron left the ground. At 1 o'clock, 253 flew off from Friston while the Spitfires of 41 Squadron left Tangmere to provide escort.

Squadron Leader John Pennington-Legh (BE502) led 175 against the Hindenburg position at 1.30, Pennington-Legh dropping his bombs successfully on the fortified position. Pilot Officer D. I. Stevenson (BE687) came diving in to the attack but saw snipers atop a church so dropped his bombs on them, seeing the steeple crumple as his bombs exploded. His Hurricane received hits from AA fire and although he struggled to get back, had finally to bale out ten miles off Dieppe. He was picked up by the Polish destroyer *Slazak* and landed at Portsmouth none the worse for his 'dunking'. Flight Lieutenant Burton Murchie (BE417) flying Yellow 1, dropped his bombs on some works with cranes, two miles in front of the fort. The following pilots attacked troop positions on the west headland: Pilot Officer A. H. McLaren (BE492), Flight Sergeants N. Howe (BE668), D. W. Westcott, A. J. Long and Sergeant F. A. Cawthray (BE394). Both Pennington-Legh and Burton Murchie were decorated in the autumn, the former receiving a bar to his DFC, Murchie the DFC.

Flight Lieutenant Denys H. H. Gathercole (BE497) led seven aircraft of 245 Squadron against the gun positions on the east headland, diving down to 300 feet to make the strafing run. Several of their Hurricanes were hit by ground fire, and in fact after this, their second sortie of the day, only three machines remained serviceable. Flight Sergeant K. Clift (AG165) was attacked by an Me109F but it was driven off and shot down by Spitfires.

Derek Yapp led 12 Hurricanes of 253 Squadron in to attack German batteries firing on the ships, arriving at Dieppe at 1.20. Many gun posts were strafed with success and it was noticed that machine-gun fire from the headlands had decreased. As the Hurricanes turned to fly out they met more return fire from both sides of the valley of La Scie. Flight Lieutenant J. L. W. Ellacombe DFC was hit but managed to gain sufficient height to bale out, landing in the water close to the last two boats leaving the general area of Dieppe. Squadron Leader Yapp's machine was also hit and one of his cannons was knocked out. Derek Sidney Yapp received the DFC for his leadership.

'For the final sortie of the day we were told that the convoy was withdrawing and the many gun batteries were the prime objective. I was flying my own Hurricane IIC BP707 and my Number 2 was Pilot Officer G. Dodson RAAF in a twelve gun IIB. As we crossed the coast to the west of Dieppe we were bounced by FW190s and forced to take violent evasive action which split the squadron into small sections. With my Number 2, I headed for some flashes on the edge of a wood to the south-west of Dieppe and saw a battery of field guns – probably 88mm's. We flew a wide circuit to attack north to south across the guns and approached at maximum throttle – Pilot Officer Dodson on my starboard side. We both had the satisfaction of seeing our cannon and machine-gun bullets detonating on the guns and scattering the gunners.

'It was too good to last – the inevitable light flak appeared from the right and my Hurricane was mortally hit. Oil and glycol smoke poured from the engine which I was unable to nurse as the tnrottle linkage was shot away. I broke to the right heading for the coast and flew through the twelve guns firing from Pilot Officer Dodson's Hurricane. He had a perfect cine film to prove it. At high speed and at tree-top height I reached the coast where the engine died with a great thud. I eased the aircraft up to about 600 feet, shedding hood and right side panel on the way, baling out as the stall approached. The jerk of my parachute opening was a relief but I was puzzled by the smoke under the canopy until I realised that tracer bullets were the cause. Within a few seconds I was in the sea about 500 yards from the cliffs. I got rid of my parachute harness and boots and set off for England with a steady side stroke, dragging my dinghy in its unopened pack and encouraged by the zipp of bullets in the sea around me.

'To my great relief I saw a small landing craft turning towards me. The ramp was lowered and I was dragged aboard *LCA 188*. I was handed a mug of cold tea which I gulped down – I nearly choked – it was neat whisky! The main convoy was some miles away and this badly damaged Landing Craft Assault with only one engine now attracted the attention of the big guns. The shells arrived in salvos of four and the great plumes of water around us were disconcerting to say the least.

'Sub-Lieutenant Hall RNZVR was the skipper and the crew were three Chief Petty Officers RN. They took it all very calmly – after all, they had been experiencing this treatment for the past eight hours. "Can't we take evasive action?" I asked.

' "Ten degrees port," shouted Sub-Lieutenant Hall, which at 4 knots did nothing to raise my spirits. Suddenly we saw a great white bow wave heading towards us. A powerful RN steam gun boat circled round and came alongside and took us in tow. Our miserable 4 knots became 15 knots and the shell fire was no longer a menace. We soon joined the main convoy which was steaming towards Newhaven.'

Flight Lieutenant John Ellacombe, 253 Squadron

No. 41 Squadron's Spitfires closely escorted the Hurricanes into the attack. Many types of enemy aircraft were seen about but 41 did not engage. Heavy flak came up to meet them and five Spitfires were hit and damaged. The CO, Squadron Leader Geoffrey Cokayne Hyde, flying his third mission of the day, was lost to view of the others whilst coming out and failed to return. Hyde had only taken command of the squadron on 28 July, coming from 64 Squadron in place of Squadron Leader Nobby Fee who had gone to command 412 RCAF Squadron.

Between this Hurricane assault and the lull before the next wave arrived, at least three Spitfire squadrons were still high above and in contact with enemy aircraft. 232 Squadron led by Squadron Leader Archie McDowell, flying in Duke-Woolley's Wing, saw nine FW190s briefly in the clouds but failed to close with them. 602 from Biggin Hill had a scrap with several Focke Wulfs, Pilot Officer Ralph Sampson sending one into the sea (the Me109 which had attacked Flight Sergeant Clift of 245 Squadron?). The Germans evened the score by shooting down Flight Lieutenant Niven but he was rescued by the Navy slightly injured, ending the day in Brighton Hospital. Niven had risen from sergeant to flight commander with 602 Squadron.

Our third patrol was made to cover the withdrawal and we arrived on the scene at 7,000 feet to have a height advantage over the enemy. By now there were a lot of German aircraft about, dive-bombing and strafing, and I vividly remember seeing ships on fire and aircraft burning on the ground. We plunged into the fray, attacking dive-bombers and, inevitably, becoming involved with defending fighters, one of which shot down one of my flight commanders, Flight Lieutenant Johnny Niven DFC. He successfully baled out and I circled him in the water to look after him until a corvette picked him up. Fortunately he suffered only from the loss of a finger, which became the subject of ribald comment.

Squadron Leader Peter Brothers, OC 602 Squadron

Harry Brown was leading 616 Squadron at 12-13,000 feet when a group of ten FW190s were seen and engaged. Pilot Officer R. G. Large and Pilot Officer Smithson each damaged one but Flight Lieutenant J. S. Fifield's machine was hit and he baled out. He was rescued by a minelayer although he had had a nasty experience during his descent when his neck became entangled in his parachute lines. Fifield was safely landed at Newhaven luckily with no more than a stiff neck.

Also above was Group Captain Harry Broadhurst flying his third sortie over Dieppe. He had left Hornchurch in company with Wing Commander Peter Powell, a former Hornchurch Wing Leader, at 12.30 arriving over Dieppe shortly before 1 pm at 25,000 feet. Below they could see the ships withdrawing. Powell broke away and dived to sea level to view the situation from low level while the Group Captain circled above.

The ships at the end of the convoy, Broadhurst could clearly see, were being subjected to enemy air attack. He could see the destroyer *Berkeley*, designated 'First Rescue Ship', in apparent difficulty. Broadhurst radioed the Hornchurch Controller asking him to request Group that the cover squadrons be concentrated over the rear of the convoy. He also contacted the Control Ship, suggesting that the lower cover squadrons be directed over the *Berkeley*.

There were several Dorniers and Focke Wulfs still about and then two 190s began to dive towards the *Berkeley*. Broadhurst dived after them but was unable to close before they let go their bombs one of which appeared to score a direct hit on the destroyer's stern. Closing finally with the rear 190, he emptied most of his cannon and machine-gun ammunition into it before returning along the line of ships to land back at RAF Kenley.

At Kenley, Broadhurst once again made a point of talking to the pilots as well as the Station Commander and the Wing Leader before once again reporting to the AOC by telephone. He again emphasised that as the Spitfires would be unable to cover the whole length of the convoy that they should be concentrated over the rear ships.

Meantime, *Berkeley* was in a bad way. According to Flight Lieutenant Kidd aboard *Calpe*, *Berkeley* was hit at 12.45 and began to sink immediately. *Calpe* and some smaller craft took off most of the crew and personnel and picked up others from the sea. *Berkeley*'s captain, Lieutenant J. J. S. Yorke RN and most of his men survived. Petty Officer Harry Brook, from Eastbourne, Sussex, was a director-layer aboard *Berkeley*. After Dieppe he was interviewed for a local newspaper in his hometown. Of the RAF he said: 'The RAF gave us a wonderful defence, but for them there would have been more casualties and a greater loss of shipping. They put up a grand show.' Brook received the DSM for his part in the Raid.

Shortly after 1 pm, HMS *Albrighton* was ordered to finish off the sinking *Berkeley* which she did with two torpedo shots. She sank at 1.08 pm.

Off Dieppe a second wave of Hurricanes were fast approaching. At 1.10 pm 87 and 174 Squadrons had received orders to rendezvous and report to the control ship and if no targets were detailed they were to proceed to strafe and bomb the western headland as soon as possible. 87 took off at 1.25 followed by 174 five minutes later, while 3 and 43 Squadrons, ordered to fly against the east headland at 1.12 took off at 1.45. 412 Squadron provided the escort for the latter, while three more Spitfire squadrons 124, 401 and 416 covered the ships.

Twelve Hurricanes of 87 Squadron, led this time by A Flight commander, Flight Lieutenant Stuart Hordern (HL864 LK–? (? for Q!)). The plan was that 87 would go in with 174 but due to the heavy smoke over Dieppe a concentrated raid was out of the question. 87 made individual attacks on targets of opportunity and some machine-gun posts and lorries were strafed. Sergeant Ronald Gibson, aged 22, failed to return.

Third sortie – very similar to (my) first run in (second sortie) but less activity visible. Again flew over east cliffs but not firing. As we flew over fields a convoy of lorries appeared ahead but although we fired I think we came on them too suddenly and certainly my aim was over the top of them. Wide turn away to port and back out. As we came to the edge of cliffs a gun position seemed to present itself right in our line of fire so we all had a go! As I passed over I saw one or two cows (Friesians) come charging out of what was a peaceful cow shed! Over the water the landing craft were returning – laden with soldiers happily waving – glad to be out of it. The weather began to cloud over and when we landed it was certainly overcast – soon started to rain.

Pilot Officer Frank Mitchell, 87 Squadron

My main recollection of Dieppe was my shooting up an enemy lorry and seeing their troops jumping out of it and returning with

5

6

15. Pilot Officer Frank Mitchell of 87 Squadron with HL864 LK-?. Flight Lieutenant Stuart Hordern flew this Hurricane twice to Dieppe. *(IWM)*

16. Flight Lieutenant C. B. Watson of 174 Squadron, who was shot down into Dieppe harbour and taken prisoner. *(J. W. Brooks)*

17. Pilot Officer John Godfrey, 412 Canadian Squadron, whose letter home written the day after Dieppe gives a first hand account of the Raid. *(J. Godfrey)*

three-quarters of my elevator wires broken by a single bullet
passing through the aircraft.

Flight Lieutenant Stuart Hordern, 87 Squadron

This was the third and final strafing run made by 87 Squadron and
its CO Denis Smallwood (a future Vice Chief of Air Staff) and
Flight Lieutenant Alex Thom were both awarded DFCs for their
part in Dieppe, and Pilot Officer Robin McNair also received a
DFC for night fighting and Dieppe.

Flight Lieutenant W. W. McConnell DFC (BE405) led ten
Hurri-bombers of 174 Squadron against the east headland – being
directed by the control ship's orders. They carried 250 lb bombs,
having run out of 500 lb bombs by this time. They attacked gun
positions, one direct hit being observed and several near misses.
Pilot Officer M. (Doofy) DuFretay (Free French) was last seen
diving on Rommel but did not come out of the attack.[1]

As 174 flew out low across the coast the pilots saw a formation of
FW190s pass right overhead flying along the coast. John Brooks
looked up at the rear 190, recalling clearly the oil streaks on its
underbelly it was so close. The Hurricane pilots had strict orders
not to engage in air combat, in order to reserve overall Hurricane
strength for possible further sorties, so left well alone. The Germans
obviously did not see 174 right below them.

This was also 174's third sortie of the day. McConnell later
received a well deserved bar to his DFC and was promoted to
squadron leader and given the squadron. Flight Lieutenant de
Soomer was also promoted and given command of 3 Squadron.
Three other pilots were decorated, Pilot Officers Harry Davies and
James W. B. Reynolds with DFCs, and Flight Sergeant John
Brooks the DFM. Reynolds, a Canadian, was later killed in a flying
accident on a Typhoon. Brooks was later shot down over France,
evaded and ten days later was back with the squadron via Spain.

Three Squadron also attacked the east headland, diving down to
the attack from 1,500 feet to 500 feet. They were, however, attacked
by 15 FW190s (perhaps the 190s that missed 174 Squadron) who
came down on them from the starboard beam to their stern. Squad-

---

[1] Lieutenant Maurice Halna duFretay, aged 22, ex French Air Force, escaped
to England in a light aeroplane after the fall of France.

18. Flight Lieutenant Stuart Hordern led 87 Squadron on the third strike made by his Squadron. *(S. S. Hordern)*

19. Squadron Leader Johnnie Johnson commanded 610 Squadron at Dieppe, claiming one destroyed and a share in another.

20. Lt Rolf Berg claimed a FW190 but was shot down by another. He was rescued but did not survive the war, being killed in action on 3 February 1945. *(Norwegian Forsvaramuseet)*

21. 174 Squadron group in 1942. (l to r): PO Mallett, Sgt Seely, Sgt James, FL McPhail, FL McConnell, PO Robinson, F/Sgt Wetere, F/Sgt Montgomery and Sgt Tye. Mallett, Seely, James, McConnell, Wetere and Montgomery all flew against Dieppe. Sgt James was killed and McConnell had to lead the squadron twice following the loss of the unit's CO. *(J. W. Brooks)*

ron Leader Alex Berry was warned of the closing 190s but pressed home his strafing run. A Focke Wulf opened fire on him, hit his Hurricane which burst into flames and crashed into the cliff face. It was this gallant CO's fourth mission of the day.

As well as Tappin's DFC, two other 3 Squadron pilots were decorated with the DFC for their part in the day, Flight Lieutenant Desmond J. Scott, and Flight Lieutenant Louis T. Spence.

No 43 Squadron also attacked the east headland and at least six gun positions were strafed. 3 Squadron was ahead and below 43 when the Focke Wulfs attacked and 43 were also attacked by half a dozen 190s. Sergeant E. Bierer's machine was hit and slightly damaged but he got home. This was 43's fourth mission.

Nobby Fee's 412 Squadron (Fee in BL632) saw six 190s attack the Hurricanes but immediately six other 190s attacked the Spitfires. There was a brief exchange but neither side inflicted much damage on each other. The 190s, however, were successfully driven away from the Hurricanes although they were rather persistent with the Canadians.

When we were about a mile offshore from Dieppe, we climbed to about 500 feet. There were FW190s all over the place around 2,000 feet, and we were the only Spits at our height. Some 190s started to dive down on the Hurries. We tore after them and they, seeing us coming, started to break away. Just then someone yelled, 'Red section, break!' There were some 190s on our tail. We went into a steep turn to the right and shook them off. I lost the others for a few seconds. The flak started to come up at us in great volume. Red balls were shooting past my nose, uncomfortably close. I spotted my Number 1 and joined him. Just then the CO yelled, 'Let's get out of here.' We dove down onto the sea, going all out and weaving as hard as we could. The Hurries were about two miles out to sea on the way home. We managed to keep the Jerries busy so that none of them had been attacked. We stayed with them on the way home, weaving around them with our head turning about 120 to the minute, looking for Huns. However, none chased us back and we landed with the whole squadron intact.

Pilot Officer John Godfrey, 412 Squadron –
from a letter home dated 20 August 1942

Fee's Spitfire had a hole blasted through his aileron about the size of a football and Godfrey's machine had a piece of shrapnel pass through his fuselage and under his seat.

While this action was taking place, 124 Squadron led by Tommy Balmforth (BR987) had left Gravesend to patrol over the returning convoy. They flew at between 10,000 and 15,000 feet, ten miles off Dieppe over the leading ships.

Pilot Officer B. J. Hull (BR319), Blue 3, became separated but joined up with White 1 and 2. All three were attacked by 190s. Hull broke and attacked one from 450 yards, which caused a fire and bits to fly off the German fighter. He then dived on another 190 he saw below flying in gentle turns over the ships. Two bursts sent the 190 into the sea between two lines of ships. Climbing back up, Hull saw and attacked a Ju88 which was being escorted by five FW190s. He attacked the bomber from a range of 350 yards, closing with it until he lost his aim as his Spitfire was buffeted by the 88's slipstream. The Junkers was last seen diving into cloud almost inverted, at 3,000 feet. This made for Hull a score of one destroyed, one probable and one damaged.

Pilot Officer A. G. Russell (BR567) Blue 4, hit a 190 at 8,000 feet and it dived inverted. Flight Lieutenant William Gregson (BR587) Red Leader, attacked a Focke Wulf which had attacked his Number 4. His fire produced strikes and flashes on the German's leading edge, wing root and engine cowling. Gregson too had had a successful day, his skill producing one destroyed and three damaged. He was awarded the DFC. Pilot Officer Mike Kilburn of 124 also received the DFC for his part at Dieppe.

The last two Spitfire cover squadrons over Dieppe as the third – withdrawal–phase of Operation Jubilee ended were the Canadians of 401 and 416 Squadrons. Both arrived on station at 2 pm.

Squadron Leader Hodson, leading 401 and his Number 2, Pilot Officer T. Ibbotson, saw two FW190s but attacked without visible results. Blue 1, Pilot Officer G. Murray attacked another 190, claiming a probable. Blue section was then bounced by four 190s and Murray turned and damaged one of them. Pilot Officer H. Westhaver, Blue 2, attacked another and finding that his cannons had packed up, hammered the German with his machine-guns, seeing strikes and claiming it as damaged.

Yellow 1, Flight Lieutenant J. Whitham, swooped down on more

190s, who scattered but he made no claim. He then saw his wing-man, Sergeant Buckley, attacked by two 190s. Whitham yelled a warning for him to break and he did in fact start a gentle weave but two more 190s attacked. Whitham tried to intervene but Buckley was hit and went down from 4,000 feet to crash. Morton Haist Buckley, aged 22, hailed from Ontario.

Whitham continued to attack the 190s, hitting one with a seven-second burst which produced smoke from the 190's engine. The 190 was last seen in a shallow dive two miles off the French coast. Whitham fought on to damage yet another 190.

Flight Sergeant R. D. Reeser, Yellow 3, attacked a 190 but he saw his wingman, Sergeant L. J. Armstrong hit and go into a spin. Armstrong baled out and was seen in his dinghy, eight miles off the French coast. He was not rescued and later his capture was confirmed.

Lloyd Chadburn led 416 Squadron over the ships at 6,500 feet. They were attacked from behind by 15 Focke Wulfs but they turned the tables on the German machines, claiming three destroyed and a fourth damaged. Flight Lieutenant H. Russel, Pilot Officer R. A. Buckham and Flight Sergeant J. D. Phillip claimed the victories, Pilot Officer J. S. McKendy the damaged. The following day, Russel, made a radio broadcast about his experiences over Dieppe and said of this kill: 'I think the pilot of the 190 I shot down had just come from an OTU.'[1] It appears he thought the victory an easy one!

As this battle raged and then ended, seven Ju88s were spotted coming in and threatening to attack the ships. The Canadians waded in and claimed one probable and five damaged. Lloyd Chadburn got the probable, the damaged going to Flight Lieutenant Foss Boulton, Pilot Officers Robert Buckham, McKendy, (who actually identified an Me110 but more likely it was an 88) and Jackie Rae (EP278), while Flight Sergeant H. McDonald made it five. Rae was flying on Chadburn's wing and saw his fire smash into his 88 and it flew away with smoke pouring from it. When this scrap broke up the Canadians continued their patrol. Chadburn received the DFC for his leadership over Dieppe.

During this final phase of the withdrawal, the last Mustang loss of the day occurred. 400 Squadron had flown their penultimate

[1] Operational Training Unit

sorties between 12.20 and 1.24 pm, by Flying Officer Duncan (Bitsy) Grant and Pilot Officer J. W. Pace. At 1.15 pm Flying Officer Frank Grant and Pilot Officer D. G. Burlingham took off to fly 400's last Tac/R mission behind Dieppe. Burlingham was flying his first mission and was last seen near St Aubin. He failed to return and was reported killed. One account says he was shot down by FW190s.

No 239 Squadron flew its last sorties of the day between mid-day and 1.05 pm. Flying Officer D. A. Lloyd and Pilot Officer P. O'Brien (AG544 and AM146) searched the roads between Le Tréport and Blangy and were attacked by four 190s but they left them behind. On their return they reported that the majority of landing craft were ten miles from Dieppe and some of the leading vessels were nearing Shoreham.

My main thought about 239's part at Dieppe was the extremely inept way the recce was planned. The person responsible was someone who should have known better. Recce was routed in at Dieppe round the course and out again at Dieppe. This was silly as what happened immediately round Dieppe was of not much value, it was reinforcements that were the target. The idea of course was to give the recce the benefit of the fighter cover around Dieppe but the fact was that the pair of recce aircraft attracted the German fighters on to a soft option. Also they had to fly low over the flak around Dieppe. We would have done better to cross the coast away from Dieppe and exit away from the town. German Air Force controllers were mainly far too busy playing with our fighters to worry about two aircraft outside the main fight.

If my memory is right it was about mid-day when it was called-off – or we were – we had three pilots left out of twelve, most of whom we got back but they were out of action at the time. . . . when we were called off I was myself due for the next trip.

This business of not getting anywhere near fighter battles was found always a good idea later in 1943-44 when recce was working in France. We rarely got intercepted even as far in as near Paris.

Wing Commander Peter Donkin, OC 239 Squadron

Routing reconnaissance Mustangs away from the main battle areas in order that they might search the areas behind the battle with less danger of interception or being hit by flak was just one of the lessons the RAF learned through the Dieppe Operation.

Officially the withdrawal cover phase ended at ten minutes past two o'clock. Yet even then enemy air activity remained high, and this activity was encompassing much of the Luftwaffe's theatre of operations in Northern Europe.

The ever-watchful British radar, continuing to monitor German air activity began to plot incoming enemy aircraft between 2 pm and 2.30 pm. And these plots originated in some cases from bases as far away as Belgium and Holland. These plots were joined by more enemy aeroplanes from Le Havre and Amiens which together totalled an estimated 75 to 80 hostile aircraft. Later, at 2.50, a further 25 to 30 arrived on the screens from St Omer.

Over the next hour 80 to 100 German aircraft came into the area of the battle from the south of Dieppe. More aircraft had come up from Lille and from Abbeville, the first time the latter base had been active since the bombing attack by the Americans earlier in the day.

Back on English aerodromes the fighter pilots were preparing for the final phase – to cover the returning ships. Although the weather was closing in it was still very warm, following the hot sunny morning. The Boston crews also stood by in case they were required.

All during the morning, the returning pilots had been greeted with the usual mugs of tea, others with refreshing lemonade. On most airfield dispersals there seemed to be an everlasting supply of sandwiches which were eaten amid excited talk about the battle while aeroplanes were refuelled, re-armed and made ready. Those who managed a quick meal in the Mess were more fortunate, at least one squadron reporting a delightful sounding delicacy of 'nearly-spam and chips!'

My squadron flew four times that day so that really we did not have much time on the ground, except to snatch a little food and several cups of the inevitable tea.

Squadron Leader Johnnie Johnson, OC 610 Squadron

I remember our temporary pitch on the far edge of Ford airfield; the tented accommodation, the five-barred gate leading into some farmer's property. There were some cows munching contentedly at the time everybody was flat-out and the battle raged across the Channel. A pressman, armed with camera, came up to me and asked if he could muster the aircrews who were at readiness (all dressed up in their flying kit, Mae Wests, et al) and take a picture with the cows in the background. I muttered that if it was going to help win the war – wan smile from cameraman – 'get clicking.'

Wing Commander James Pelly-Fry, OC 88 Squadron

Yet it was the ground crews who worked the miracles, turning round aircraft in the shortest possible time, working on strange machines or at unfamiliar airfields. It was like the Battle of Britain all over again for many of them. Get them down, check them, rearm and refuel them, polish the cockpit hoods and windscreens, patch the acceptable bullet holes, etc etc. Warrant Officer M. W. Young, the Armament Warrant Officer on 226 Squadron, had his work mentioned in Group Routine orders, for the Bostons had bomb loads changed at dispersal several times and he was working at a strange base.

However, all aircraft were always ready, and as the afternoon began the pilots too were ready to go out again and bring the Canadians home.

CHAPTER TEN

The Way Home
2 pm to 5 pm

The evacuation was over. The raid was over. The main task now was to bring the Canadians, the small ships and the larger vessels, home. It was obvious that the Luftwaffe was not going to let this happen without a fight and with the amount of aircraft that showed on the radar screens, the RAF fighter pilots would have their hands full in covering the journey back.

Wing Commander Denys Gillam led his three Typhoon squadrons off from West Malling at exactly two o'clock. The Duxford Wing this time was detailed to sweep from Le Touquet to Le Tréport. 56 Squadron, led by Cocky Dundas (R7714) flew as top cover, Charles Green's 266 Squadron in the middle while Paul Richey's 609 Squadron (R8221) flew below. 609 left one Typhoon behind due to engine trouble. The pilots had been waiting in their cockpits for the green signal flare to take off, and when it came . . .

. . . it resulted in an eruption of starter cartridge reports, smoke, exhaust flame and dust as thirty-six 2000 hp Sabre engines fired. Taxiing out over the dry grass airfield caused problems as the big three-bladed propellers churned dust and debris into the eyes of pilots straining to see through their cockpit side windows which were open until take off to try and avoid excessive heat. Then the CO's section was away in a rising cloud of dust and I was leading my flight in hot pursuit. With no preliminary circuit to join up the formation we set course at low level for Beachy Head closing to 'search formation' and then crossed out over the chalk cliffs with climb power, ignoring the enemy radar on this occasion and going directly up to 10,000 feet.

Immediately the VHF became noisy with menacing sounds of enemy radio interference and with spasmodic instructions and excited observations from other squadrons already in action.

Levelling over mid-Channel at 10,000 feet, Denys Gillam, leading the Wing with 56 Squadron, maintained high power until we
were indicating 300 mph for fast target penetration, and then the
enemy coast was in sight through a layer of broken cumulus
cloud at about 2-4,000 feet. Turning west from the Somme Estuary the three Typhoon squadrons made an impressive sight with
their blunt nose radiators and aggressive overall shape, and then
the action began.

Confused radio chatter suggested enemy aircraft inland
somewhere, then almost simultaneously I saw unidentified aircraft below momentarily through gaps in the cloud, and the
harbour and sea front of Dieppe. It was ringed in smoke and fires
with white tracks off-shore of weaving naval vessels and assault
craft and the unmistakable white splashes of sticks of bombs. We
could see no immediate target, although at some point a section
of 266 broke away and dived after some Dorniers, and then
Gillam led the Wing in a long diving sweep at 400 mph round
behind Dieppe and down through the broken cloud layer to look
for activity; and I again had a fleeting glimpse of some 190s or
109s (or Spitfires) before they disappeared into cloud. The rear
section of our squadron saw 190s in and out of cloud for long
enough to attack them and claimed three damaged.

Flight Lieutenant Roland Beamont, 609 Squadron

The Wing was off Le Tréport, Gillam flying at 15,000 feet,
(R7698) when control warned of the approach of enemy bombers.
These bombers, they were informed, were approaching the with-
drawing armada of little ships from the direction of Merville and all
eyes scanned the sky in that direction. 266, flying at 16,000 feet,
then spotted three Dornier 217s some five miles inland behind Le
Tréport with about 20 FW190s as escort, flying in loose formation.
The Germans were at 5,000 feet. 266 reported the sighting to the
Wing Leader but Gillam could not see them so he ordered them to
go after them.

Flight Lieutenant R. H. L. Dawson, Yellow 1, and his Number 2,
Pilot Officer Wilfred Smithyson of 266 dived to the attack, accompanied by Pilot Officer Munro, White Leader. Munro closed
behind one Dornier loosing off 100 rounds of cannon fire from 300
yards, closing in to 50 yards. Smoke poured back from the Dor-

nier's port wing from between the engine and the fuselage, then the bomber dived steeply. Munro claimed it as probably destroyed. The action of Dawson and Smithyson was not observed but chatter over the R/T was heard. Smithyson reported a Dornier crashing and Dawson said that it was one he had just shot down. However, Smithyson was not heard again and he failed to get home. His death was later confirmed.

Munro, meantime, was unable to follow his Dornier down for he was attacked by the Focke Wulfs, tracer shells passing over his wings as he broke away. He dived towards the coast and joined up with another Typhoon, piloted by Dawson. Flight Lieutenant A. C. Johnston and his wingman, Blue 1 and 2, with Green 1, saw ten FW190s below at two o'clock. Johnston dived and eight of the Germans pilots broke downwards, leaving two flying on seemingly oblivious of the fast approaching danger. Johnston, his Typhoon flying at full boost, caught up with one 190 and he opened fire at 600 yards, in a series of short bursts down to 400 yards. The Focke Wulf went down vertically with white glycol smoke pouring from the engine. Johnston followed at terrific speed but had to pull out when his speed reached 480 mph and he was almost into some low ground haze. The 190 was still going down and Johnston claimed a probable.

Gillam led 609 down and saw four FW190s almost a mile off to port. The 190s saw the Typhoons approaching and rapidly turned to port to dive through some clouds. 609 followed and Gillam fired at one from 400 yards and knocked some pieces from it, claiming it damaged. Sergeant A. C. de Saxce (R7845) (Free French) also fired at a 190 which was formating on Flying Officer R. E. J. Wilmet's Typhoon. 'Fifi' de Saxce yelled a warning at Bob Wilmet (609's piano playing Belgian) but his French was not understood by the Belgian pilot. However, the Frenchman's fire, although producing no result, deterred the 190.

Wilmet then became separated from the squadron, so he flew inland to seek out targets. South-east of Le Touquet he passed a 190 head-on but made no contact with it before it was gone. On returning out over the coast he was attacked by a Spitfire IX but it missed him.

Fifty-six Squadron had remained above during these actions, at 17,000 feet for more enemy fighters were spotted at high altitude.

Some approached but they were held off by 56 making steep turning counter attacks.

Between 2.15 and 2.25 pm, 331 and 332 Norwegian Squadrons took off from Manston to fly cover for the convoy. 331 was led by Major Mehre, 332 by Captain F. Thorsager (EP283). Five miles off the English coast enemy aircraft were reported and the Norwegians were vectored towards them. However, the plot was not only enemy aircraft but friendly Typhoons.

Flight Lieutenant Dawson and Pilot Officer Munro, who had joined up after Smithyson had gone missing, were flying towards England with other Typhoons. 331 Squadron suddenly came upon them about half way across the Channel. The Spitfires came in from the starboard quarter but they saw they were Typhoons and broke away. Most of the Typhoons used full boost to get away and some weaved, but one pilot of 332 found an aircraft flying towards him head-on. Having expected to see hostile fighters, and seeing the big air intake of the Hawker Typhoon he opened fire almost by instinct. Dawson's machine shed some pieces, half rolled and plunged straight into the sea from 100 feet. The Norwegian pilot sat horrified as he recognised the fighter as a Typhoon, but it was too late. The 'Tiffie' hit the sea, exploded and disappeared. Several machines circled but there was little or no wreckage and no sign of the pilot. Roland Herbert Leslie Dawson, from Salisbury, Southern Rhodesia, was 26. Four Spitfires made aggressive moves on four other Typhoons at 14,000 feet led by Squadron Leader Green, but they did not open fire.

Failure to brief the Spitfire Squadrons adequately concerning the presence of Typhoons caused considerable difficulties. Subsequently a greater margin of height was allowed between Spitfire Squadrons and Typhoons.

Wing Commander Denys Gillam, OC Duxford Wing

The Norwegians reformed and were then vectored onto German bombers over the convoy, finding several Dornier 217s escorted by FW190s. Lieutenant M. Ree of 331, emptied his guns into one Dornier diving and making a head-on pass, and damaged it. Sergeant Helmer Grundt-Spang shot down a Focke Wulf and damaged another, the former hitting the ground north-east of Dieppe.

Second Lieutenant Svein Hegland set another 190 on fire and was credited with its destruction.

> ... I took part in two of [331 Squadron's] missions, the first one as cover over the beach-head and the second one as cover for the convoy returning from Dieppe. On the second mission I shot down one FW190 attacking one of our MTBs. I ... believe it was the last time in the war that the Luftwaffe showed up in real force. I particularly remember my second mission escorting the convoy of ships on its return journey across the Channel. The Luftwaffe and the Allied fighter squadrons formed up like two great swarms of bees circling the convoy. Leaving the swarm was connected with the greatest risk, and when attacking an enemy aircraft you were certain to find two or more enemy aircraft trying to blast you out of the sky.
>
> In this situation I discovered one of our motor torpedo boats or rescue launches being attacked by a FW190. I dived and caught the FW190 with a burst of cannon shells around the cockpit area. By this time he was running all out for the French coast at sea level and must have flipped into the sea as soon as he was hit. Myself I had to turn my full attention to several FW190s on my own tail. By twisting and turning I managed to get in a head-on attack on one of my adversaries. We were both firing continuously and none of us wanted to break off. I tilted my right wing showing that I meant to pass him on his left, and I felt the shake in the aircraft as he passed underneath. If I hit him or not I never knew. Afterwards I had the struggle of my life taking evasive actions and at the time trying to gain altitude to join my own swarm of bees. This ended up in several dog-fights with large numbers of enemy aircraft in the air circling and attacking the convoy.
>
> *Second Lieutenant Svein Hegland, 331 Norwegian Squadron*

Lieutenant Roffe A. Berg shot down a 190 into the sea and damaged another but he was then hit in the glycol tank and had to bale out. His wingman radioed a May-Day call. Berg came down in the sea and was rescued by a motor launch, *ML 190*, which landed him safely at Newhaven.

No 332 Squadron also engaged the German fighters. Sergeant

22. Flight Sergeant R. L. 'Dixie' Alexander of 133 Eagle Squadron claimed three victories during the fighting. *(R. L. Alexander)*

23. 2/Lt Sven Hegland of 331 Norwegian Squadron, destroyed a FW190. *(Norwegian Forsvaramuseet)*

24. Wing Commander Denys Gillam who led his Typhoon Wing at Dieppe. *(D. E. Gillam)*

25. Squadron Leader Stanislaw Skalski, CO of 317 Polish Squadron.

26. A post-war picture of Mike Maciejowski who won the DFC at Dieppe flying with 317 Polish Squadron. *(M. Maciejowski)*

Olav Djonne attacked one but was himself attacked by another, shot up and forced to take to his parachute. He was picked up by a gunboat, *SGB 9*, commanded by Lieutenant Peter Scott DSC (better known today as a naturalist and artist). Scott had had a busy day as most of the small ships had. His boat had been attacked by two bomb-carrying FW190s at 7.20 am but they missed. The second 190 had been hit by his gunners and it flew off leaving a trail of smoke. *SGB 8* saw it crash into the cliffs. Scott's boat picked up several soldiers from the sea, also a German flyer, as well as the Norwegian pilot and later an American pilot with a broken leg. All were put below, the German being placed under armed guard.

No 81 Squadron led by Squadron Leader Berry (BM351) left Fairlop at 1.53 pm to fly their mission over the convoy. They arrived on station at 2.20 but saw nothing of the enemy until it was time to turn for home. Pilot Officer W. S. Large, a Canadian, (BM376) was attacked by a FW190 and his Spitfire was badly shot-up. He landed at Shoreham without either flaps or brakes and with his glycol tank virtually empty. The Spitfires mainplane had to be replaced. One cannon shell had entered his cockpit, being deflected off one of his boots.

The convoy of ships now stretched almost the whole breadth of the Channel between Dieppe and the English ports. Over the next hour several squadrons upheld the air umbrella above them and for some it was the first lull in the great air battle that they had seen. The Luftwaffe, or a large part of it, was obviously refuelling and rearming for a final attack. Now that Dieppe itself was no longer under direct threat and the weather was closing in, they could choose their moments more carefully. This made the vigilance of the Spitfire pilots all the more necessary, for the Dorniers were coming out yet again.

Nos 122 and 154 Squadrons patrolled over part of the convoy, having crossed the English coast above Bexhill, but after forty minutes of seeing nothing they returned home. For both squadrons it was their last action of the day.

Wing Commander Pat Jameson (BM232) led 411 and 485 Squadrons out shortly after 2 pm, finding heavy clouds in close layers. 485 at 5,000 feet saw nothing of the enemy nor did 411 flying at 12,000 feet.

Dolly Dolezal's 310 Czech Squadron and Squadron Leader Cermak's 312, also patrolled above the ships at about the same time as Jameson, both being led by Wing Commander K. Mrazak DFC. 310 saw four 190s but did not engage. 312 flew at 7,000 feet at mid-Channel. They saw a number of Dorniers. Flying Officer J. Keprt (EP432) destroyed one, Sergeant Liskutin (EP660) another while Flight Segreant J. Pipa damaged a third. Cermak (EN841) saw Keprt's Dornier fall into the sea and Sergeant Liskutin used his camera gun on his Dornier's burning wreckage on the sea. Liskutin had shared his kill with another Spitfire with code letters he identified as either BX or PX. Possibly this was in fact 131 Squadron, code letters NX, which was the only other squadron to engage Dorniers at this particular time.

Calpe was attacked and bombed by three Dorniers who came in from the west at 8,000 feet, diving down to 6,000 before releasing their bombs. *Calpe* was hardly moving as they were looking for a downed pilot but luckily the bombing was not good. Yet the bombers did score near misses which damaged the ship's stern, killed some men and blew six more overboard. They were rescued by Peter Scott's *SGB 9*.

Immediately afterwards a Focke Wulf 190 came in from the east and raked the starboard side of the destroyer's bridge with cannon fire. One starboard oerlikon gunner was killed and Air Commodore Cole was wounded. This was not the only casualty of the day of RAF personnel aboard either the *Calpe* or the *Berkeley*, for on the latter Wing Commander Stanley Skinner DFC, a former night-fighter pilot who had served with 604 Squadron, acting as observer on the raid was killed. He was with the American Colonel L. B. Hillsinger also an observer, who had his foot blown off. For his gallant work at Dieppe, Cole, the First War air fighter, was awarded the Distinguised Service Order.

Wing Commander Michael Pedley DFC led 131 Squadron out at 2.45 flying at 3,000 feet. They saw three Dornier 217s flying one thousand feet above, attempting to dive-bomb the ships. 131 attacked and broke them up. Flight Lieutenant Ray Harries (BL600), Flying Officer N. S. Wilson, Pilot Officer A. Eckert, an American, and Sergeant A. W. Bower, a South African, together destroyed one of them, while Pedley (B,420 NX–A), Pilot Officer H. G. Copeland, a New Zealander, Sergeant J. D. Thorogood and

Sergeant J. L. Davidson claimed another. Pilot Officer Copeland damaged the third. Some of their Spitfires received some slight damage from return fire.

No 64 Squadron also became involved in the action against raiding Dorniers. They had been warned of their approach from Le Touquet and had climbed to 23,000 feet. Shortly after 3 pm, Squadron Leader Duncan-Smith saw two sections of Dorniers numbering two and three respectively, flying at 10,000 feet. He led his men down and sent one bomber into the sea but his Spitfire was hit by its rear gunner and he had to leave his Spitfire (3.20 pm). He came down close to two Naval vessels who confirmed that his Dornier had gone into the drink 1½ miles away. Duncan-Smith was awarded the DSO for his part in Jubilee.

Flight Lieutenant C. Thomas and Flight Sergeant G. A. Mason attacked some escorting FW190s, Thomas seeing one which he attacked crash into the sea. Mason claimed his as damaged. Pilot Officer H. F. Withy had a long chase after another Dornier but could only claim it as damaged.

Pilot Officer J. K. Stewart, who took over the lead of Blue Section when Don Kingaby's engine gave trouble, forcing him to return to base, was in the thick of the action. At one moment he was heard to yell over the radio: 'Be careful! You are firing at me!' This young Rhodesian failed to return and was presumed lost in the Channel.

The last Boston action of Operation Jubilee was mounted by 226 and 88 Squadrons at 2.14 pm. Five crews were briefed, four from 226 and one from 88, being escorted by 66 Squadron. Their mission was a low level attack to place a final smoke screen in front of Dieppe (two Bostons carried smoke curtains). The Bostons were led by Squadron Leader Digger Magill, his companions piloting the other Bostons being Flying Officer D. T. Smith, Flying Officer R. A. Marks and Pilot Officer B. R. Miles. The 88 machine was piloted by Flight Sergeant Attenborough (Z2217 RH–G). Their mission would provide one last screen to cover those few ships still within gun range from German batteries. 66 Squadron was led by Squadron Leader R. D. Yule (EP688).

One Boston failed to make the rendezvous, so it was only four bombers that 66 picked up. These four made eleven runs in front of the cliffs from east to west. Anti-aircraft fire was still very heavy and one Boston flown by Flying Officer Marks was hit and came down in the sea two miles off Dieppe. He and his crew, Pilot Officer K. A. I. Warwood and Pilot Officer L. K. Brownson were reported missing.

> The trip ... was the last of the day. It was in answer to an urgent call for protection of the withdrawing naval forces which were being severely harassed by fire from the shore. The idea was to put down a curtain of smoke from cliff to cliff either side of the town and down to sea level. I think we can justly claim to have succeeded. It meant running in flat out from the east under the cliff, between the lighthouse and the beginning of the jetty, along the line of the beach and withdrawing under the western cliff. We had quite a view of the water-front and the shambles on the beach. Unfortunately, we lost Flying Officer Marks and crew in the process. I have little doubt that he collected the fire aimed at me. He was flying to seaward of me and a bit lower (to give depth to the screen) and should have been hidden to the enemy by the smoke from my aircraft. Hit as he was at nought feet he had no chance.
>
> *Squadron Leader Graham Magill, 226 Squadron*

Flying Officer Donald Smith was also on the receiving end of the flak. As he began to make one of his run-ins a shell hit his Boston (MQ–H) and shattered his windscreen. Pieces of broken perspex became embedded in "Smithy's" right eye but undaunted, this 'tall, lanky, laconic Canadian, rarely separated from his beloved pair of Scotch Terriers ..' carried on to lay his smoke. On the return flight his left eye became affected by powdered perspex which constantly swirled about the cockpit, swept up by the constant gale of cold air which streamed through the broken windscreen but he managed to fly back to Thruxton and land safely. For this action Don Smith received the DFC.

No 66 Squadron reported seeing two Bostons shot down, one crashing into the sea off the harbour, the other going into the sea beside the convoy eight miles off Dieppe. Perhaps the latter was either Smith flying very low, or it was a Dornier going in. 66 escorted the remaining two (sic) Bostons home but they were bounced by four Focke Wulf 190s who shot down two Spitfires, one being seen to dive into the sea five miles north of Dieppe. These two were piloted by Sergeant R. Lyons, a Canadian and Lieutenant Victor Robinson Engelstaff Nissen SAAF, aged 21, from the Transvaal, South Africa. Both were killed. Flight Sergeant Attenborough landed at Ford at 4.10 pm, Magill (Z2281 MQ–B) landing at RAF Manston at 4.30.

No 277 Squadron were kept busy with all this activity over the convoy, several Air Sea Rescue flights being flown. Pilot Officer R. F. F. Harris and Pilot Officer J. Adamson flying a Defiant (AA312) on one search, were attacked by a Messerschmitt 109F but Adamson got in an accurate burst from his turret, claiming the German fighter as damaged.

Luftwaffe air activity now began to increase. The clash with the Dorniers and Focke Wulfs was just the first of several prolonged engagements above the convoy. They were fought above and below and in the clouds as the bombers tried desperately to penetrate the fighter umbrella to get through to the ships without being spotted by the ever watchful Spitfires. The RAF fighter-pilots however, had no intentions of relaxing their vigilance even after such a long and tiring day of intense air activity.

Nos 129 and 501 Squadrons left their bases shortly before 3 pm and both engaged enemy aeroplanes. 129, still led by Rhys Thomas DFC were no sooner over the Sussex coast than they saw the huge flotilla of ships stretching for twenty miles between Beachy Head and Dieppe. As they flew over the vessels they saw two Dorniers escorted by six 190s just above them. Flight Lieutenant B. Ingham dived towards the twin-engined bomber's starboard and chased one of them. He fired two bursts into it which set the bomber's starboard motor on fire, then smoke poured from the fuselage. Other Spitfires then joined in and attacked it and when it was well alight it fell away and exploded upon hitting the sea. Squadron Leader Thomas opened his throttle and went after the other Dornier, seeing it fall away as his De Wilde ammunition splattered over it but he could only make claim for a damaged.

Wing Commander P. Gibbs (EP120 'Y') flying with 501 Squadron, joined by 118 Squadron of his Ibsley Wing, plus other squadrons from the Tangmere Wing, 41 and the 309th USAAF Squadron, flew out to the ships. 501 flew to the end of the convoy which was about eight miles from Dieppe. These tail-end ships were being attacked by Dornier 217s, Ju88s and FW190s.

Gibbs and his pilots reached the area at 3.10 and were immediately in combat with eight to ten FW190s. Flight Lieutenant Philip Stanbury DFC (EP538) damaged one but then lost it in dense cloud. Four Dorniers broke from cloud at 5,000 feet at the south end of the convoy. Gibbs chased one of these which began dropping its bombs as it reached the ships. Gibbs' fire smashed into the Dornier which was then finished off by a Spitfire of 118 Squadron. Gibbs was then attacked by a 190 which damaged his machine in its port aileron and starboard mainplane. It was probably Gibbs, who when interviewed by a newspaper reporter stated that he had shot down one Dornier but was '... then attacked by a FW190 who put two cannon shells up my whatnot,' ... he got away and force-landed at another aerodrome.

Flight Sergeant G. A. Mawer (EP191 SD–P), an Australian, chased two Dorniers and damaged one. As he broke away, his ammunition finished, a cannon shell exploded above his cockpit canopy, stunning him. The explosion shattered the perspex hood cutting his head slightly. He jettisoned the canopy but stayed with his Spitfire and got home.

Pilot Officer W. R. Lightbourne had his Spitfire badly shot-up and decided to leave it. As he struggled to get out his parachute pack caught in the cockpit and he was draped around the tailplane when he eventually pulled free. His leg was broken, he was dazed, in pain and had sustained a cut right hand but as he fell free managed to pull the rip-cord. A few moments later he splashed down into the sea. Being right above the convoy he came down very near the ships and was quickly picked up and laid out on the deck of the small vessel. In spite of his injuries he had little time to worry about his problems with 'Dornier attacks keeping his mind off things.' Two hours later he was transferred to a larger ship and for the first time had treatment for his broken leg.

118 Squadron led by Squadron Leader Bertie Wootten (AP129) also found enemy air activity on arrival over the convoy, 217s and 88s being seen dropping bombs. Flight Lieutenant John Shepherd (AR453) destroyed a Dornier in company with Flying Officer I. G. Stewart and Flight Sergeant S. A. Watson, while Sergeant T. J. De

Courcey finished off the Dornier already hit by Wing Commander Gibbs.

Six aircraft of 41 Squadron patrolled Selsey Bill and were not engaged while the 309th had only a brief encounter with the bombers, claiming one as damaged.

The weather began to close right in and the squadrons were recalled. Only four of 129's Spitfires managed to land back at Thorney Island, others landing where they could, the CO landing at Ford. Sergeant S. G. Jonssen (Norwegian) was heard over the radio to call for an emergency heading at ten minutes past four o'clock but he did not reach base. His burnt-out Spitfire and his body were later found at Rowland's Castle, just four to five miles north of Thorney island, the Norwegian having, evidently, flown into some trees.

No 501 Squadron had much the same problem. They reached the English coast at 4.10, the visibility at Tangmere being down to 600 yards with 10/10th cloud below 300 feet. Four pilots got in at Tangmere, Gibbs and six others getting down at Shoreham. Sergeant A. Lee was unable to locate base and crashed into a hillside at Billinghurst, twelve miles north of Tangmere. The impact of his crash broke his harness and he received head and leg injuries which resulted in death within a very few minutes.

At ten minutes past three o'clock the Belgian pilots of 350 Squadron left Redhill and were over the ships thirty minutes later. They too found Dorniers and Focke Wulfs flying in and out of the rain clouds and engaged. Pilot Officer F. A. Venesoen claimed his second 190 of the day. Flying Officer A. M. Plisnier also claiming his second victory when he shot down a 190. Other 190s were damaged by Pilot Officers G. M. Seydel, E. J. Plas, Sergeants Flohimont, R. A. Alexandre (two). Sergeant J. L. Vanterberge damaged a Dornier. Venesoen had his Spitfire's wing-tip shot away while one of Sergeant Alexandre's cannons exploded and pieces of his shells damaged the engine.

Nos 111, 308, 402 and 611 Squadrons were next over the convoy. Flight Lieutenant F. Vancl was again leading 111, but visibility had deteriorated due to both lowering cloud and drifting smoke. They saw six 190s but the Germans made no attempt at an attack although they were in a good position to do so. Vancl got in a quick burst at one before it disappeared. 111 Squadron's CO, Pete Wickham, again led the American 308th Fighter Squadron (EP166) but they saw nothing. 402 also found an empty sky and high cover, flying at 26,000 feet where they reported 7/10ths cloud. 611 patrolled three thousand feet lower, later dropping down to 13,000 feet but again made no contact.

At 3.15 Group Captain Broadhurst lifted off from Kenley on his fourth sortie of the day. He flew directly to Dieppe. At 19,000 feet he was attacked by two FW190s but after jettisoning his belly fuel tank he managed to shake them off. Then four more engaged him but by taking violent evasive action and then diving into thick cloud he lost them.

Emerging below the clouds he found the ships steaming home in apparent good order. He cruised over them for some time before heading back to England. He tried to get into Tangmere but the weather prevented this so he returned to Hornchurch. For the fourth time he put a call through to the AOC suggesting that as the weather was closing in, high patrols should cease and that the strength of lower patrols could be reduced. At 4.56 pm an order went out reducing the cover squadrons to three at any one time.

Harry Broadhurst had flown more than eight hours during the day, destroyed one FW190 and damaged three others. He had brough back much valuable information. He had been there, he had seen it. He had started the day in the dog-house for his outspoken opposition to certain planning details but by the end of the day . . .

. . . the fourth [sortie] was from Hornchurch. This last must have been very late, because I remember escorting a shot-up Blenheim back to Tangmere just at the end of the operation. I found when I got back to 11 Group that night, that I was no longer in the doghouse!
Group Captain Harry Broadhurst, Deputy SASO 11 Group

Sixty-seven Spitfires of the Polish Wing reached the convoy just after four o'clock and flying at various heights and over varying parts of the line of ships, had differing results. 303, 306 and 317 patrolled below the clouds, 302 and 308 above. Among the Polish pilots of this patrol were Wing Commander Rolski, Squadron Leader Nowierski (BL627) and Squadron Leader S. Kulaczewski from HQFC.

No 302 led by Julian Kowalski (EN865) saw nothing. His squadron had flown four patrols during this hectic day, yet had seen no enemy aircraft to speak of, and had not fired a single round in anger. 303 patrolled in very poor visibility led by Squadron Leader Zumbach (EP594). They saw some ships firing at two twin-engined aeroplanes which they identified as Heinkel 111s. Zumbach led the attack and both bombers were shot down, one being shared with 317 Squadron, although one Spitfire disappeared during the attack. Pilot Officer Adam Damm failed to return.

No 306 saw several FW190s but Squadron Leader Czerwinski was unable to make contact. However, one Spitfire was seen to climb up after two 190s. This was thought to be Flying Officer E. Landsman who also failed to return. His capture was confirmed by the Germans over a month later. Flight Lieutenant Tadeusz Koc, who had shot down the last German aircraft destroyed in the Polish campaign in 1939, led 308 Squadron as top cover to the Wing, 17-18,000 feet, but saw nothing of the enemy.

However, 317 Squadron, led by Flight Lieutenant Kazimierz Rutkowski, did find the enemy. Several FW190s were seen and then Dorniers and Heinkels attacking the convoy from two different directions. Rutkowski led the Poles down, himself sending one He111 into the sea, while Pilot Officer Stanislaw Brzeski claimed a second. Flying Officer Lukaszewicz claimed a Focke Wulf and Pilot Officer Mike Maciejowski and Sergeant A. Kolczynski shared the destruction of a Dornier 217. Flight Sergeant K. Stramko assisted 303 in the destruction of one of their two Heinkels. Maciejowski's Spitfire received some damage and he had to belly-land back at Northolt.

The Polish fighter pilots had done well at Dieppe, claiming 18% of the German aircraft claimed. They flew 224 sorties. Wing Commander Stephan Janus was awarded the DSO, while Zumbach and Skalski received bars to their DFCs. Rutowski and Maciejowski received DFCs.

Flight Sergeant P. K. Marsden and Sergeant W. T. Gregory, the crew of a 277 Squadron Lysander IIIA (V9485) were out looking

7

29

27. A pair of Mustangs of No. 400 RCAF Squadron. This unit flew 20 recce sorties behind Dieppe on this day.

28. Roland Beamont flew three missions with 609 Squadron during the Dieppe Operation. *(R. F. Watson)*

29. Boston of 88 Squadron Z2233 RH–K flying inland from Dieppe on 19 August. Pilot Officer Campbell flew this machine three times during the Raid. Smoke is from the burning tobacco factory. *(IWM)*

for a downed pilot off Selsey Bill when a German fighter took an interest in them.

They were chased inland but safely evaded the German's unwelcome attentions.

Some enemy fighters and bombers were indeed right over the southern coast of England at this time, obviously taking advantage of the cloudy weather. At 3.45 two separate groups of enemy aircraft were reported between the Needles and Shoreham, numbering between seven to ten aeroplanes. They did not penetrate very far inland but Squadron Leader Yapp of 253 Squadron and two of his pilots scrambled from Friston to patrol their base. Soon after making his forced landing at Shoreham with his shot-up Spitfire, Pilot Officer W. S. Large of 81 Squadron was bombed and machine-gunned by one of these marauding German raiders.

No 412 Squadron also scrambled two Spitfires to patrol St Catherine's Point, but they saw no sign of any Germans.

At Ford, 141 Squadron, a Beaufighter night-fighter unit, had taken no part in the day's activities but its personnel had watched all the hustle and bustle with much interest. They had fervently wished that they had not been a night-fighter outfit and could join in. However, at ten minutes past four o'clock with the scattered enemy aircraft in the area and especially as the weather and cloud were worsening, an order was sent to 141 to send off a Beau. Sergeant R. O. Cleo with his navigator/radar operator, Sergeant G. Grant (V8264) scrambled to assist, coming under 'Blackgang' control. They were vectored and guided for some time and had several chases. We shall come back to this crew later.

We had a magnificent view of the air battle as German fighter-bombers tried to attack the convoy which was protected by circling squadrons of Spitfires, and we saw a number of FW190s and Messerschmitts shot down, some crashing into the sea quite close to the convoy.

We disembarked at Newhaven after dark, I arrived back at RAF Friston at dawn, wearing borrowed boots and still clutching my unopened dinghy. After all I had to salvage something from my poor old Hurricane BP707 – the best aircraft in B Flight, 253 Squadron.

Flight Lieutenant John Ellacombe, 253 Squadron

It will be remembered that John Ellacombe had been brought down during 253 Squadron's last cannon attack, at approximately 1.30 pm, being rescued by *LCA 188*.

Nos 19, 121 and 165 Squadrons took off to take station over the convoy, arriving at ten minutes to five. At the same time 242 and 403 also flew out over the ships.

Squadron Leader Patrick Davies took his 12 Spitfires right out into the Channel, flying at 1,500 feet. Twenty miles out they found ten FW10s above and ahead of them at 3,000 feet. The two fighter formations met head-on and several indecisive combats took place. Flight Lieutenant C. F. Bradley (EN971) attacked the last one as it passed overhead and saw a large piece of the 190 fly off. The Focke Wulf turned onto its back and dived vertically towards the water. Bradley had to turn away but looking back he saw a splash on the sea. He claimed a damaged but requested a destroyed.

Red 2, Sergeant I. M. Mundy, a Rhodesian, (AR422) attacked the centre of three 190s, seeing strikes on its starboard wing but as another 190 came down behind him he had to break away. Pilot Officer Jack Henderson fired at two 190s and so did Pilot Officer Royer, but they saw little effect from their fire. Sergeant J. W. Foster, Blue 2, (BL573) received hits in his starboard mainplane, also sustaining a slight cut on his right leg from a cannon shell splinter but was otherwise all right. 19 Squadron reformed and later returned to base via Beachy Head.

Squadron Leader Bill Williams (AD199) led 121 Eagle Squadron over the sea. The Spitfires were subject to attacks by FW190s who dived in and out of the clouds taking pot-shots at them but no serious attacks were made. Pilot Officer J. M. Osborne (P8589) caught a burst in his engine, however. He struggled hard but his engine caught fire and he had to bale out when down to 550 feet, five to ten miles inland from Beachy Head. He got down safely and waved back to his circling comrades.

No 165, led by Squadron Leader Hallowes, flew as low squadron but saw nothing of the German fighters. 242 and 403 Squadrons from Manston, gave further cover but Squadron Leader Parker's (BM539) pilots saw little. The Canadians of 403, however, patrolled at mid-Channel. Seeing little of interest, Squadron Leader Les Ford flew to the French coast but on the way saw several FW190s. Ford attacked one which burst into flames. Its pilot took to his parachute, landed in the sea and clambered into his dinghy. Sergeant M. K. Fletcher fired into another 190 which began to trail smoke before it disappeared in the cloud.

Squadron Leader Desmond McMullen patrolled with 12 Spitfires of 65 Squadron over the Channel at between 3,000 and 5,000 feet. One Dornier 217 .was encountered and attacked by McMullen (AB902 YT–N). He dived upon it, fired and observed strikes on its fuselage as both his cannons hit home and his machine-guns shredded its wings. He was unable to finish it off, due to the amount of flak being thrown up by the ships and had finally to break away and leave it.

Nos 401 and 602 Squadrons came out shortly after 5 pm but again the sky appeared empty. Although the sky appeared empty, the Luftwaffe was not finished yet. Jubilee was still far from over.

Our fourth patrol followed but by then the ships were well on their way home; all seemed surprisingly quiet and there was no sign of enemy aircraft. By now we were operating at 16,000 feet.

Squadron Leader Peter Brothers, OC 602 Squadron

CHAPTER ELEVEN

Battles in the Clouds
5 pm to 9 pm

The convoy of small ships was nearly home – some had in fact already reached the safety of their home ports. The weather had not improved. Thick clouds and occasional rain showers made visibility poor over much of the remaining convoy.

Jubilee was nearing its end, only the safe return of the ships with the survivors of the raid had still to be completed. Fighter Command continued to cover the last phase as they had covered the operation throughout the day.

At exactly 5 pm, the Typhoon Wing took off from West Malling for its last patrol of the day. Again the Typhoons were led by Wing Commander Gillam and all three squadron commanders took part, Squadron Leader Dundas (R7825), Squadron Leader Green and Squadron Leader Richey. Their task was to sweep the area from the Somme Estuary to Cap Gris Nez. During this sweep Gillam's port wing gun panel came open and he had to abort. He radioed to the others but being on the wrong radio button there was some confusion. In consequence and also because Paul Richey's machine also developed some trouble, eight of 609's pilots followd Gillam back to England. Squadron Leader Green of 266 took over the sweep and with the remaining Typhoons crossed the French coast north of the Somme at 12,000 feet but 10/10ths cloud forced them to return instead of going on to St Omer. Green led them back to their home base of Duxford.

Ninety-one Squadron had continued its Jim Crow activities each hour as briefed. Pilot Officer I. G. S. Matthew and Pilot Officer A. M. leMaire searched for a high speed launch (HSL) and were nearly jumped by eight FW190s which were attacking another launch, having set it on fire. The two Spitfire pilots tried to attack but the 190s flew off. Half an hour later Pilot Officer R. M. Batten and Sergeant M. K. Eldred, also searching for a missing HSL, found two HSLs on fire and then escorted three others back to England. The burning boats were in fact the same as the previous two pilots found.

In the air over the convoy was an extremely dangerous place to be at this hour. With rain showers and low cloud the German Focke Wulf fighters were able to take advantage of hiding in these clouds and pouncing on the patrols of Spitfires. If the Spitfires got too low under the cloud then they could be shot at by the ever-ready Naval gunners.

Sergeant V. Evans (BL673) of 222 Squadron, was flying withdrawal cover with his squadron which was led by Squadron Leader Oxspring and included Wing Commander E. H. Thomas. A FW190 swooped down from the cloud, shot up Evans' Spitfire and dived away. Sergeant Evans struggled back to England to crashland at Hawkinge successfully.

Other FW190s were ranging over the northern area of the Channel but the combats were fast coming to an end. The 307th Fighter Squadron saw four 190s about to attack some Spitfires but they drove them off, claiming two as damaged. Squadron Leader Tommy Balmforth, leading 124 Squadron, saw six Me109Fs but they turned tail when his 12 Spitfires approached. Johnnie Johnson leading 610 Squadron also saw some 190s who also turned and flew off. 610 gave chase but left them. They then gave air cover to some ASR boats they found five miles off Dieppe still searching for missing pilots.

Some Dorniers and Junkers were still about, one Dornier being found by Squadron Leader Grant of 485 Squadron. He attacked it but it rapidly disappeared into the clouds. Some other Dorniers were seen but they also slipped into the clouds and out of sight. Flight Lieutenant R. W. Baker chased one, using 16 lbs of boost to catch it. His fire from 300 yards produced some strikes on the bomber's wings and fuselage but Baker had to give up the chase near the French coast when his ammunition gave out.

No 411 Squadron also found a Dornier over the convoy, it being attacked by Flight Sergeant Matheson and then by Squadron Leader Newton. The bomber was forced to jettison its bombs about one mile from the convoy but it got away although damaged.

Duke-Woolley led 71, 232 and 124 Squadrons out, Gus Daymond leading 71 (BM510) with Bob Sprague leading one section. Oscar Coen led the third section which comprised Sergeant P. J. E. Evans, Strick Strickland and William O'Regan. Strickland later recorded in his diary:

> We arrived over Dieppe to find all of our assault boats and transporters away from the beaches and on course for England. Destroyers, however, were still firing at long range and Dieppe itself was ablaze. A large force of 190s appeared. Wing Commander Duke-Woolley ordered the Debden Wing to prepare for attack. We manoeuvred into the sun and climbed above. When we turned towards them from below, they retreated headlong towards Le Touquet. Shortly before dusk the assault craft, transports, tank-carriers were within sight of Beachy Head with a rear-guard of destroyers and E-boats. We set course for home and landed at Gravesend, refuelled, re-armed, prepared for night fighting.

124 Squadron also saw six Messerschmitt 109Fs but they quickly turned tail and retreated when the Spitfires turned towards them. 232 also saw some 109s briefly in the clouds.

At 5.45 pm, 'Blackgang' control located another 'bandit' and radioed to Sergeants Cleo and Grant still on patrol in their 141 Squadron Beaufighter. The bandit was said to be flying north-west and Cleo, guided to the location by his radar-man, obtained a visual contact with it ten minutes later when it was five miles ahead of him. For a moment he lost sight of it in 9/10ths cloud but quickly found it again at 6.10 pm, just one mile ahead. It was raining quite heavily in places. Cleo closed to a range of 1,000 yards, then closed still further until he was just 250 yards away. At this range he fired three bursts of cannon and machine-gun fire of one, three and five seconds' duration, closing right in to 150 yards. Strikes were observed on the enemy aeroplane, which had been identified as a Ju88, and both of its engines caught fire. The Junkers went down slowly, hit the sea in flames and sank, four miles south of Selsey Bill.

No 131 Squadron, led by Michael Pedley was also successful. They scrambled to intercept an incoming raid at 5.55 pm, control vectoring them towards enemy raiders plotted near Selsey Bill.

Two DO217s and a Ju88 were encountered and attacked. The Junkers were attacked by Pedley, Flying Officer H. S. Jackson and the New Zealander, Pilot Officer H. G. Copeland, shot down and destroyed. Flight Lieutenant J. C. S. Doll, Flying Officer Jackson, Pilot Officer E. A. J. Williams and Pilot Officer I. K. Crawford, severely damaged one of the Dorniers which they claimed as probably destroyed, while Squadron Leader R. H. Allen damaged the other Dornier. For the 23 year old former New Zealand farmer, from Mataura, Copeland, it was his fourth sortie of the day. He had shared in the destruction of two enemy aircraft during the battle and damaged another. However, the rear gunner of the Junkers succeeded in putting hits into both Copeland's and Pedley's Spitfires. Copeland (AD348) staggered away with his engine knocking and made for the coast. As he reached it his engine failed but he managed to glide the last half mile to crash land in a field damaging his mainplane.

Having landed from what we believed to have been our final sortie we were scrambled yet again, this time to intercept an enemy raid heading for Tangmere itself. The weather which had been sunny and bright all day, had by now deteriorated and we climbed up through layer after layer of cloud under directions of the fighter controller. At last we spotted a motley assortment of aircraft comprising a Dornier 217, a Ju88, He111 and possibly a few more of one or another. Blue and Yellow sections went after their chosen targets whilst I took Red section after the Ju88. All the EA jettisoned their bombs and dived for cloud cover. We followed the Ju88 in a very steep dive, catching glimpses of it between the cloud layers and closing on it slowly, it was a dead stern chase and when we were near enough to open fire we could see a light winking back at us, the significance of which we did not initially fully appreciate! Firstly my Number 2 called up saying he had been hit; turning away he crash-landed safely near Selsey Bill. Next, my cockpit filled with the smell of cordite as an explosive shell went through the wingroot, the rudder bar then 'kicked' so violently that it nearly broke my ankle. Then Number 3 of section called up, 'Watch it, Peerless Leader, your rudder is coming off!'

Not being cast in the mould of heroes I decided it was time to give the Ju88 the best of it so I also turned back gingerly, for base where I performed a highly entertaining ground loop on landing due to my hydraulic system having been shot away. We claimed the Ju88 as a probable as both its engines were smoking when we saw it last. However, an anti-aircraft unit on the Isle of Wight reported it going in to the sea. I felt really sorry that it had gone down for the rear gunner in it must have been not only an excellent shot but also a cool-headed and very courageous man.

Wing Commander Michael Pedley, OC 131 Squadron

These raiding bombers were taking every advantage of the rain and cloud to slip across the south coast and bomb RAF bases now that the convoy was all but home. At 4.30 one enemy bomber had been damaged by anti-aircraft fire over Southampton. At approximately 6 o'clock two or three bombers flew over Ford and dropped bombs near 605 Squadron's office, damaging two of their Bostons, although no personnel were hurt. At 6.30 a FW190 attacked Ford, dropped three bombs and machine-gunned 141 Squadron's crew room. Two of the squadron's Beaufighters were slightly damaged by blast and one airman, Aircraftman Pridding, who had been working on a Beaufighter, was buried up to his neck in debris while running for cover.

Yet another raider attacked Ford at around 7 pm, its bombs destroying a Boston of 418 Squadron. Further enemy aircraft came over during the next hour or so. A Ju88 was damaged by gunfire over the Isle of Wight at 7.10, and the Portsmouth AA batteries destroyed another 88 at 7.40. The Isle of Wight gunners damaged a Heinkel at 8 pm.

We were in the midst of baths, shaving etc, when we were told to get back to the flights immediately. The Jerries were taking advantage of the bad weather to bomb us. We all took off again but the weather was so bad we couldn't locate any. One Ju88 flew over the aerodrome [Tangmere] just as we took off, but we lost it in the clouds and rain.

Pilot Officer John Godfrey, 412 Squadron.
From a letter home dated 20 August 1942

The final patrols of this day were flown between 6.10 and 8.55 pm. There were also several scrambles in order to protect south coast bases and ports but little contact was made against these raiders.

Over the Channel the activity was quickly dying down. One of the last combats of the day was by 340 Squadron. The Frenchmen, led by Wing Commander Dutch Hugo, patrolled around 5,000 feet in 8/10ths cloud. One Dornier was seen and attacked and damaged by Capitaine Bechoff (EN889 GW–Z). It was 340's fourth mission.

The Canadians of 416 Squadron led by Lloyd Chadburn saw this combat taking place five miles from their position but saw little else. Other final patrols over the remaining ships were flown by 303, 331, 332 and 616 Squadrons. 331 orbited the ships at 3,000 feet, now only 16 miles or so south of Beachy Head. After five minutes, Blue section went off to chase a Dornier which had been spotted seven miles east of the ships. Blue 3 and 4, Lieutenant Einar Sem-Olsen (BL987 FN–Z) and Sergeant E. Fossum (AD509 FN–P) attacked the Dornier, both seeing cannon and machine-gun strikes on the German's fuselage and port engine nacelle. Pieces flew off but then they lost it in the endless mass of clouds.

Nos 118, 242, 32 and 245 as well as 412 Squadron, were all scrambled at this late hour to try and locate elusive hostile raiders, Me109s even having been reported dropping bombs near Selsey Bill, and machine-gunning trawlers off the Sussex coast. None of these squadrons made contact.

Squadron Leader Jean 'Moses' Demozay, the French leader of 91 Squadron, led (DL–J) ten of his pilots on one last defensive patrol between Folkestone and Hastings from 7.15 to 8.15 pm but they found little activity. His unit had flown 73 patrols during the day covering a total of 61 flying hours.

Throughout the afternoon, crowds of people had begun to line the coastal high grounds along the south-coast opposite Dieppe. On the high vantage point of Beachy Head, between Eastbourne and Newhaven, many locals made the trek to the top to view the whole panorama of the returning armada of ships. 611 Squadron made mention of this spectacle in its diary. They also recorded: 'Last sight of landing craft (on their) way home, brown jobs lying down and the occasional fighter pilot standing in the front waving.'

30

32

30. Group Captain Harry Broadhurst, deputy SASO at 11 Group, flew four reconnaissance sorties over the Raid, bringing back valuable information for which he received a bar to his DFC. He also destroyed a FW190.

31. Wing Commander David Scott-Malden won the DSO at Dieppe leading the North Weald Wing. *(IWM)*.

32. Squadron Leader Peter Brothers, CO of 602 Squadron brought his unit from a rest to fly at Dieppe. *(P. M. Brothers)*

Several local newspapers would also report the story over the next few days.

> The planes in their hundreds made the sky alive with action, speed and noise. Bombers and fighters were seen, some engaged with enemy 'planes and many a swift aerial battle was fought out within sight of the eager watching crowds.
>
> *Brighton and Hove Herald, 22 August 1942*

Don Blakeslee led 133 Eagle Squadron over the last of the convoy, taking off at 7.55 pm. Little was seen but one pilot had a brief moment of excitement.

> On the fourth show of the day we were attacked by two FW190s who came from above and fired on us. From a tight turn I went over on my back after them, and continued to fire down to about 3,000 feet; I observed strikes at long range, but was forced to pull out at around 3,000 feet. I barely missed going in because we were at maximum speed and I blacked out pulling out of the dive. I am reasonably sure that the 190, who was probably six or seven hundred yards ahead of me by then, had less chance of pulling out than I did. I claimed a probable.
>
> *Flight Sergeant Richard Alexander, 133 Squadron*

The Eagle Squadron pilots were the last ones down. They landed back at RAF Lympne at 8.55 pm.

Operation Jubilee was at an end.

*

Special mention must be made of the Air Sea Rescue operations which were carried out tirelessly throughout the day. With so much planned aerial activity the ASR service was naturally well to the fore in the planning of the raid and all concerned carried out their duty with a high degree of skill and courage.

A total of 34 rescue launches were employed, and during the day they investigated approximately fifty distress calls and rescued 15 airmen, mostly fighter pilots. They lost three boats sunk with others damaged and had two officers and 18 airmen killed or missing as a result.

The basic plan had been for nine launches to patrol 'Inshore', between Fairlight and Littlehampton, four more to patrol further out on what was the 'Intermediate' line, fifteen miles out from Beachy Head. The 'Advanced' line of six launches patrolled 30 miles south of Beachy Head.

At 4.30 am high speed launches (HSLs) 104, 106, 116, 117 and 177 from Newhaven, were at their pre-arranged 'Intermediate' rendezvous point and remained here until between 6 pm and midnight. *HSL 177* rescued one pilot at 11.15 am, this being Pilot Officer Don Morrison of 401 RCAF Squadron who had been in the water about 15 minutes. Later, at 4.50 pm, *177* went to the assistance of *HSLs 122* and *123* of the Advanced Group, who were being attacked by Focke Wulf 190s and in distress. *RML 513* assisted No *177* in beating off several determined Focke Wulf attacks and in the subsequent rescue of 14 survivors of Nos *122* and *123*, seven of whom were wounded. 122 and 123 were left burning furiously and lost. *177* suffered no casualties although it suffered some superficial damage from strafing, being hit by both cannon and machine-gun fire. The launch's skipper, Flying Officer F. Conway, was awarded the MBE while his coxswain, Corporal Fellick and Leading Aircraftman Hermitage were both Mentioned in Dispatches.

From Littlehampton, *HSL 442*, received a call at 6.20 am from the Walrus of 277 Squadron, requesting them to rescue the crew of the downed Boston of 418 Squadron, captained by Sergeant Buchanan, who had been shot down by FW190s.

Between 5.55 am and 6.22 pm, the Air Sea Rescue Service received over 40 reports, the majority from 11 Group, Fighter Command, and a few from Shore Signal Stations. Several of these calls were duplicated. Newhaven ASR dealt with 26 crash calls, two being too near the French coast to be dealt with, two more proving ficticious. Ten successful rescues were made during this time although two pilots died following rescue.

The third launch lost was *HSL 147* from Dover. Dover was informed at 1.10 pm by Air Sea Rescue Headquarters, of a Mayday at position 173°, 43 miles off Dungeness. *HSLs 147* and *186* were ordered to this position at 1.12 and proceeded out to sea. At 2.40 pm, *HSL 186*, which had become separated from *147*, rescued a pilot at position 174°, 46 miles off Dungeness. On the return to a pre-arranged rendezvous, *186* was attacked by German aircraft at 3.35

pm and sustained some casualties. A 'help' call to base brought two Spitfires from 91 Squadron who escorted this launch back to Dover. Meanwhile, *HSL 147* had also been attacked by hostile aircraft at 3.03 pm and was assumed sunk five or six miles from the Somme Estuary. At 3.50 two Spitfires, again from 91 Squadron, flew out to search for the missing launch but their search mission was in vain.

RML 495 was also attacked by a Ju88 in the afternoon which dropped bombs then commenced to strafe it. The launches' crew returned the German's fire with their oerlikon guns and succeeded in driving it away damaged – possibly even destroyed.

ASR launches were amongst the last boats to leave the battle area off Dieppe, staying for as long as possible in case further rescues were needed. 91 Squadron escorted launches back well after 6.30 pm and 610 Squadron on their last patrol saw ASR launches five miles off Dieppe at the same time. Many pilots had cause to thank the crews of the ASR launches during the war, and 19 August 1942 was no exception.

CHAPTER TWELVE

The Luftwaffe

The Dieppe Raid was, from the point of view of the German
fighter pilots, one of the happiest days since the days of the Battle
of Britain.

Hans Ring – Historian of the German Association of former Fighter Pilots

This is an accurate assessment, especially as it was the biggest air
battle in which German fighter pilots in the West had been engaged
for well over a year. Throughout 1941-42 the Royal Air Force's
constant offensive actions over Northern France, Belgium and Holland had brought continual action but in the main it was no more
than just nibbling at the large British formations of bombers and
Spitfires. The RAF's Sweeps, Circuses, Ramrods and Roadsteads
were all designed primarily to bring the Luftwaffe to battle but
more often than not only a relative handful of German fighters
would be able to get in position to attack and with sometimes over a
hundred British Spitfires buzzing around a dozen or so twin-
engined medium daylight bombers, made it difficult to engage in an
all-out, old-fashioned dog-fight. Above Dieppe, however, there was
a continual stream of aeroplanes and the action remained over this
general area for hours. Thus the Luftwaffe fighter pilots were able
to bring all of its available aeroplanes to do battle over this one
locality.

As previously mentioned, there were only two *Jagdesgeschwaders* in
France, JG2 and JG26. JG2's area of operations was generally to
the west of the River Seine – Normandy and Cherbourg, while
JG26 operated east of the Seine, over Northern France and Belgium.

Major Gerhard Schopfel was *Kommodore* of JG26. He was a pre-
war pilot, had shot down his first RAF fighter over Dunkirk and by
the end of the Battle of Britain had 29 kills and the Knight's Cross.
His fighters were the first to be involved in the Dieppe Operation
due to their bases being in close proximity to the harbour town.

The *Jagdesgeschwader's* Staff *Staffel* was based at St Omer/Wizernes, its I Gruppe, commanded by Hauptman Johannes Siefert, at St Omer/Arques. II Gruppe led by Oberleutnant Wilhelm-Ferdinand Galland, was at Abbeville/Drucat and III Gruppe headed by Hauptman Klaus Mietusch had its base at Wevelghem, near Courtrai.

Major Walter Oesau's JG2's I Gruppe under Oberleutnant Erich Leie was at Tricqueville, its II Gruppe commanded by Hauptman Helmut Bolz at Beaumont-le-Roger. III Gruppe led by Hauptman Hans Hahn were stationed at Maupertus. All these units were equipped with the Focke Wulf 190 A–2 and A–3s. Both of the *Jagdesgeschwaders* had their No 10 'Jabo' (fighter-bomber) *Staffeln*, equipped with FW190 A–3U1, and both had their *Staffeln* equipped with Messerschmitt Me109G–1s, and some 109Fs.

Gerhard Schopfel, by 19 August 1942, had nearly 40 victories. Siefert, also a holder of the Knight's Cross (*Ritterkreuz*), also had 40 victories and had also been with JG26 since before the war. 'Wutz' Galland, was the brother of Adolf Galland, and had 12 victories to date. Klaus Meitusch was another experienced fighter pilot and had been with JG26 since 1938. Erich Leie, another Knight's Cross holder, had 42 kills. He had flown with two of the finest German pilots of the 1940-41 period, Helmut Wick and Walter Oesau. He had taken over the command of I/JG26 in May 1942. Hans 'Assi' Hahn had 65 victories, the Knight's Cross with Oak Leaves and a wealth of experience. He was another pre-war pilot who had been with JG26 since the outbreak of war.

The bomber force which became committed against the ships of the British and Canadian forces came mainly from Kampfgeschwader 2 who were mostly based in Holland. KG 2 'Holzhammer' was equipped with the Dornier 217E. Other units that became involved in the battle were the Junkers 88s of 1 Staffel of KG77, Dornier 217s of KG40's II Gruppe plus Heinkel 111s of III/KG53.

1 Staffel of JG26 were the first fighters to fly against Jubilee. Before 6 am, this *Staffel* scrambled all available aircraft – just ten. Shortly afterwards the 2 and 3 Staffels put up eight Focke Wulfs each. One of the first successes fell to Oberfeldweber Heinrich Bierwith of II/JG26 who claimed the destruction of a Spitfire.

Despite the fact that 19 August came during one of the periods the Germans considered it possible for the Allies to launch an attack on the French coast, due to tides etc; the Luftwaffe commander for the Dieppe Area had not maintained a readiness state. It seemed apparent from the weather predicted for the 19th, cloud and rain following later in the day, that there would be little risk of such an attack taking place. He had, therefore, allowed many of his pilots leave until noon of the 19th. In fact one pilot in three had been granted 24-hours' leave passes. There was some rapid return to airfields and squadrons when it was known that the 'Tommies' were over Dieppe in force.

As the day progressed and the scale of the raid became apparent more and more Luftwaffe aircraft began to take off to join the battle with the RAF. These aircraft were monitored by British radar. At between 8.29 and 9.14 am fifty German aircraft were reported climbing up from the St Omer and Desvres area, then 12 more from Lille followed by 12 to 15 from Dunkirk – probably from the airfield at Mardyck. What was also apparent was that so far nothing was reported from the area covered by JG2. At this hour there was a total of fifty or more enemy aircraft to battle with the RAF in the general vicinity of the town of Dieppe.

The first reported reaction of the Le Havre – JG2 – area was recorded at approximately 9.40 am. At 9.41, twenty or more fighters appeared from Abbeville – Wutz Galland and his II Gruppe was taking the air. Five minutes later a further gaggle lifted off from Abbeville.

The peak of German fighter cover came between the two hours 9.30 to 11.30 am, during the time they covered and escorted the Dorniers, an estimated 100+ being recorded. Over the hour 12 noon to 1 o'clock over fifty fighters escorted further Luftwaffe bombers. One hour later, at 2 pm, radar picked up reinforcements coming in from Belgium and Holland, these being joined by a further group of aircraft from Le Havre and Amiens – an estimated 75 to 80 aircraft. At 1.50 pm 25 to 30 came up from St Omer.

Abbeville was out of the battle for some time following the American Fortress raid. Only three minutes warning of this raid was received by the 'Abbeville Boys' before the first bombs began to rain down. Several 190s, as observed by the American crews and their Spitfire escort, were caught on the ground and destroyed. This was at approximately 10.30 am and it was not until after 3 pm that radar picked up activity from this base. This was part of the 80 to 100 aircraft reported from bases to the south of Dieppe.

From British radar reports it was estimated that German bombers, mostly Dorniers 217s, had carried out 125 sorties, while FW190s and Me109s had flown 500 sorties, 350 of which had been over Dieppe itself. In actual fact bombers had flown some 145 sorties, and the fighter pilots about 800, of which JG26 flew 377 in 36 separate missions. Many individual fighter pilots had flown up to three and some as many as six missions during the day.

The most outstanding Luftwaffe fighter pilot of the day was 25-year-old Josef 'Sepp' Wurmheller. As *Staffelkapitän* of 9/JG2 he had had a successful early start to 1942, having destroyed ten Allied aircraft in May, and a further 12 in June. On the morning of 19 August he was in fact suffering from a broken foot and had his lower leg encased in plaster bandage. However, when the alarm came and the huge Allied effort was revealed, Wurmheller was helped into his Focke Wulf and took off. Not long after take off his machine developed engine trouble and he had to force-land in a field. He hobbled to a German command post from where he was returned to his airfield by car. He had banged his head in the landing but in spite of a raging headache, climbed into another 190 and headed for the battle. Over Dieppe he claimed one Blenheim and two Spitfires, before returning home to refuel and rearm. On his second sortie he claimed three Spitfires and then later on his fourth flight over the ships shot down another Spitfire. These seven victories brought his score to 60 and won for him the *Eichenlaubs* (the Oak Leaves) to his Knight's Cross, the 146th Luftwaffe pilot so honoured. During his final sortie his headache had got so bad that he flew with a veil before his vision. At the end of the day a doctor discovered that his head injury had in fact caused a concussion. Wurmheller ended the war with 102 victories, the vast majority claimed in the west and he had received the *Schwertern* (the Swords) to his Knight's Cross.

Another successful day was had by Oberleutnant Siegfried Schnell, *Staffelkapitän* of 9 Staffel of II Gruppe, JG2. 'Wumm' Schnell had already been decorated with the Knight's Cross and Oak Leaves in 1940 and 1941 respectively. He claimed the destruction of five Spitfires over Dieppe, bringing his score to 70. Later in the war he commanded III Gruppe of JG54 but died in action on the Russian front in February 1944 having achieved 93 victories.

JG26's most successful pilot was Oberleutnant Kurt Ebersberger who claimed four Spitfires, victories 25 to 28. Oberleutnant Fuelbert Zink gained his 24th, 25th and 26th victories by claiming two Spitfires and a Mustang while Ofw. Emil Babenz of 2 Staffel I/JG26 claimed three Spitfires to bring his personal victories to 21. For Oberleutnant Egon Mayer, *Staffelkapitän* of 7/JG2 and Knight's Cross winner, it was a special day – his 25th birthday. He had been with JG2 since December 1939 and had gained his first victories over France in 1940. His two Spitfire kills over Dieppe brought his score to a round 50. He was to gain 102 victories in the west, and received the Oak Leaves and Swords, before his death in combat in March 1944.

At least 19 holders or future holders of the coveted Knight's Cross were successful over Dieppe and at least 30 of the pilots who made claims were what is more popularly known as 'aces', the *Experten* of the German Luftwaffe.

Also successful had been 10 Jabo Staffel of JG2 commanded by 26 year old Oberleutnant Fritz Schröter. He had been with JG2 since March 1941 but *Staffelkapitän* of 10 Staffel since only July 1942. For his outstanding leadership over Dieppe on 19 August he was awarded the Knight's Cross. His *Staffel* claimed to have bombed and sunk one destroyer, two landing craft, and damaged another destroyer, two trawlers, two landing craft and also to have shot down one RAF aircraft. Whether the destroyer claim was the *Berkeley* is not known. In one report the *Berkeley* was hit by bombs jettisoned by a harassed Ju88, in another it was hit by a bomb-carrying FW190.

Wing Commander Michael Pedley recalls the Luftwaffe tactics and his own side's as seen from the standpoint of a Spitfire squadron commander.

The Tangmere Wing being equipped with Spitfire Vs had been ear-marked for low level and medium cover whilst Spitfire IXs ... were to provide the high cover, although in the event we seldom actually saw them over the beach-head. Whilst the RAF Wings had to relieve each other in rotation the enemy fighter force could choose its own moment to strike and in fact came in waves at unpredictable timings. We could generally watch the FW190s building up overhead like a swarm of bees before they started diving down to try and engage our shipping and assault forces.

The Tangmere Wing would be stepped up by squadrons from about 5,000 feet to 12,000 feet with their sections weaving about in battle formation ('finger-four' or line astern depending on choice). The tactic adopted was to break formation just as the enemy was coming within range and climbing steeply, engage the EA head-on. Occasionally it was possible to get after a FW190 that had hesitated in its dive but usually the EA were going too fast to follow down. Nevertheless, our form of attack was highly effective in diverting the enemy fighters from their target and from time to time achieved 'kills'; thereafter, having lost their advantage of height the EA seldom stayed below us but instead dived away clear of the danger area.

We were happiest when the bombers showed up, usually in twos or threes or even as single aircraft; these we attacked with great gusto and generally succeeded in shooting down before they could do any damage.

By mid to late afternoon the Luftwaffe fighter force had been considerable reduced in number due to losses, battle damage etc, and it was almost 'grounded'. Eighteen Focke Wulfs at the Luftwaffe's Forwarding Centre at Welveghem, being its total spare machines, were all issued to units during the day. Also by the late afternoon all the stocks of 20mm ammunition had been expended and was not replenished until the next day and then by special air-lift. This also affected serviceability of the Focke Wulf fighters. One wonders what the casualty figures on both sides might have been if the Focke Wulfs had been higher in number.

At Dieppe the 190 pilots had, for the first time, encountered the new Mustangs, although it was not appreciated that the latter were flying reconnaissance missions, and not part of the overall fighter force. They had mixed fortunes when in combat with the Mustang. One which was attacked caught a burst in the port wing tank and promptly exploded in mid-air. Another was chased from near Dieppe to almost Eastbourne but the German pilot could not close nearer than 150 yards.

CHAPTER THIRTEEN

Speaking Personally

'Looking back over the intervening years, the Dieppe Raid, so far as the Allied Air Forces were concerned, was a reasonably successful operation; not so much by what was achieved on the 19 August 1942, but from the lessons learnt, which made the later invasion successful. As is well known now, the German reaction was massive and swift, and the air fighting was said to have been the fiercest of any single day during the war. Losses in the air on both sides were heavy, and although the Allies were able to accept their casualties because of ready replacements, the Germans could not – or so we were told. No doubt there was some truth in this!

'Possibly because of Dieppe, the Mulberry Harbour idea was finalised, since Dieppe confirmed that it was not possible to take a vital port on the French coast without its being made useless by the Germans.

'Speaking personally, it was just another 'op', another daylight raid over occupied Northern France, although this time the army and the navy were taking part. There was plenty going on once the other side was reached. We, as fighter-bombers were under orders not to seek any combat since we had a specific job to do, and to let the 'Spit' squadrons get on with tackling the Luftwaffe.

'But what impressed me most was all the debris of war, not only on the beaches but far out to sea. There were bright yellow dinghies and bits of aircraft floating about, apart from rubbish of an unknown character. The small German coaster which accidentally ran into our landing fleet earlier that morning was still afloat and burning. Ashore there appeared to be the utter random confusion of a junk yard. The whole panorama was canopied by a pall of smoke.

'Yet a few days later when we went to the same area, the whole mess had vanished, as though swept clean with a new broom. Once more the quiet and placid conditions prevailed along the French coast, with hardly a movement anywhere, yet we were well aware that many pairs of eyes – French and German – were watching us!'

John Brooks, 174 Squadron

'Somebody found a supply of orange-headed pins (as used on plotting maps), and on our return to Charmy Down and to the pubs in Bath, we were all to be seen wearing 'Dieppe Pins' awarded for our part in this heroic action! They lasted a few days, I think.'

Frank Mitchell, 87 Squadron

'I think that we were all quite exhausted by the end of the day which I believe was the greatest single air battle of the war with losses in excess of ninety aircraft on both sides. Certainly the squadron flew more sorties than on any occasion previously and that we got through the day without losing a single pilot was certain proof that the unit was by then a very experienced outfit.

'Returning to my digs that evening I told my wife that it had been better than going to the pictures whereupon I fell asleep. My mother, who was rather deaf, had been telephoning during the day for news and that evening she again called; to be told that I was in bed. "I knew it all along," she said, "He's dead!" '

Michael Pedley, OC 131 Squadron

'The issue of the *Daily Mirror* the following morning carried the whole of the front page with one picture, the boys of 88 Squadron. But the caption! The usual awful blurb, for the benefit of the factory girls and others, about 'Cows grazing peacefully in the field and our brave heroes in the air just before take-off for Dieppe, where Death is the order of the day! When I telephoned the Editor, congratulating him about the picture, but grumbled about the caption, he said, "Quite right, but that's what the girls like." You cannot win.

'In retrospect, I feel that the contribution made by squadrons of 2 Group was all that was expected. Whatever concept of the Dieppe Raid might have been – it was thought to be a try-out for D-Day – there is no doubt that many lessons were learned for the future reference. Air tactics; the co-ordination needed between bomber force, fighter force, and both with land forces. It must be remembered that at that point we had not, by any means, reached the refinements of sophisticated Tactical Air Force expertise. Dieppe was a damn good try at it. Despite the ground losses, it was probably invaluable in order to get the necessary know-how for the Big

Thing later. And of course, the Spitfire boys had a field day.'

James Pelly-Fry, OC 88 Squadron

'About two years later, on D+10, I arrived in Normandy with our US IX Tactical Air Command HQ (Advanced). As the Allied forces consolidated their positions, poured in thousands of tons of supplies and reinforcements and engaged the enemy on that relatively small sector, strategists were puzzled by the inactivity of a crack German Army on the Allied left flank. As you know, the enemy sat there for week after week. Historians now know that, in addition to the excellent intelligence deception and Patton's Third Army (still) in the UK, Operation Jubilee in 1942 had conditioned the German strategists to believe that the logical site for the main landing of the invading forces would be in the Pas de Calais area, and Normandy was a diversion. So I think it is pretty well understood that the heavy sacrifices at Dieppe in 1942 saved thousands of other Allied lives directly and indirectly during June 1944 in Normandy, especially on that longest day which also profited from Dieppe experience.'

Harold Strickland, 71 Eagle Squadron

'It was a long day for the squadron beginning with a maximum effort first light attack with smoke to blind gun positions threatening the first stages of the assault. That preplanned effort was followed by quick reaction responses throughout the day to calls for assistance from the beach-head. It concluded with the laying of the defensive screen. It was a day of truly direct co-operation with the other forces – a classic Combined Operation.

'We in 226 were fortunate in that we did not suffer more aircrew casualties for our aircraft took a great deal of punishment in the course of the day; not a little from our own side. I think I am correct in recalling that only three aircraft were fully serviceable at the beginning of the following morning for our return to Swanton Morley Base. The remainder followed us if and when they could. 226 Squadron got a special mention for its smoke laying in the message received from No 2 Group Headquarters on the following day. We were proud of that but we had already 'celebrated' on the night of the 19th immediately it was all over.'

Digger Magill, 226 Squadron

'A big fighter effort went into the support of the Dieppe Raid. Many of us talked about it after the event and I remember fairly well the general reaction of my contemporaries in Fighter Command. From our point of view we thought the whole operation was an extraordinary nonsense. The Commando Raid led by Lord Lovat to the west of Dieppe made sense to us. We thought that a raid in some force like Lovat's with a specific objective, even though by itself it proved only that that sort of operation could be done, that it might be repeated elsewhere, and so would have served to worry the Germans about their coastal defences, would probably divert over-large resources to a wasteful and extended defensive exercise. But the raid itself on Dieppe baffled us. It was large enough to invite heavy casualties, but too small for the Germans to consider it an 'invasion' of any sort. It had to have only limited objectives, and we could not see what there could be to justify the effort. We would have liked to have set about the nearest German airfields in a big way, notably that at Abbeville with whose fighters we often tangled on Sweeps, and to have made life thoroughly unpleasant by repeated attacks on and around them – instead of anchoring ourselves to the immediate area of Dieppe in the strength that we did. To maintain the Dieppe cover we all had a pretty sweaty day – I did four sorties covering seven hours or so – and I suppose that around fifty squadrons must have taken part to keep that localised cover going.

'In saying this I would not wish to detract anything at all from our admiration and respect for the troops who carried out the raid. They were brave men and we wouldn't willingly have swopped places. But we also could not see how they could avoid being on a beating to nothing. Some weeks, or months, before Dieppe I had located and escorted back towards England the small commando force which attacked the Bruneval radar station. To my mind that sort of operation – the stiletto rather than the blunt and heavy cutlass – was what we ought to be about. But we were just up at the sharp end and didn't have to plan the War. Maybe it all made, or makes, sense. I wonder, sometimes, though . . .'

Myles Duke-Woolley, OC Debden Wing

'One of the subsequent incidents which meant a lot to me was a special ceremony in their ex-patriate HQ in Kensington when the

33. Squadron Leader D. C. Carlson, CO of 54 Squadron received the DFC for his part in the Dieppe Operation. *(IWM)*

34. John Brooks of 174 Squadron flew two fighter-bomber sorties to Dieppe and received the DFM. *(J. W. Brooks)*

35. Squadron Leader Pete Wickham flew five missions to Dieppe, leading his own 111 Squadron twice and the 308th US Squadron three times. He won a bar to his DFC. *(IWM)*

33

35

squadron commanders and I were presented with the Norwegian War Cross by King Haakon. An informal party had been arranged afterwards, on which Prince Olaf (as he then was) was coming with the Norwegian Air Force boys. "I'd better just tell my father where I'm going," he said. The response from King Haakon was, "Oh, no you don't. If there is going to be a party with these chaps I'm coming too." So it had to be hastily reorganised into an official lunch at Claridges.'

David Scott-Malden, OC North Weald Wing

'I was in operations as a fighter pilot from the autumn of 1941 until the end of the war. Of all the fighting I took part in I believe the Dieppe Raid proved to be one of the hardest tasks. My personal score of one FW190 shot down was a modest result (that day), but the Luftwaffe was at its very best and the Norwegian Wing was fairly inexperienced. I feel the Dieppe Raid was a turning point in the war. The German losses were high, and more German forces were deployed to the Eastern Front. The quality and the perseverance of the average German pilot was on the decline.'

Svein Heglund, 331 Norwegian Squadron

'I completed three tours of operations during the war, was shot down four times, served 34 years in the RAF which included many other tough assignments, but I am sure that this was the most dramatic of them all.'

Jchn Ellacombe, 253 Squadron

'From the air defence point of view the main differences between Normany and Dieppe were:
  1 the whole of the resources of the air forces in UK were devoted to smashing the enemy airfields, communications and sea defences.
  2 Fighter Command were responsible for the air defence of the beach-head until I got ashore with airfields and HQs etc., and took over control of the whole of the beach-head until we were well established and the Americans took control of their sector.
'In the event, there was practically no enemy air opposition because of the effect of the bombing and our offensive patrols over his airfields.

'There is no doubt that the Army and Navy gained some useful experience at Dieppe and put it to good use during the landings in North Africa, and the landings in Sicily and Italy. Taking the operation as a whole, Dieppe was very small fry compared with the subsequent operations, and in the interim all three services had gained a mass of experience both in seaborne operations, airborne operations and tactical air force operations. To say nothing of manipulating Signals Intelligence.'

Sir Harry Broadhurst, Deputy SASO, 11 Group

'I led my squadron on all four missions and the Wing on one of them that day, so when the evening came and daylight was dwindling away we were tired, but we were happy. Especially happy, because two pilots we lost came back safely, having baled out over the Channel and being rescued by the Navy. Comparing our losses with the enemy's gave us a satisfaction which was equally shared between the pilots and their ground personnel. It was with proudness I could talk to the men before we turned in for the night and thank them. My pilots and I had every reason to praise their work. All aircraft worked perfectly, four squadron missions, all of them with 12 aircraft each, not one engine failure, not one gun jammed, not one radio failed, indeed an engine change was performed within six hours. And the next morning 12 aircraft ready for a fighter Sweep over Northern France, where not a single Luftwaffe 'plane was seen. We all slept well that night.'

Helge Mehre, OC 331 Norwegian Squadron

'During the day's operation, our patrol heights had increased to keep on top of the enemy and thus the air battle had become ever more remote from ground activity yet still played a vital part. It was also good to remember that despite our losses we (in 602) had destroyed four aircraft and damaged eleven. On our return to No 14 Group, we were all delighted to receive a signal from the AOC, Air Vice Marshal Raymond Collishaw as follows:
"I saw 602 Squadron's Dieppe combat films today and congratulate the squadron on the way pilots closed the enemy to decisive range before opening fire."
A fitting end to a busy day.'

Peter Brothers, OC 602 Squadron

At the end of the day when we landed back at Duxford in the quiet, warm dusk of the Cambridgeshire countryside, we had lost one Typhoon with engine failure, and another missing; we had claimed two probable victories and three damaged and had taken a very small part in a great and heroic raid. The enemy may have been as frightened by the Typhoons as we were at the time though I doubt it – but the day of the Typhoon was still to come.

Roland Beamont, 609 Squadron

*

There can be little doubt that the Royal Air Force in general and the fighter pilots in particular had a terrifically exciting day and successful day, despite the subsequent realisation of their overall losses. On the evening of 19 August, the fighter pilots' tails 'were well up'. For many months they had wanted a really big, decisive confrontation with their counterparts in the German Luftwaffe and over Dieppe their wish had come true. For many of the pilots who had reached operational units after 1940, this was the first occasion that any of them had seen German bombers in the air; and many did not see or encounter bombers again in the war.

Although it has been mentioned already, by August 1942 many of the wing, squadron and flight commanders were veterans of the 1940 air battles fought over Southern England. What is also true is that many of the more junior pilots at Dieppe were seeing their first big actions, several future successful air fighters, in terms of German aircraft brought down, claimed their first aerial victories on that day.

It is little wonder, therefore, that in the vast majority of squadron messes, hotel bars, or pubs that evening, these same pilots proceeded to have some tremendous parties. Many of them turned into quite a 'thrash'. During some of these the occasional pilot who had been missing, would suddenly turn up. At Manston, the Norwegians were in full swing when their wounded CO, Wilhelm Mohr, hobbled in with his leg encased in plaster. This delighted his pilots who proceeded to sign the plaster in the time-honoured manner. Then Rolf Berg turned up, smiling sheepishly, and wearing an enormous white sailor's polo-neck pullover.

One of the most incongruous sights was aboard Peter Scott's *SGB–9 Grey Goose* as it finally returned home. It will be remembered that Scott had rescued several soldiers and airmen from the water, including a German flyer and the Norwegian fighter-pilot, Olav Djonne. Scott went below to see how everyone was getting along. He found the German with the ship's cat on his lap, sitting quite happily next to Djonne, who only hours before would quite happily have killed him in the air, while the German's armed guard, sitting on the other side of his prisoner, was fast asleep with his head on the German's shoulder. It is sights like this that makes one wonder why people go to war with each other in the first place.

In the mess of 71 Eagle Squadron, a different scene was taking place, much to the delight of those watching. Wee Michael McPharlin, it will be recalled, was pulled out of the sea shortly after he had swallowed his entire supply of benzedrine tablets.

We didn't realise for some time that he was still full of benzedrine, but when we did it accounted for his liveliness and lack of apparent need for sleep even after propping up the bar until 2 am. When I had consulted the MO about the effects of a dose of the size he had so happily gobbled, we estimated that he might continue at full throttle for, maybe, 48 hours. He would then go out like a light. And so it was. We could not leave him unattended because this was all guesswork, so we arranged for relays of pilots to keep him company. He stayed on full song all night, all the next day, all that night again, and showed no sign whatever of slowing up as the third night approached. Suddenly, and in mid-pint, he crumpled like a wet flannel – in the space of perhaps a minute, out to the wide and apparently filleted. We poured him into bed, and he slept the clock round, suffering no apparent ill-effects when he woke up. Our faith in benzedrine as an escape aid zoomed.

Myles Duke-Woolley, OC Debden Wing

*

On the morning of 20 August, 91 Squadron were out early looking for any signs of missing pilots who might still be bobbing about in their dinghies. German aircraft too were out over the Channel on similar missions. Pilot Officer E. Tonge (DL–L) was known to be near some enemy aircraft and failed to return from his search sortie. Flight Lieutenant J. R. Heap (DL–B) found a Dornier 24 flying-boat near Dieppe and attacked. It went down, hit the sea and exploded. The battle of the previous day might be over, but the war was continuing.

*

Thursday, 20 August, 1942. 6 am – Dawn Readiness:

'Here I am after the most hectic and exciting day of my life. We were in the thick of things at Dieppe yesterday and no doubt you are anxious to know how we made out. . . .'

Pilot Officer John Godfrey, 412 Squadron

CHAPTER FOURTEEN

Summing Up

Initially it was thought that the honours between the Royal Air Force and the Luftwaffe, in terms of casualties inflicted on the other, were about even. Fighter Command soon knew that they and 2 Group, Bomber Command, had lost just over 100 aeroplanes during the day, but that indications from claims submitted by its fighter pilots plus those shot down by the Navy, also showed nearly 100 German aircraft destroyed. After the war, however, Luftwaffe records showed that they had lost only 48 aircraft. Naturally many more had been damaged, and in fact by the morning of 20 August, the Luftwaffe had only 70 fighters in a serviceable state. Had Dieppe been just the first in a series of such actions, the Luftwaffe's fighter arm in the west would have been almost wiped out. Fortunately for them Dieppe was a one-off. In contrast, on D-Day, 6 June 1944, the Luftwaffe opposed the huge landings with just two FW190s flying one strafing run.

Yet the British news media heralded a great victory, the biggest since the dark days of the Battle of Britain. And despite the losses, the fighter pilots were well pleased.

It has always been difficult to assess with any real accuracy the actual losses of any battle, or to verify, the claims made by either side in a given conflict. The Dieppe Raid's casualties and claims are no exceptions. For those interested in such figures, the attacking force lost approximately 1,000 men killed, 600 wounded (other than those wounded and taken prisoner) and 1,900 captured. By comparison the RAF's losses in lives was small – 64.

The vast majority of air combat claims were always made in good faith, but in any air battle with aeroplanes twisting and turning, climbing and diving and all at high speed, it had to be virtually impossible to know for certain the results of a fighter pilot's attack. Unless the target blew up, lost a wing, was actually seen to crash, ie seen to fall from perhaps several hundred or thousand feet, and watched all the way down (a bad thing for a fighter pilot to attempt), or see the pilot take to his parachute, he could only claim what he believed his attack had done to the aeroplane he fired at. From the study of combat reports, including those concerning Dieppe, it is often clear that firing at an enemy aircraft, losing it, then seeing an aircraft go into the sea was claimed as a definite kill. The fact that several pilots were shooting at several aircraft and that possibly they all saw this one machine go into the sea, easily boosted claims – but they were made in all good faith. Above Dieppe, especially, with such a concentration of aeroplanes over a limited area it is little wonder that claims exceeded actual losses. It happened on both sides, for the Luftwaffe claimed over 100 victories on the 19th yet no more than 70 RAF aeroplanes were actually brought down by German aircraft, possibly less. Flak accounted for at least 30 and German bomber gunners at least four.

An analysis of RAF fighter claims for the 19th indicate the following totals.

Type	Destroyed	Probable	Damaged
FW190	47	27	76
Me109	3	1	2
Do217	33	8	46
Ju88	8	3	11
He111	5	—	—
	96	39	135

Actual losses admitted by the Luftwaffe:

Fighters	23	—	8
Bombers	25	—	16
	48	—	24

Of these:

	Destroyed	Damaged
Jagdesgeschwader 2	14	3
Jagdesgeschwader 26	5	1
Kampfgeschwader 2	16	7
	35	11

Almost every 'official' list of RAF casualties for 19 August differs in some respect. While I do not claim that the following list is 100% accurate, I have compiled it from basic squadron records and added to it from subsequent knowledge. Undoubtedly these figures could be fractionally higher if a damaged aircraft was later deemed to be unrepairable or struck-off. The totals for damaged are merely an indication, for some were seriously damaged, others only superficially hit. Many more with only very minor damage are not even noted or listed anywhere.

Royal Air Force losses – aeroplanes:

Type	Lost to enemy action	Lost in accidents	Damaged by enemy action	Damaged in accidents
Spitfires	59	3	31	9
Hurricanes	20	—	12	2
Mustangs	10	—	4	1
Typhoons	2	—	—	—
Bostons	4	—	6	—
Blenheims	2	—	1	—
	97	3	54	12

Royal Air Force losses – aircrew:

Pilots:	Killed in action	Killed in accidents	Captured	Wounded	Injured
Spitfire	27	2	11	14	2
Hurricane	12	—	3	1	1
Mustang	6	—	3	1	—
Typhoon	2	—	—	—	—
Boston	3	—	—	1	1
Blenheim	1	—	—	1	—
	51	2	17	18	4
Boston Observer/ Navigators	3	—	—	5	—
Boston Air Gunners	3	—	—	1	—

	Killed in action	Killed in accidents	Captured	Wounded	Injured
Blenheim					
Observer/					
Navigators	2	—	—	—	—
Boston					
Air Gunners	2	—	—	—	1
Passenger	1	—	—	—	—
Totals	62	2	17	24	5

Luftwaffe pilot losses:

	Killed in action	Missing	Wounded	Killed in accidents
JG 2	2	6	7	—
JG 26	5	—	—	1
	7	6	7	1

Statistics on bomber crew losses are not available.

The Royal Air Force flew a tremendous number of operational sorties on 19 August 1942 – 2,955. This figure is broken down as follows:

Type	sorties	
Spitfires	2050	171 patrols
Hurribombers	61	6 attacks
Hurricanes	205	18 strikes
Typhoons	72	9 patrols
91 Squadron (Spits)	39	38 patrols
Mustangs	72	35 tasks
Blenheims	16	3 raids
Bostons (2 Group)	62	15 raids
Bostons (Ftr Command)	3	1 raid
Fortresses	24	1 raid
	2604	balance of scrambles,
		defensive patrols,
	351	– ASR, etc:

Of these, 120 sorties were carried out by USAAF fighters of 31st Fighter Group – 8th Air Force. The 97th Bombardment Group, 8th Air Force flew 24 B17 sorties.

Luftwaffe sorties totalled:

JG 2	423*
JG 26	377
Bombers	145*
	945
* approximate	

Tangible recognition of the gallantry, courage, dedication and determination shown by the airmen during the Dieppe Raid was given to many of them. Several of these have already been mentioned in the main narrative but the list is a long one. All of the following received awards for Dieppe or for a previously successful period of operational flying culminating with the Dieppe show.

Group Captain Harry Broadhurst DSO DFC AFC, who flew four times on that day, received a bar to his DFC for destroying one enemy aircraft and for his valuable information on the progress of the air effort, gleaned during eight hours of active participation. Wing Commander Eric Hugh Thomas DFC, Biggin Hill's Wing Leader, also received a bar to his DFC. Wing Commander David Scott-Malden DFC, who led his Norwegians three times over Dieppe (his Wing claimed a total of 21 victories), received the DSO – 'a brilliant pilot and a fine tactician ...'. Fellow Wing Leader, Peter Russell Walker DFC, Tangmere Wing, who had led two sorties, also received the DSO.

As well as Flight Lieutenant Herbert Tappin of 3 Squadron, who '... despite fierce enemy opposition he pressed home his attacks...', Flight Lieutenant Desmond J. Scott and Flight Lieutenant Louis Thomas Spence of the same squadron, received DFCs. 19 Squadron collected three DFCs, Squadron Leader Patrick Davies '... his fine qualities were well to the fore ...', Flight Lieutenant Ivor H. Edwards and Pilot Officer Jack Henderson. Squadron Leader E. R. Thorn DFM, CO of 32 Squadron was awarded the DFC for his leadership and for when he '... continued his attack although warned that an enemy aircraft was attacking him.' Squadron Leader W. G. G. Duncan-Smith DFC and bar, CO of 64 Squadron, a '... brilliant pilot and fine leader ...' received the DSO. Flight Lieutenant Colin R. Hewlett of 65 Squadron, '... flew with distinction ...' at Dieppe and won the DFC. Squadron Leader Chesley Peterson DFC, CO of 71 Eagle Squadron whose '... devotion to duty has been outstanding ...' also received a well earned DSO. James Elmslee Walker RCAF of 81 Squadron collected a DFC after Dieppe, mostly for his work in Russia. 87 Squadron's 'boss', Squadron Leader Denis Smallwood who led '... in the face of strong opposition from ground defences; his leadership proved a valuable asset' and Flight Lieutenant Alec Thom, and Pilot Officer Robin McNair of 87, '... at Dieppe his cool and courageous work set an inspiring example ...' all won the DFC. Squadron Leader Desmond Griffiths and Pilot Officer Alan C. Baxter (RNZAF Navigator) of 88 Squadron received DFCs.

Squadron Leader Peter Wickham DFC, who flew five times during the day, leading his own 111 squadron twice and leading the American 308th Fighter Squadron on three missions, was awarded a bar to his DFC. Flight Lieutenant John Shepherd '... at all times displayed great skill and determination ...' and Pilot Officer Frank T. Brown of 118 Squadron received DFCs. Flight Lieutenant Selden R. Edner, 121 Eagle Squadron collected a DFC. Flight Lieutenant William Gregson '... led his flight with skill and courage ...' and Pilot Officer Michael P. Kilburn of 124 Squadron, the latter flying four sorties, were awarded DFCs. Squadron Leader R. H. Thomas DFC, CO of 129 Squadron '... an outstanding squadron commander ...' received a DSO – his squadron's low level attacks winning the admiration of the attacking forces. Wing Commander Michael Pedley, for his outstanding ability and Flight Lieutenant Ray Harries both of 131 Squadron, received DFCs. Pilot Officer William H. Baker and Flight Lieutenant E. G. Brettell, '... an excellent flight commander who has completed 111 sorties ...', of 133 Eagle Squadron received DFCs. Squadron Leader Donald Carlson, the New Zealand CO of 154 Squadron also got a DFC. In 174 Squadron Flight Lieutenant William Winder McConnell DFC received a bar to his decoration and was promoted to squadron leader. Pilot Officers Harry Davies and James Reynolds both got DFCs, John Brooks the DFM. Their sister squadron, 175, collected two 'gongs', the CO, John Pennington-

6.   Flight Lieutenant Foss Boulton, 416
CAF Squadron, flew during the Dieppe
how and damaged a Ju88. *(IWM)*

7.   Flight Lieutenant Don Kingaby
laimed a Do217 at Dieppe flying with 64
quadron.

8.   Wing Commander Peter Donkin,
O of 239 Mustang Squadron during the
ieppe operation. He is seen being pre-
ented with the DSO from the King later
the war. *(P. L. Donkin)*

Legh DFC, received a bar, Flight Lieutenant Burton D. Murchie, a Canadian, a DFC.

In 222 Squadron, Bobby Oxspring, the CO got a bar to his DFC. Wing Commander Wilfred Surplice's 226 Squadron were well rewarded, Surplice having a DSO, Squadron Leader J. S. Kennedy DFC, a bar, and DFCs to Flying Officer Harold Asker DFM, George A. Casey, and Pilot Officers Don Smith, Leonard H. Longhurst and Renton S. Rutherford. Flight Lieutenant Denys H. H. Gathercole of 245 Squadron won the DFC and so did the CO of 253 Squadron, D. S. Yapp, for his ' . . . low level attacks on gun positions and strong points . . .' Squadron Leader Jean Zumbach, CO of 303 Squadron, received a bar to his DFC as did Squadron Leader S. F. Skalski of 317 Squadron. Flight Lieutenant K. Rutkowski and Pilot Officer Mike Maciejowski DFM, both of 317, received DFCs. Sergeant Marius Erikson of 332 Squadron was awarded the DFM. Squadron Leader F. (Dolly) Dolezal, CO of 310 Squadron, received a DFC. The Canadians too received decorations. Keith Louis Bate Hodson, CO of 401 Squadron, and George B. Murray of the same unit collected DFCs and Squadron Leader Norman Hobson Bretz, boss of 402, ' . . . led his squadron in four sorties and destroyed one enemy aircraft and damaged another . . .' was given a DFC. Squadron Leader Les Ford DFC, 403 Squadron received a bar for his ' . . . inspiring example . . .' and so did Clarke John Fee, CO of 412, together with one of his flight commanders, Fred Ernest Green, who ' . . . completed three sorties, two of which were low level escort duties . . .' Squadron Leader Robert Newton leader of 411 Squadron got a DFC for his ' . . . zeal and courage . . .', and Lloyd Chadburn of 416 also got a DFC. Squadron Leader R. J. C. Grant DFM, CO of 485 received the DFC and Flight Lieutenant Dennis Crowley-Milling DFC of 610 was awarded a bar to his DFC, for his ' . . . outstanding keenness to inflict losses on the enemy.'

Those RAF personnel aboard the control ships were also decorated. Air Commodore Adrian Cole CBE MC DFC, who controlled on the *Calpe* until he was wounded, received the Distinguished Service Order. Acting Squadron Leader Gerald Le Blount Kidd also on No 1 Control Ship, received the MBE, while Squadron Leader James Humphrey Sprott on the second control ship, was awarded the OBE. Acting Squadron Leader James Booth Reynolds, who planned, briefed and then flew with 226 Squadron on the first raid, received the OBE.

Finally a list of the number of flying personnel engaged in Operation Jubilee, not including ASR crews:

	pilots	*aircrew*
Single seater fighters	730	—
Bostons – Fighter Command	4	8
Bostons & Blenheims – 2 Group (smoke)	30	60
Bostons – 2 Group (bombing)	28	56
Army Co-operation Mustangs	47	—
USAAF Fortresses	24	192
	863	316

On 1 September 1944 troops of the 2nd Canadian Division returned to the harbour town of Dieppe. On that occasion the port and its defences were given up without a fight, but this time they came from the land – not the sea.

Report by Group Captain Broadhurst on his reconnaissance missions over Dieppe on 19 August 1942, and on the results of his visits to the various sectors on that day.

The following sorties were carried out:–

        0600 – 0800
        0940 – 1145
        1230 – 1430
        1515 – 1645

First Sortie

2. I took off from Northolt at 0600 hours and flew straight to Dieppe arriving at approximately 0630 at 25,000 feet. The weather was clear over the area but there was some cloud to the east and west.

3. I cruised round observing the general picture and made a short reconnaissance of the sea area between Dieppe and Le Havre and Dieppe and Boulogne. No shipping was seen. In the battle area the landings on the flank beaches had obviously taken place whilst that on the main beaches at Dieppe was still in progress and appeared to be meeting with considerable trouble.

4. The anchorage just to the north of Dieppe was rapidly taking shape and the majority of the Spitfire cover could be seen maintaining their patrol in its vicinity.

5. I had by now lost height to 20,000 feet, and was in a position up sun – ie. to the northeast of the battle area. From here I soon gained a complete picture of the air situation. In general it appeared that Focke Wulf 190s were coming out from France in pairs and fours

from Le Tréport area at about 15,000 feet, and when in a position directly up sun of our patrols would dive straight down towards the ships and the beaches, some dropping bombs, some attacking the Spitfires, and some shooting up the ships with their forward armament.

6. These attacks seemed to be achieving very little, however, although an occasional Spitfire was shot down and no doubt the attacks against ships and beaches caused some casualties. The bombing was extremely inaccurate.

7. After watching these attacks for a short period of time I started to lose height down towards Le Tréport area, and eventually picked on the No 2 of one of the attacking Focke Wulf pairs and shot it down into the sea. I then returned to Biggin Hill where I met the Station Commander and visited all the squadrons at dispersal points and from conversations with the pilots I was able to confirm what I had seen from the air.

8. I thereupon rang up the Group Operations Room and spoke to the Commander-in-Chief, and having given him an outline of the situation asked him to pass a message to the AOC suggesting that patrols of Spitfire IXs in pairs be instituted in the area which I thought would tend to baulk the Focke Wulfs' approach to the main patrol area.

Second Sortie

9. After breakfast I took off from Biggin Hill at 0940 in order to make rendezvous with the Fortresses and Spitfire IX Squadrons at 23,000 feet over Beachy Head with the intention of accompanying them on their bombing expedition to Abbeville-Drucat.

10. I was at 25,000 feet over Beachy Head at 1000 hours when Hornchurch Controller (by whom I was being controlled) informed me that dive bombing was reported from Dieppe and that the situation was very warm. I therefore hastened to Dieppe in time to find a force of Dornier 217s and Ju88s accompanied by about thirty to fifty Focke Wulfs attacking the beach areas and shipping at Dieppe.

11. The Dorniers appeared to be between 10,000 and 12,000 feet with their escorts stepped up to about 15,000 feet. I attacked one of the escort but both cannons failed to fire and after emptying nearly

all my machine-gun ammunition into him I broke off the combat and climbed back towards Abbeville where I joined the bombers at 23,000 feet just as they were turning off their bombing run.

12. I was able to witness the bombs bursting on Abbeville aerodrome with extreme accuracy.

13. I accompanied the bombers back to the English coast and landed at Hornchurch for refuelling and rearming.

14. I met the Wing Commander Flying and went with him round the dispersal points where I spoke to all the pilots, discussing their tactics and German tactics, and generally talking over the situation with them.

15. I telephoned the Group Operations Room and spoke to the AOC giving him a description of the bomber attacks at Dieppe and suggesting an alteration to the patrol, heights of our fighters, and also gave a description of the Fortress bombing at Abbeville.

Third Sortie

16. I took off from Hornchurch in company with Wing Commander Powell at 1230 hours and flew direct to Dieppe arriving there at about 1300 hours at 25,000 feet. The withdrawal was now almost complete and with the exception of a few ships two or three miles off Dieppe, which included the destroyer *Berkeley*, the convoy was in full progress back towards the English coast.

17. After cruising around for a few minutes, Wing Commander Powell separated from me, and went down to sea level to see the situation from a low altitude while I circled the Dieppe area gradually losing height down to 18,000 feet. I noticed one or two attacks by Dornier 217s whose bombing appeared to be extremely inaccurate, many of them jettisoning their bombs as soon as they were attacked by Spitfires.

18. I noticed that the rear of the convoy, i.e. that part of it nearest to the French coast, was being subjected to the most severe attacks and latterly the majority of these were being directed against the destroyer *Berkeley* which was apparently in difficulties. I called up Hornchurch Control and asked them to suggest to Group Operations that the patrols be concentrated over that area, at the same time calling up the ship control and suggesting that he moved the bottom cover squadron to the immediate vicinity of the *Berkeley*.

The ship controller was continuously reporting the presence of Dorniers 217, but I noticed that there were several Focke Wulf 190s about, some of them carrying bombs. Towards the end of my patrol I saw two Focke Wulfs drive towards the *Berkeley*. I dived after them but could not intercept them until after they had dropped their bombs, one of which appeared to score a direct hit on the stern of the *Berkeley*. I closed to the rear of the Focke Wulf as he pulled away from his dive and emptied most of my cannon and machine gun ammunition into him with good effect, and then returned along the line of the convoy to Kenley where I had lunch.

19. Whilst at Kenley I met the Station Commander and Wing Commander Flying and visited the squadrons at their dispersal points. After this I rang up Group Operations and made my report to the AOC, in which I emphasised that the patrols, which obviously could not cover the whole of the convoy should be concentrated on that part of it nearest the French coast.

Fourth Sortie

20. I took off from Kenley at about 1515 hours and flew direct to Dieppe where at 19,000 feet whilst jettisoning my extra tank I was attacked by two Focke Wulfs. After shaking these off I again came into combat with four more Focke Wulfs and had to take severe evasive action into cloud which was then almost 10/10ths over the whole area at varying heights in the region of 5,000 feet.

21. I emerged below cloud to find the convoy well clear of the French coast and apparently steaming along in good order and with very little interference. As I was almost out of ammunition I cruised back along the convoy to the English coast and endeavoured to land at Tangmere, but as the weather had closed right in I returned to Hornchurch.

22. From here I rang up the Group Operations Room and spoke to the AOC suggesting to him that owing to weather conditions, high patrols were not necessary and that in my opinion the patrols could be considerably reduced in strength. We also discussed the state of the pilots and I told him that although they were in tremendous heart they were beginning to show signs of tiredness.

23. After refuelling and rearming I returned to Northolt, landing at 1900 hours, having flown a total of 8¼ hours during the day.

Conclusions

24. In general I think that the tactics of the cover patrols were very effective and only need slight modification to counter the heights and direction of approach by the German fighters and bombers.

Reconnaissance Patrols

25. It is my firm opinion that in future operations an experienced pilot complete with a Number Two should be employed for reconnaissance over the battle area in order to bring back tactical information for the immediate use of the AOC.
26. Several pairs of these senior pilots could be employed so that a continuous watch on the situation could be maintained.

Ship Control

27. With regard to the ship control, it is considered that their RT set should be much more powerful so as to drown idle chatter by individual aircraft.
28. Whilst the present system only controls a limited number of aircraft it is considered that the leaders of the top squadrons working on their own frequencies should occasionally press the button which gives them the frequency on which the ship controller is working in order to get a picture of what is going on below them.

Visits to Sectors

29. From visiting sectors I discovered the following:–
    (i) The morale of the pilots was without exception extremely high but it was found that in most cases three sorties had taken the edge off them and that after four sorties they were visibly tiring.
    (ii) The arrangements for refuelling and rearming varied in the sectors, some being extremely rapid, others being only a little faster than in the ordinary day to day operations.
    (iii) By visiting dispersals after units had returned it was possible to pick up tactical information and telephone it back to Group within a few minutes, particularly as I had been over

the area myself and I was able to get into the picture very rapidly. It is suggested that the reconnaissance mentioned in Paragraph 25 should be combined with the duties of visiting units after landing.

German Tactics

30. I gained the impression that the Germans did not adapt themselves very rapidly to the situation and that they were trying to compete with our patrols in the same way as they do when we give close escort to bombers. Only on rare occasions did they display any determination to press home their attacks, usually when our patrols were thin, either as a result of heavy combats or latterly when the patrols were spread over a large area of convoy.

(Public Record File Air 16/765)

Report made by Flight Lieutenant Gerald Le Blount Kidd RAFVR, close support controller aboard HMS Calpe. *Dated 24 August 1942*

Communications worked excellently throughout and great credit is due to Flight Lieutenant Hall for his work in this connection. He also rendered invaluable assistance throughout the day as liaison officer between Air Commodore Cole and me and in other capacities.

No signals were received by me from Uxbridge so that it was not known what targets had been accepted and what squadrons were on their way.

The view enjoyed by the controller from the bridge was excellent and was invaluable in exercising control over aircraft. HQ ships 1 and 2 were often a good distance apart – as there were no fighters under the direct control of HQ 1 interceptions could not be made in several instances. Difficulty was experienced in locating the fighters actually under ship control. It was noted that aircraft in loose pairs and fours had a much better chance of making interceptions than aircraft in Squadron formation, – (This was seen only once). Fighters rarely, if ever, saw enemy aircraft before they were warned by the controller. Too often they were down sun of the convoy and too low and the attacks would be made from up sun and above.

Fighters were often too low and got fired at by the convoy gunners who were naturally very light on the trigger.

There was a lot of RT chatter between aircraft. As things turned out this did not matter but if closer control of close support squadrons or control of fighters had been required, intercom would have to be cut to a minimum.

Close support at Dieppe had little apparent effect on the houses which were evidently reinforced.

My aircraft recognition was very weak indeed, it is essential that controllers doing this type of work should be adept at this.

It was observed that enemy aircraft were often chased home by large numbers of our fighters, many of whom could have had very little hope of catching up. Cover over the convoy was left very thin on these occasions.

Excellent co-operation and assistance was at all time received from Squadron Leader Sprott on HQ 2. Apart from the fact that owing to the unforeseen strength and preparedness of enemy resistance the objectives were not gained and casualties were high. Nevertheless viewed as a combined operation the raid was a success of timing and close-co-operation between the services. The next combined attack will have a much better chance of success as a result of the great deal of experience gained by all who took part.

Much gratitude is felt for the pilots who looked after the convoy with such tireless resolve from the moment of first light until after the weather had closed down and for the organisation and pre-planning that made that possible.

The Navy's efficiency and courtesy was much appreciated and the calm and cheerful courage of the Canadian Officers and men was an inspiration.

(Public Record File Air 16/765)

Report by the Air Force Commander on the combined operation against Dieppe – 19 August 1942

General Outline

1. Operation Jubilee was a raid against occupied territory with the purpose of capturing, by assault, and occupying for a limited period, the town of Dieppe. Military tasks in the area of Dieppe included the destruction of local defences, power stations, dock installations – the capture of prisoners and the destruction of the aerodrome installations near the town. It was also intended to capture and to remove German invasion barges and other craft in the harbour.

2. The operation was planned to take place on the first suitable morning for such a landing between 18 and 23 August. The expedition sailed from the area of the Portsmouth Command in a succession of groups starting at civil twilight on the evening of 18 August.

3. The Naval, Military and Air Force assigned to this operation are set out in Appendices.

4. The plan prepared jointly by the three Force Commanders involved a landing on the outer flanks of Dieppe at Orange and Yellow Beaches by Nos 4 and 3 Commandos, whose tasks were to neutralise enemy battery positions 6 miles to the east and west of Dieppe. At the same time a Regiment of the 2nd Canadian Corps was to be landed to secure Green Beach three miles to the west of Dieppe, and to attack objectives on the west outer perimeter of the town (Hindenburg). Simultaneously the Royal Regiment of Canada was to secure Blue Beach 1½ miles to the east of Dieppe, and objectives on the east flank of the outer perimeter, ie; Bismarck. Half an hour later the Royal Hamilton Light Infantry and Essex Scottish Regiment with the Camerons of Canada were to make a

frontal assault on Red and White Beaches in front of the town of Dieppe. This frontal assault was to have been supported by an armoured detachment of tanks. Later a Royal Marine Commando was to land near the harbour of Dieppe to demolish objectives in the dock area. A further echelon of tanks was then to be landed making a total of 28 tanks. It was intended, when the tasks ashore had been completed to withdraw the whole force for re-embarkation at about 1100 hours.

Air Support

5. Air support was to be provided throughout the operation as follows:–

Fighter Cover

(i)   Fighter cover and general protection for the expedition throughout the hours of daylight. The primary task of this cover was to protect the expedition against air attack. It was considered that the two most dangerous periods in regard to attack from the air would be the landing and withdrawal. It was, therefore, decided that the strength of this fighter cover should vary from 2 to 6 Squadrons during the different phases of the operation, with such reinforcements as might prove necessary.

Close support

(ii)   (a)   Close support, bombing and low flying fighter attacks on selected targets were to be made in direct support of the assault, occupation and withdrawal.

(b)   Smoke laying aircraft were to be used to neutralise defences, both in accordance with the pre-arranged plan and subsequently as required at the request of the Military Force Commander.

(c)   Day Bomber Squadrons were to be employed to attack both pre-arranged targets and requested targets.

Reconnaissance

(iii)   (a)   Tactical Reconnaissance was to be made over the area of the operation including the lines of approach of any enemy reinforcements.

(b) Coastal ASV reconnaissance from Cherbourg to Boulogne was to be maintained throughout the night prior to the assault.

(c) Fighter anti-surface vessel reconnaissance patrols were to be maintained throughout daylight hours.

Strategical Bombing

(iv) It had been agreed between the three Force Commanders not to lay on any preliminary or diversionary effort with bombers prior to the assault in order not to jeopardise surprise. A strategical bombing attack was, however, planned against the enemy aerodrome of Abbeville, with a view to interfering with the operation of his defending fighters. This attack was to coincide with the main withdrawal from the beaches at which time considerable interference was anticipated from fighters operating from the Abbeville area.

Disposition of the air forces in No 11 Group

6. The following forces were available:–

Day Fighter forces	—	50 Squadrons Cover
		6 Squadrons Close support
Day Bomber forces	—	2 Squadrons
Hurricane Bombers	—	2 Squadrons
Army Co-operation	—	4 Squadrons
'Smoke' forces	—	3 Squadrons

7. The assembly of these forces involved internal moves of Squadrons within No 11 Group and the reinforcement of the Group by 15 Squadrons from outside. These extensive movements were carried out on 14 and 15 August.

Detail of the squadron and necessary maintenance unit moves were as follows:

	Intake of Units into No 11 Group	Internal movements in No 11 Group
Fighter Squadrons	17	17
Servicing Echelon	—	8
Squadron Transports	4½	9½
Petrol Tankers	7	12
Starter Trolleys	32	116
Echelons without air lift	—	6
Squadrons without air lift	—	6
Squadrons with air lift	—	11

8. The following supplies of ammunition and petrol were accumulated at stations in No 11 Group immediately prior to the operation:

Ammunition	20mm Ball	20mm HE/1	.303 AP	.303 Incend	20mm Links
	727,200	727,200	7,484,400	2,474,800	1,454,400
Petrol	100 Octane Galls.	712,000.			

Enemy Dispositions

9. The German Air Force had approximately 260 front line single engined aircraft between Brest and Texel. These were disposed as follows:–

Holland	40
Pas de Calais	125
Brest to Fécamp	95

10. The German policy since June this year has been to concentrate these air forces on a few aerodromes along the Western Front. The German system of reinforcement in flexible up to a point, with extreme mobility of units from one place to another. On the other hand he finds difficulty in adapting his control areas quickly to these reinforcements.

11. Apart from reconnaissance units and a small number of aircraft used for anti-shipping, the whole of the German bomber force on the Western Front has been in use by night only. This force was

disposed in the Dutch bases at Eindhoven, Soesterberg, Gilze Rijen and Deelen. It numbered some 120 long range bombers with a further 100 at Beauvais, Creil, Châteaudun, Chartres and Rennes. Reports from pilots during the operation Jubilee indicate that a small number of bombers from reserve training units were brought into action. It was considered unlikely that he would be able to bring his fighters from as far west as Brest or as far north as Holland early in the operation. Thus the fighter forces likely to oppose us in the early stages were from the Abbeville area – 50, Beaumont – Lé-Royer area – 50, Cherbourg area – 20, together with possible reinforcements from St Omer and Courtrai – approximately 30 and 45 respectively.

Command

12. Captain J. H. Hallett RN was the Naval Force Commander.
Major General F. N. Roberts MC was the Military Force Commander
Air Marshal T. L. Leigh-Mallory CB DSO Air Officer Commanding No 11 Group, was the Air Force Commander

Operational Control

13. Control of all air forces was exercised direct by the Air Force Commander from his operational headquarters at Uxbridge. Aircraft were despatched on instructions issued from No 11 Group Operations Room through the normal Group to Sector, Sector to Squadron Dispersal point channels. The Force Commanders afloat were able to ask at any time for special air support from bombers or fighters by means of the W/T link provided between Portsmouth and the Headquarters Ship, and a listening watch maintained at No 11 Group Headquarters.
14. The lowest squadron in the fighter cover operated on No 11 Group Guard No 1 frequency so that the fighter controller in either of the headquarters ships could communicate with the squadrons of the fighter cover.
15. All outgoing close support fighter sorties called the Headquarters Ship by VHF R/T when approaching the enemy coast. The Fighter Controller in the Headquarters Ship then, at the request of

either the military or naval Commanders, re-directed fighter sorties to attack any suitable alternative targets which the situation demanded.

16. Despite the fact that a very large number of squadrons were being used throughout the operation (over 60 Squadrons) this method of control worked admirably. During the whole course of this very gruelling test of the normal ground control organisation in No 11 Group there was no breakdown.

17. This proved conclusively that the existing fighter ground control organisation, although primarily designed for defensive purposes, provides all the facilities required for the direction of offensive operations within normal fighter range. The co-ordination of the Air Force effort from a central point is essential. The Group Operations Room with its extensive network of communications augmented by advanced W/T and R/T communication with local Commanders in the expedition proved to be ideal.

18. The local control by the Headquarters Ships proved equally successful. The bottom Squadron of all Fighter cover formations operated on No 11 Group Guard 1 frequency and were directed on to enemy aircraft by a Controller in Headquarters Ship No 2. Close support Squadrons operated on a Tangmere Sector Operational frequency and were directed on to targets as required by the Military Commander by a Controller in Headquarters Ship No 1. Thus the two Headquarters Ships accompanying the expedition were used to assist in the control of air forces as would an AASC during a land battle.

19. In the majority of cases Close Support Fighter Pilots had been briefed as to the targets to be attacked, before leaving the ground, but experience gained during the operation showed conclusively that it was possible to redirect fighters or to give them assistance in finding their target by local direction. Similary, fighters were frequently assisted in sighting enemy aircraft by the running commentary given by the controller in Headquarters Ship No 2. There is no doubt that this local control was largely responsible for the high percentage of interceptions made on enemy aircraft, thus greatly minimising the effectiveness of enemy air attacks on ships and troops.

20. To summarise – the system of control from the Group through Sectors, and through the Headquarters Ships, adequately met all

requirements. The excellent communications and flexible control facilities of the normal Fighter organisation at home proved most efficient for such combined operations.

Tactical Reconnaissance

21. Tactical reconnaissance units suffered a higher casualty rate than any other type. This was due to the deep penetration required of them which necessitated their patrolling well beyond the area of fighter cover. The coast roads leading to Dieppe were reconnoitred every half hour, and those from Amiens, Rouen, Yvetot, and Le Havre, places from which reinforcements might be expected, every hour.

22. Aircraft took off from Gatwick, flew to the Dieppe area via the Beachy Head route, made contact with the command ship, and then proceeded on their allotted tasks. On completion of each sortie tactical reconnaissance pilots flew sufficiently near to the ship to ensure satisfactory R/T transmission of any information they had. They then returned immediately to Gatwick and passed their information by telephone to the Air Force Commander.

23. The only movement worthy of note was that of about five light tanks approaching Dieppe reported at 1210 hours.

24. The range of the HF fitted in the tactical reconnaissance aircraft proved inadequate.

ASV Reconnaissance Patrols

25. Aircraft of Coastal Command maintained ASV search patrols throughout the hours of darkness on the flanks of the expedition during the passage. No sightings were made.

General Narrative

26. The operation is conveniently divided into five distinct phases. The first covers the outward passage and the landings on various beaches. The second covers the period when progress was being made towards the predetermined objectives ashore. The third phase covers the withdrawal of landing parties to their beaches. The fourth period extends to the time when the withdrawal was

complete. The fifth phase covers the return passage to England.

27. The expedition sailed from the area of Portsmouth Command in a succession of Groups on the evening of 18 August, headed by the destroyer *Calpe*.

28. Shortly before dark the convoy which consisted of 217 craft in all, steamed past the *Calpe* (Headquarters Ship No 1) to be checked.

29. In the early hours of the 19 August, the *Calpe* led the way through an enemy minefield, which had already been swept by a flotilla of minesweepers from Newhaven. A quarter of an hour later the whole convoy was safely through the minefield but it was noticed that the LCTs had lagged some way behind.

30. Shortly after 0300 hours the first landing craft were lowered from their parent ships. The lighthouse on the cliff outside Dieppe was then visible. Up to this time the outward passage was comparatively uneventful, but a misfortune now occurred.

31. The landing craft conveying No 3 Commando, which had been detailed to attack Yellow Beach (6 miles east of Dieppe) came into contact with an enemy convoy which included armed trawlers, and a number of our small craft were sunk. These losses resulted in the failure to subdue coast defence batteries to the east of Dieppe.

32. There was no other enemy activity throughout the night and no attempt was made by the enemy to reconnoitre for our approaching expedition. It would seem, therefore, that the force was assembled and dispatched without disclosure. It would have achieved complete tactical surprise if No 3 Commando had not unfortunately been intercepted by the enemy trawlers en route.

Narrative Phase 1 0445 – 0550

33. Despite the chance contact with enemy ships en route, the forces arrived at Dieppe approximately on time, and the initial naval bombardment of selected objectives was carried out as arranged.

34. In the opening attack, escort was provided for smoke carrying aircraft of bomber and Army Co-operation Commands laying a smoke screen over the cliff headland to the east of Dieppe Harbour. This was most effective lasting from 0510 to 0600 hours. Intruder aircraft engaged each of the two gun batteries to the south of

Dieppe with bombs and machine guns. Hurricane Bombers, Fighters and Fighters and Spitfires attacked the coastal emplacements, and beach defences. Cannon fighters provided direct support to our troops as they landed at Red and White Beaches in front of Dieppe and were successful in centralising enemy fire along the front from 0515 to 0525. During the landings there was little opposition from enemy aircraft.

35. In phase 1 our surface forces kept to their time table despite shelling by enemy shore batteries. Batteries situated to the south of the town were slow to commence firing but when they did were particularly destructive. Further smoke screens were requested to cover our landings, a necessity which had already been anticipated and additional smoke aircraft were already on their way to the scene of action.

Phase 2 0550 – 0730

36. By the second phase landings had been effected successfully on Yellow (East Commando) Green (West flank) and Orange (West Commando) Beaches and progress had been made towards the surrounding houses.

37. The Western Commando had been completely successful in overcoming the battery position at Hess and killing all the personnel. The final assault on this position was assisted by a squadron of Spitfires which attacked Hess battery at 0620 just before our men were due to attack. This assistance was successful and the attack was made immediately our Spitfires had finished. The OP of this battery was in a lighthouse close by which had been attacked by two Spitfires at first light. The landing on the beach 1½ miles to the west of Dieppe (Green Beach) was also successful, capturing the RDF station and destroying their other objectives.

38. The eastern flank (Blue Beach) initial attack had, however, failed. A second attack made at approximately 0740 resulted in a small penetration which, however, did not succeed in silencing the guns on the Eastern Headland. In the main landing on Red and White Beaches the tanks were held up by the inability of the engineers to land the explosives necessary to blast a passage through the promenade wall, with the result that the majority of the tanks were stranded, and the infantry were disembarked whilst the

tanks were still immobilised. Large white houses overlooking the beaches gave considerable trouble and bombardment by destroyers was requested from our troops ashore.

39. In view of these difficulties a further smoke screen was called for on the eastern headland Bismarck but no aircraft were immediately available for this. The smoke carrying aircraft were at once ordered to load up with smoke and take off as soon as they were ready.

40. Earlier attacks had failed to silence the eastern headland defences and the gun positions (Hitler and Göring) south of Dieppe continued to shell the beaches.

41. Twelve Bostons had already been ordered off to bomb Hitler and were quickly airborne.

42. Rommel was also still giving trouble and the landing on Blue Beach had in consequence failed. The only remaining Bostons were, therefore, detailed to attack Rommel followed by a further six when they became available. All these batteries continued to harass our troops and an attack was called for on Bismarck. A squadron of Cannon Hurricanes had already been despatched to be 'on call' to the headquarters ship by 0740 and a second squadron of Cannon Hurricanes was despatched to be 'on call' to the headquarters ship 20 minutes later.

43. Thus at the end of the second phase the RDF Station, 5 light AA positions had been captured and the gun battery behind the Orange Beach had been demolished. Throughout this period air cover was afforded to the troops against moderate enemy fighter opposition; the number of enemy aircraft patrolling the area at any one time during this period did not exceed one Squadron.

Phase 3 0730 – 1050

This third phase covers the withdrawal to the beaches.

45. At 0752 two Cannon Hurricane Squadrons were ordered to engage enemy E-Boats which had been reported proceeding south from Boulogne. Two fighter cover squadrons accompanied these Hurricanes. At the same time a message was received cancelling the support on Bismarck and Rommel. The Air Force Commander was always doubtful whether this latter message was genuine, but had to act on it as information was received within a few minutes

that a second landing on Blue Beach had been successful. At this time one Bomber Squadron was also on its way to bomb Rommel and was beyond range of recall. Aircraft were also on their way to drop smoke bombs on the eastern headland; these were recalled.

46. The situation had meanwhile deteriorated on the western flank. Heavy opposition was also coming from the western headland and the houses behind the beach. Machine gunning and shelling continued undiminished from the headland and from Hindenburg.

47. A squadron of Hurricane Bombers and a squadron of Cannon Fighters covered by two Spitfire Squadrons were ordered to attack these positions.

48. The situation in various areas continued to grow critical and due to various delays the time scheduled for the evacuation was deferred from 1030 hours to 1100 hours.

49. At 0956 the following reply was received to the Air Force Commander's request for a situation report: 'Situation too obscure to give useful report. Air co-operation faultless. Enemy air opposition now increasing. Have you any questions.'

50. A few minutes later a request was received for a 30 minute smoke screen along Red and White Beaches from 1100 to 1130 hours: Thruxton was ordered to prepare as many aircraft as possible with SCI and as many aircraft as could be fitted were ordered off for this purpose. The Military Commander gave Green Beach third priority after Red and White Beaches for smoke and 3 Blenheims with an escort squadron were detailed to this task.

51. At 1039 a request was made for maximum fighter support against machine gun positions on both headlands.

52. Four close support squadrons were ordered to these attacks with two squadrons as cover.

53. A further call for support against the headland came in 20 minutes later, by which time squadrons were already on their way. At this time it appeared that the LCAs were arriving at White Beach, ready to re-embark the forces on shore. Thus at the beginning of this third phase the right wing of our landing forces had made progress but those in the centre including the tanks were held up.

54. Enemy air opposition had by now increased considerably, 20 to 30 fighters being seen continuously in the area until 1000 hours

when enemy bombers appeared escorted by fighters.

55. The enemy employed a considerable number of bombers from aerodromes in Holland in addition to small numbers from Beauvais. To counter this increased enemy activity and in order to cover re-embarkation, which was about to commence, the strength of fighter cover over Dieppe was increased from 3 to 6 Squadrons. Heavy casualties were inflicted on the enemy bombers who were now concentrating on shipping and landing craft.

Phase 4 1050 – 1410

56. The fourth phase marks the withdrawal from the beaches. During this time the gun batteries Bismarck and Hindenburg on the east and west headlands continued their intense bombardment, and in many areas the situation was more than critical.

57. Until the expedition had safely withdrawn, frequent and urgent requests were received for bombing and close support attacks on enemy gun positions, and calls for smoke screens were made.

58. At 1030 hours a most successful pre-arranged attack was made by 24 Fortress Bombers escorted by four Spitfire IX Squadrons, on the enemy fighter aerodrome at Abbeville-Drucat. Some twenty-five tons of high explosives and a large number of incendiaries were dropped. Many bursts were seen in the north-west dispersal areas and on the runways whilst fires were started in woods adjoining the dispersal areas. Bursts were also observed on storage sites and clouds of black smoke were seen rising from the whole target area. This very accurate bombing of dispersal area and runways – bombs fell near to at least 16 aircraft in these areas – caused considerable confusion to the enemy, and he was denied the use of his aerodrome for probably 2 hours, his aircraft being instructed to land at alternatives. The Abbeville control was out of action until the evening, when a new and unfamiliar voice came on the air.

59. This attack on Abbeville was followed by a diversionary feint made towards Ostend by a Typhoon Wing in an endeavour to draw enemy air forces away from Dieppe.

60. The enemy air activity by this time had increased and he had altered his form of attack. The tactics of our fighter cover were changed to meet this situation by adding a high squadron of Spitfire IXs at 23,000 feet.

61. During this period bombing attacks were made by Boston Squadrons on Bismarck and Hindenburg.

62. Further attacks were also made by three close support squadrons and smoke was laid between the east and west headlands across the port of Dieppe to cover the final withdrawal.

63. The constant requests for bombing, close support and smoke were met to the limit, demands frequently being anticipated as a result of the clear picture available in the Fighter Control Room at Uxbridge. All types of squadrons were called on to operate a shuttle service.

64. It was decided that tactical reconnaissance aircraft could serve no further useful purpose and their operational flights were discontinued.

65. In the final withdrawal a maximum effort was directed to protect our re-embarking forces from both ground and air attack.

66. By 1310 it appeared doubtful whether any more troops could be evacuated. An hour later the last craft was reported 3 miles from the French coast. The withdrawal from Dieppe had been completed.

Phase 5 1410 – 2245 hours

67. As our forces cleared the enemy coast smoke-laying aircraft laid a protective screen between them and the enemy's defences.

68. The Typhoon Wing was then reinforcing our Spitfires in intercepting enemy bombers coming from the direction of Holland.

69. Fighter Cover was maintained throughout the long voyage home.

70. There was considerable deterioration in the weather and the enemy took advantage of the increasing cloud cover to send out single bombers to attack our ships as they neared the English coast. One or two formations of FW190s were also employed for this purpose. In addition to standing cover over the returning convoy, 86 interception sorties were made.

Appreciation of the Enemy's Air Effort

71. The enemy reacted almost as had been foreseen; at first he did not appear to appreciate the scale of our effort and he used only

25/30 fighters in each sortie. As the day went on the strength of his sorties increased to between 50/100 aircraft. At first fighter bombers, and later, when the moves from Holland had been effected, night bombers in increasing numbers were used until all his resources on the Western Front were in action.

72. Early in the day enemy air effort was confined entirely to fighters patrolling the area in small numbers. Occasionally dive attacks on our ships were made from height. The German control merely instructed his aircraft to go to the Dieppe area where large numbers of British bombers and fighters were operating.

73. It was not until about 1000 hours, some six hours after our assault, that our patrols encountered enemy bombers. It would seem, therefore, that these had not been at a high state of readiness.

74. The first bombers came in small numbers and were escorted by FW190s. Later larger formations up to 15 in number operated under the main German Fighter Force which was engaging our cover patrols. Reports from pilots indicate that a small number of reserve training bombers were included.

75. The German Bomber Force throughout confined its attentions to our convoy and did not harass our troops ashore. A bomber jettisoned its bombs and crippled HMS *Berkeley* shortly before 1300 hours. She was later sunk by our own forces. The attack on Abbeville-Drucat at 1030 hours was undoubtedly successful in striking at the enemy's most congested aerodrome at a critical period in the operation. This attack was timed and prearranged to this end and it undoubtedly succeeded in considerably reducing the efforts of the GAF against our expedition.

Casualties

76. (Details of casualties were noted in an appendix to this report – N.F.)

77. The very low rate of casualties suffered in all types of squadrons during such intensive day-light operations in close support of a combined operation are of particular interest.

Administration

78. The concentration and redisposition of Air Forces in No 11

Group was for security reasons undertaken as a reinforcing exercise, under the title of Venom.

79. No serious administrative difficulties were experienced throughout the operation, though the shortness of the period of activity did not perhaps bring to light some of the difficulties which might have arisen had it been more prolonged.

Communications

80. Communications on the whole were excellent. Signals were promptly and clearly received at Uxbridge. The majority of outgoing messages from Uxbridge to the headquarters ship retransmitted by Portsmouth, did not reach the Military Commander afloat, so that requests for close support from the ship were often repeated unnecessarily.

81. The control organisation in the ships worked very efficiently and this system is capable of further expansion and development.

82. Additional land line links to Uxbridge for the operation worked fairly satisfactorily, although some of the temporary lines were not up to the high standard necessary.

83. The operations and Intelligence Teleprinter Operators worked at high pressure but were able to handle the traffic without serious delays.

Conclusions

84. (i) This operation showed that such expeditions can be successfully supported and protected by home defence fighters operated by the normal Home Defence Fighter Organisation, assisted by forward direction through R/T in ships. This efficient organisation is fully capable of so operating air forces to the limit of present fighter range and is bound to be superior to any alternative forward control scheme which could never provide anything like equal facilities.

(ii) Landings on such a scale in occupied territory in daylight effectively pin the enemy air forces to an area enabling our supporting fighters to operate at height and in conditions best suited to them. In existing circumstances the enemy is forced to employ his night bombers in daylight, at times unescorted by fighters thus sacrificing an appreciable part of his limited bomber resources.

(iii) Close Support attacks by cannon fighters are effective only whilst they are engaging their targets, but they have no lasting material effect on well protected defensive positions. They are extravagant in as much as each aircraft is in action for a few seconds only. To achieve any lasting moral effect would demand such a large expenditure of these Fighters that our efforts in other directions would be reduced to unacceptable proportions.

(iv) A very much higher standard of interservice recognition is essential in combined operations. As modern aircraft are all so alike, it is important that all personnel have a very thorough knowledge of and frequent practice in recognition.

(v) Airborne smoke is extremely valuable in combined operations. Smoke is often likely to have better effect than bombing, particularly if it is intended to protect surface forces against well placed gun positions. It is essential however, to speed up the present rate of turn round for smoke carrying aircraft and to be able quickly to alternate between SCI and bombs and to change over from one to the other on the ground in the shortest possible time.

(vi) Some difficulty was experienced at times in obtaining detailed target requirements from the Headquarters Ship. This problem of locating and selecting suitable targets for Air attacks, together with methods for defining, to the Air Force Commander requires careful interservice study so that the Air effort is always profitably employed.

Certain major conclusions together with my recommendations for awards are being forwarded by me in a separate letter.

T Leigh-Mallory
Air Marshal
Air Force Commander

(Public Record Officer File Air 25/204)

Squadrons which took part in the Dieppe Raid

SPITFIRE SQUADRONS

No	Commanding Officer	Code	Base on 19 Aug
19	SL P. B. G. Davies	QV	Southend
41	SL G. C. Hyde	EB	Tangmere
64	SL W. G. Duncan-Smith, DFC	SH	Hornchurch
65	SL D. A. P. McMullen, DFC	YT	Eastchurch
66	SL R. D. Yule, DFC (NZ)	LZ	Tangmere
71	SL C. G. Peterson, DFC (US)	XR	Gravesend
81	SL R. Berry, DFC	FL	Fairlop
91	SL J. E. F. Demozay (FF)	DL	Hawkinge
111	SL P. R. W. Wickham, DFC	JU	Kenley
118	SL E. W. Wootten, DFC	NK	Tangmere
121	SL W. D. Williams, DFC (acting)	AV	Southend
122	SL J. R. C. Kilian (NZ)	MT	Hornchurch
124	SL T. Balmforth, DFC	ON	Gravesend
129	SL R. H. Thomas, DFC	DV	Thorney Island
130	SL P. J. Simpson, DFC	PJ	Thorney Island
131	WC M. G. F. Pedley	NX	Merston
133	FL D. J. M. Blakeslee (US) (acting)	MD	Lympne
154	SL D. C. Carlson (NZ)	HT	Fairlop
165	SL H. J. L. Hallowes, DFC, DFM	SK	Eastchurch
222	SL R. W. Oxspring, DFC	ZD	Biggin Hill
232	SL A. McDowell, DFM	EF	Gravesend
242	SL T. C. Parker	LE	Manston
302	SL J. Kowalski (Pol)	WX	Heston

303	SL J. Zumbach, vm, kw, dfc (Pol)	RF	Redhill
306	SL T. Czerwinski, kw (Pol)	UZ	Northolt
307th	Maj M. L. McNickle	MX	Biggin Hill
308	SL W. Zak, vm (Pol)	ZF	Heston
308th	Maj F. M. Dean	HL	Kenley
309th	Maj H. R. Thyng	WZ	Westhampnett
310	SL F. Dolezal (CZ)	NN	Redhill
312	SL J. Cermak (CZ)	DU	Redhill
317	SL S. F. Skalski, dfc (Pol)	JH	Northolt
331	Maj H. Mehre, dfc (Norg)	FN	Manston
332	Maj W. Mohr, dfc (Norg)	AH	Manston
340	Cdt B. Duperior, dfc (FF)	GW	Hornchurch
350	SL D. A. Guillaume, dfc (Bel)	MN	Redhill
401	SL K. L. B. Hodson	YO	Lympne
402	SL N. H. Bretz	AE	Kenley
403	SL L. S. Ford, dfc	KH	Manston
411	SL R. B. Newton	DB	West Malling
412	SL C. J. Fee	VZ	Tangmere
416	SL L. V. Chadburn	DN	Hawkinge
485	SL R. J. C. Grant, dfm	OU	West Malling
501	SL J. W. Villa, dfc	SD	Tangmere
602	SL P. M. Brothers, dfc	LO	Biggin Hill
610	SL J. E. Johnson, dfc	DW	West Malling
611	SL D. H. Watkins, dfc	FY	Redhill
616	SL H. L. I. Brown, dfc	YQ	Hawkinge

HURRICANE SQUADRONS

No	Commanding Officer	Code	Base on 19 Aug
3	SL A. E. Berry, dfc (NZ)	QO	Shoreham
32	SL E. R. Thorn, dfm	GZ	Friston
43	SL D. A. R. G. LeR. DuVivier, dfc (Bel)	FT	Tangmere
87	SL D. G. Smallwood	LK	Tangmere
174	SL E. M. L. Fayolle, dfc, cdg (FF)	XP	Ford

No	Commanding Officer	Code	Base on 19 Aug
175	SL J. R. Pennington-Legh, DFC	HH	Warmwell
245	SL H. H. B. Mould	MR	Shoreham
253	SL D. S. Yapp	SW	Friston

TYPHOON SQUADRONS

No	Commanding Officer	Code	Base on 19 Aug
56	SL H. S. L. Dundas, DFC	US	Duxford
266	SL C. L. Green (Rhod)	UO	Duxford
609	SL P. H. M. Richey, DFC	PR	Duxford

BOSTON III SQUADRONS

No	Commanding Officer	Code	Base on 19 Aug
88	WC J. E. Pelly-Fry	RH	Ford
107	WC L. A. Lynn, DFC	OM	Ford
226	WC W. E. Surplice, DFC	MQ	Thruxton
418	WC A. E. Saunders	TH	Bradwell Bay
(1 a/c)			
605	WC P. W. Townsend, DSO, DFC	VY	Ford
(2 a/c)			

BLENHEIM IV SQUADRONS

No	Commanding Officer	Code	Base on 19 Aug
13	WC J. W. Deacon	OO	Thruxton
614	WC H. C. Sutton	YX	Thruxton

MUSTANG SQUADRONS

No	Commanding Officer	Code	Base on 19 Aug
26	SL E. M. Goodale	RM	Gatwick
239	WC P. L. Donkin	HB	Gatwick

No	Commanding Officer	Code	Base on 19 Aug
400	SL R. C. A. Waddell	SP	Gatwick
414	SL R. F. Begg	RU	Gatwick

B17 SQUADRONS

97th Bomb Group – Lt Col Frank A. Armstrong Jr

No	Base on 19 Aug
340th	Polebrook
341st	Polebrook
342nd	Grafton Underwood
414th	Grafton Underwood

BEAUFIGHTER SQUADRON

No	Commanding Officer	Code	Base on 19 Aug
141	WC G. F. W. Heycock, DFC	TW	Ford

Missions flown by RAF Squadrons at Dieppe

3 Squadron – Spitfires	4	
13 Squadron – Blenheim	2	(1 recalled)
19 Squadron – Spitfires	3	
26 Squadron – Mustangs	8	(16 sorties)
32 Squadron – Hurricanes	4	(including one E-Boat search)
41 Squadron – Spitfires	3	(plus 2 defensive patrols and one Air Sea Rescue search)
43 Squadron – Hurricanes	4	(including one E-Boat search)
56 Squadron – Typhoons	3	
64 Squadron – Spitfires	3	
65 Squadron – Spitfires	4	
66 Squadron – Spitfires	2	
71 Squadron – Spitfires	4	
81 Squadron – Spitfires	4	
87 Squadron – Hurricanes	3	
88 Squadron – Bostons	5	
91 Squadron – Spitfires	73	(total sorties – including Jim Crow, ASR searches and patrols)
107 Squadron – Boston	4	
111 Squadron – Spitfires	4	
118 Squadron – Spitfires	3	(plus one defensive patrol)
121 Squadron – Spitfires	3	
122 Squadron – Spitfires	4	
124 Squadron – Spitfires	4	
129 Squadron – Spitfires	4	
130 Squadron – Spitfires	2	

131 Squadron – Spitfires	4	(plus two defensive patrols and one ASR search)
133 Squadron – Spitfires	4	
141 Squadron – Beaufighter	1	(one sortie)
154 Squadron – Spitfires	4	
165 Squadron – Spitfires	4	
174 Squadron – Spitfires	3	
175 Squadron – Spitfires	3	
222 Squadron – Spitfires	4	
226 Squadron – Bostons	4	
232 Squadron – Spitfires	3	
239 Squadron – Mustangs	8	(14 sorties)
242 Squadron – Spitfires	4	
245 Squadron – Hurricanes	2	(plus two defensive patrols)
253 Squadron – Hurricanes	3	(plus one defensive patrol)
266 Squadron – Typhoons	3	
302 Squadron – Spitfires	4	
303 Squadron – Spitfires	4	
306 Squadron – Spitfires	4	(one recalled, plus one defensive patrol)
307th Squadron – Spitfires	4	
308th Squadron – Spitfires	4	
309th Squadron – Spitfires	4	
308 Squadron – Spitfires	4	
310 Squadron – Spitfires	4	
312 Squadron – Spitfires	3	
317 Squadron – Spitfires	4	
331 Squadron – Spitfires	4	
332 Squadron – Spitfires	4	
340 Squadron – Spitfires	4	
350 Squadron – Spitfires	4	
400 Squadron – Mustangs	10	(20 sorties)
401 Squadron – Spitfires	3	
402 Squadron – Spitfires	4	(plus one two-man patrol)
403 Squadron – Spitfires	3	
411 Squadron – Spitfires	4	
412 Squadron – Spitfires	3	(plus two defensive and one ASR patrol)

414 Squadron – Mustangs	9	(17 sorties)
416 Squadron – Spitfires	4	
418 Squadron – Bostons	1	(one aircraft – aborted and shot down)
485 Squadron – Spitfires	4	
501 Squadron – Spitfires	3	
602 Squadron – Spitfires	4	
605 Squadron – Bostons	1	
609 Squadron – Typhoons	3	
610 Squadron – Spitfires	3	
611 Squadron – Spitfires	4	
614 Squadron – Blenheims	3	(one recalled)
616 Squadron – Spitfires	4	

APPENDIX F

RAF Casualties 19 August, 1942

Squadron	Name	Nationality	P/O/AG		Machine Type	Serial Number	Code (where known)	Category
3	SL A. E. Berry	NZ	P	Killed	Hurricane II	AM286		Lost Cat E
3	Sgt S. D. Banks	Can	P	Killed	,,	BD867	QO–Y	Lost Cat E
3	FL H. E. Tappin	Br	P	Unhurt	,,	BE371		Cat B dam
3	Sgt Armstrong		P	Unhurt	,,	Z3358		Cat A dam
3	FO E. J. Pullen		P	Unhurt	,,	AG665		Cat B dam
13	PO C. L. Woodland	Br	P	Killed	Blenheim IV	V5380		Lost Cat E
	Sgt A. S. Boyd	Irish	OB	Killed				
	Sgt H. G. Neville	Aust	AG	Killed				
13	FL E. L. Beverley & Crew	Br	P	Unhurt	,,	Z6089		dam
19	Sgt E. A. Blore	Br	P	Killed	Spitfire Vb	EP523	OO–F	Lost Cat E
19	Sgt E. R. Davies		P	WIA	,,	BM542		Lost Cat E
19	PO J. Henderson		P	Unhurt	,,	BL380		Cat A dam
19	Sgt J. W. Foster		P	Slightly WIA	,,	BL573		Cat A dam
26	SL E. M. Goodale	Br	P	Unhurt	Mustang 1a	AG148	RM–G	dam
26	FL G. N. Dawson	Br	P	Killed	,,	AG418		Lost Cat E
26	FL D. N. Kennedy		P	Killed	,,	AG536		Lost Cat E
26	PO E. E. O'Farrell		P	PoW	,,	AG463		Lost Cat E
26	PO A. G. Christensen	NZ	P	PoW	,,	AL977		Lost Cat E
26	Sgt G. D. M. Cliff	Br	P	Killed	,,	AG584		Lost Cat E

Squadron	Name	Nationality	P/O/AG		Machine Type	Serial Number	Code (where known)	Category
32	FL H. Connolly	Br	P	Killed	Hurricane II	HL860		*Lost* Cat E
32	Sgt H. Stanage		P	Unhurt	,,	HL605		Cat B dam
41	SL G. C. Hyde	Br	P	Killed	Spitfire Vb	BL777		*Lost* Cat E
41					,,	EN836		Cat AC dam
43	FS H. Wik	Can	P	Killed	Hurricane II	BD712	FT–Z	*Lost* Cat E
43	PO A. E. Snell		P	Unhurt (baled)	,,	BP703	FT–O	*Lost* Cat E
43	FL F. W. Lister	Br	P	Unhurt	,,	BN234	FT–U	Cat B dam
43	Sgt E. Bierer		P	Unhurt	,,	Z2641	FT–R	Cat A dam
43				Unhurt	,,	Z5153	FT–H	dam
43				Unhurt	,,	Z3687	FT–E	dam
64	Sgt E. N. McCuaig	Scot	P	Killed	Spitfire IX	BR604		*Lost* Cat E
64	PO J. K. Stewart	Rhod	P	Killed	,,	BR977		*Lost* Cat E
64	SL W. G. D. Smith	Br	P	Unhurt	,,	BR581		*Lost* Cat E
66	Sgt R. Lyons	Can	P	Killed	Spitfire Vb	AB517		*Lost* Cat E
66	Lt V. R. E. Nissen	SA	P	Killed	,,	AB514		*Lost* Cat E
71	PO W. B. Morgan	US	P	Unhurt	,,	AB199		Cat B dam
71	SL C. G. Peterson	US	P	Unhurt (baled)	,,	BM361		*Lost* Cat E
71	FO M. G. McPharlin	US	P	Unhurt (baled)	,,	W3767		*Lost* Cat E
81	PO W. S. Large	Can	P	Unhurt	,,	BM376		Cat B dam
87	FO A. S. M. Waltos	Pol	P	Killed	Hurricane II	Z2497		*Lost* Cat E
87	PO J. Baker		P	Unhurt	,,	Z2979		*Lost* Cat E
87	FO A. Thom	Scot	P	Unhurt	,,	BN219		Cat B dam
87	Sgt R. Gibson	Br	P	Killed	,,	Z3485		*Lost* Cat E

No.	Name	Nat	Crew	Status	Type	Serial	Code	Disposition
88	WO C. A. Beach	Can	P	Killed	Boston III	AL692	RH-S	*Lost* Cat E
	Sgt D. F. J. Hindle		OB	Killed				
	Sgt L. Senour		AG	Unhurt				
	Sgt P. S. Woolston		AG	Unhurt				
91	PO A. M. leMaire	Belg	P	Unhurt	Spitfire V	BM541	DL–S	Cat A dam
91	Sgt C. H. Evans		P	Unhurt (baled)	"		DL–A	*Lost* Cat E
107	Sgt G. E. Nicholls		P	Unhurt	Boston III		OM–J	Cat A dam
	Sgt R. J. Hathaway		OB	Slightly WIA				
111	Sgt F. H. Tyrrell		P	Unhurt (baled)	Spitfire Vb	W3814		*Lost* Cat E
111	Sgt E. J. Hindley	Br	P	Killed	"	P8699		*Lost* Cat E
118	FSgt S. A. Watson		P	Unhurt	"	EN964		Cat B dam
121	PO J. T. Taylor	US	P	Killed	"	AD569		*Lost* Cat E
121	PO J. B. Mahon	US	P	PoW	"	BM405		*Lost* Cat E
121	PO G. B. Fetrow	US	P	Unhurt (baled)	"	BM401		*Lost* Cat E
121	FL S. R. Edner	US	P	Unhurt	"	EN918		Cat A dam
121	FL W. J. Daley	US	P	Unhurt	"	AA841		Cat A dam
121	PO J. M. Osborne	US	P	Unhurt (baled)	"	P8589		*Lost* Cat E
122	SL J. R. C. Kilian	NZ	P	Slightly WIA	"	BL812		Cat A dam
124	Sgt J. B. Shanks		P	PoW	"	BR588		*Lost* Cat E
129	FO H. G. Jones	Welsh	P	Killed	Spitfire V			*Lost* Cat E
129	Sgt R. L. Reeves		P	Slightly WIA	"			Cat A dam
129	PO J. B. Shillitoe		P	Unhurt	"			Cat B dam
129	Sgt S. G. Jonssen	Nor	P	Killed (acc)	"			*Lost* Cat E
130	WC M. V. Blake	NZ	P	PoW	"	W3561	M–B	*Lost* Cat E
130	Sgt A. W. Utting	Br	P	Killed	"	BL356	PJ–Q	*Lost* Cat E
130	FS Cane		P	WIA	"			dam
131	WC M. G. F. Pedley	Br	P	Unhurt	"	BM420	NX–A	dam

Squadron	Name	Nationality	P/O/AG		Machine Type	Serial Number	Code (where known)	Category
131	PO H. Copeland	NZ	P	Unhurt	,,	AD348		Cat B dam
133	PO G. G. Wright	US	P	Unhurt				dam
174	SL E. M. L. Fayolle	Fr	P	Killed	Hurricane II	HV557		*Lost* Cat E
174	PO R. L. N. Van Wymeersch	Fr	P	PoW & WIA	,,	BP299		*Lost* Cat E
174	FS C. B. Watson	Aust	P	PoW	,,	BE505	XP–L	*Lost* Cat E
174	Sgt C. F. James	Br	P	Killed	,,	BP649		*Lost* Cat E
174	PO M. H. du Fretay	Fr	P	Killed	,,	HL705		*Lost* Cat E
175	Sgt D. S. Conroy		P	Unhurt	,,	BE404		dam
175	PO D. I. Stevenson		P	Unhurt (baled)	,,	BE687		*Lost* Cat E
222	Sgt V. Evans		P	Unhurt	Spitfire Vb	BL673		Cat A dam
226	Sgt R. Parsons & Crew		P	Unhurt	Boston III	Z2264	MQ–F	Cat B dam
226	Sgt M. A. H. Demont		P	Unhurt	,,	AL688	MQ–Y	Cat B dam
	Sgt G. Bates		OB	WIA				
226	SL J. S. Kennedy		P	Unhurt		AL278	MQ–W	Cat B dam
	FO H. A. Asker		OB	Unhurt				
	FO G. A. Casey		AG	WIA	,,			
	FL O. G. E. McWilliam		Pass	Killed				
226	PO W. R. Gellatly		P	Unhurt		L710	MQ–Z	Cat B dam
	PO F. G. Starkie		OB	WIA	,,			
	PO L. J. Waters	US	AG	Killed				
226	PO R. J. Corrigan		P	Killed		L736	MQ–P	*Lost* Cat E
	Sgt S. Moth		OB	WIA	,,			
	FSgt W. Osselton	Br	AG	Killed				

	Name	Nat	Role	Fate	Aircraft	Serial	Code	Status
226	FO R. A. Marks		P	PoW	Boston III	L680	MQ–L	*Lost* Cat E
	PO K. A. I. Warwood		OB	PoW				
	PO L. K. Brownson		AG	PoW				
226	PO D. T. Smith		P	WIA	"	Z2258	MQ–H	dam
	FS J. C. Bicknell		AG	Unhurt				
	PO G. B. Tolputt		OB	Unhurt				
226	SL G. R. Magill & Crew	Br	P	Unhurt	Boston III	Z2295	MQ–A	dam
232	FL P. D. Strong		P	Killed	Spitfire Vb	EN845	EF–Y	*Lost* Cat E
232	Sgt K. G. Walker	Br	P	Killed	"	AB134	EF–M	*Lost* Cat E
239	PO J. R. Cruickshank		P	Killed	Mustang Ia	AG537		*Lost* Cat E
239	FO W. T. McKeown		P	PoW	"	AM533		*Lost* Cat E
239	SL H. P. McClean		P	Unhurt	"	AG557		dam
239	FO P. A. L. Gompertz	Br	P	Killed	"	AM134		*Lost* Cat E
242	PO D. Fowler		P	WIA	Spitfire Vb	BL992		Cat B dam
242	SL T. C. Parker		P	Unhurt	"	BM539		Cat A dam
245	FS C. G. Cummings		P	Unhurt	Hurricane II	BD959		Cat A dam
245	FL G. R. Bennette	Br	P	Killed	"	BP741		*Lost* Cat E
245	PO J. F. Barton	NZ	P	Killed	"	BD766		*Lost* Cat E
245	PO A. E. Scott	Br	P	Killed	"	HL669		*Lost* Cat E
245	SL H. H. B. Mould	Br	P	Unhurt	"	BN233		Cat B dam
245	PO C. L. Gotch		P	WIA	"	BE495		dam
245	PO I. L. Behal		P	Unhurt	"			Cat A dam
253	FO H. D. Seal	Br	P	PoW	"	BP771		*Lost* Cat E
253	FS J. C. Tate	US	P	Injured	"	BP769		*S/off* Cat E
253	FL J. W. L. Ellacombe	Br	P	Unhurt (baled)	"	BP707		*Lost* Cat E
266	PO W. S. Smithyson		P	Killed	Typhoon 1A	R7813		*Lost* Cat E

Squadron	Name	Nationality	P/O/AG		Machine Type	Serial Number	Code (where known)	Category
266	FL R. H. L. Dawson	Rhod	P	Killed	,,	R7815		*Lost* Cat E
303	FO L. Majewski	Pol	P	Unhurt	Spitfire V	EN912		dam
303	PO A. Damm	Pol	P	Killed	,,	BL574		*Lost* Cat E
306	Sgt S. Czachla	Pol	P	Injured	,,	AD581		*S/off* Cat E
306	FO E. Landsman	Pol	P	PoW	,,			*Lost* Cat E
307th	Lt E. A. Tovrea	US	P	PoW	Spitfire V			*Lost* Cat E
307th	Lt R. G. Wight	US	P	Killed	,,			*Lost* Cat E
308th	Lt R. D. Ingrams	US	P	PoW	,,			*Lost* Cat E
308th	Lt W. A. Dabney	US	P	PoW	,,			*Lost* Cat E
309th	Lt S. Junkin Jr	US	P	WIA (baled)	Spitfire Vb			*Lost* Cat E
309th	Lt Collins	US	P	Killed	,,			*Lost* Cat E
309th		US	P	Unhurt (baled)	,,			*Lost* Cat E
312	Sgt J. Liskutin	Cz	P	Unhurt	,,	EP559		Cat B dam
317	FO M. Cholewka	Pol	P	WIA	,,			dam
317	PO M. K. Maciejowski	Pol	P	Unhurt	,,	BL927	JH–L	Cat B dam
317	Sgt W. Powlowski	Pol	P	Unhurt	,,			dam
331	2/Lt J. Greiner	Nor	P	WIA (baled)	,,	BL903	FN–L	*Lost* Cat E
331	Lt R. A. Berg	Nor	P	Unhurt (baled)	,,	BL579	FN–B	*Lost* Cat E
332	Sgt P. Bergsland	Nor	P	PoW	,,	AB269		*Lost* Cat E
332	Sgt J. Staubo	Nor	P	PoW	,,	BL819		*Lost* Cat E
332	Maj W. Mohr	Nor	P	WIA	,,	EN901		dam
332	Sgt B. Raeder	Nor	P	Unhurt	,,	BL894		dam
332	Sgt J. Lofsgaard	Nor	P	Unhurt (baled)	,,	BL985		*Lost* Cat E

No.	Name	Nat		Status	Aircraft	No.	Code	Result
332	Sgt O. Djonne	Nor	P	Unhurt (baled)	,,	AD325		*Lost* Cat E
340	S/Lt Kerlan	Fr	P	Unhurt	,,	W3457	GW–K	*Lost* Cat E
340	Adj R. G. Darbin	Fr	P	Killed	,,	BL262	GW–U	*Lost* Cat E
350	PO H. E. Marchal	Bel	P	Unhurt	,,	AR380		*Lost* Cat E
350	FL A. L. Boussa	Bel	P	WIA	,,	EN769		dam
350	PO F. A. Venesoen	Bel	P	Unhurt	,,	AD475		dam
350	Sgt R. A. Alexandre	Bel	P	Unhurt	,,	AR373		dam
400	PO D. G. Burlingham	Can	P	Killed	Mustang 1a			*Lost* Cat E
401	FS B. M. Zobell	Can	P	WIA	Spitfire IX	BS120		Cat B dam
401	PO D. R. Morrison	Can	P	Unhurt (baled)	,,	BS119		*Lost* Cat E
401	Sgt M. H. Buckley	Can	P	Killed	,,	BS157		*Lost* Cat E
401	Sgt L. J. Armstrong	Can	P	PoW	,,	BS107		*Lost* Cat E
403	PO J. E. Gardiner	Can	P	Killed	Spitfire Vb	AR439		*Lost* Cat E
403	PO L. A. Walker	Can	P	Killed	,,	EN850		*Lost* Cat E
403	PO N. Monchier	Can	P	Killed	,,	AR437		*Lost* Cat E
411	PO Reid	Can	P	Unhurt	Spitfire Vb	BM652		dam
411	PO P. R. Eakins	Can	P	Killed	,,	BM406		*Lost* Cat E
411	PO D. Linton	Can	P	Killed	,,	BL542		*Lost* Cat E
411	FS S. A. Mills	Can	P	WIA	,,	AD263		dam
412	PO J. N. Brookhouse	Can	P	Killed	,,	EN831		*Lost* Cat E
412	FS W. F. Aldcorn	Can	P	Unhurt	,,	BL587		*Lost* Cat E
414	FL F. E. Clarke	Can	P	WIA (ditched)	Mustang 1a	AG375		*Lost* Cat E
414	PO C. H. Stover	Can	P	Unhurt	,,	AG601		Cat B dam
414	FO C. L. Horncastle	Can	P	Unhurt	,,	AG459		dam
414	FO R. C. MacQuoid	Can	P	Unhurt	,,	AG582		dam
416	PO P. G. Blades	Can	P	Unhurt	Spitfire Vb	EP581		Cat B dam

Squadron	Name	Nationality	P/O/AG		Machine Type	Serial Number	Code (where known)	Category
418	Sgt W. L. Buchanan	Can	P	Injured	Boston III			
	PO P. C. McGillicuddy	Can	OB	PoW				Lost Cat E
	Sgt C. G. Scott	Can	AG	Injured				
501	FS A. R. MacDonald	Br	P	Unhurt	Spitfire Vb	EN974	SD–D	dam
501	WC P. Gibbs		P	Unhurt	,,	EP120	SD–Y	dam
501	FS G. A. Mawer	Aust	P	Slightly WIA	,,	EP191	SD–P	dam
501	PO W. R. Lightbourne		P	Injured	,,	AB402	SD–K	Lost Cat E
501	Sgt A. Lee		P	Killed (acc)	,,	EN963	SD–E	S/off Cat E
501	PO M. F. Goodchap		P	PoW	,,	BL932		Lost Cat E
602	FL J. B. Niven		P	Injured	,,	BM451		Lost Cat E
602	FS S. C. Creagh		P	Unhurt	,,	EP198	DW–H	Lost Cat E
610	PO L. E. Hoken		P	Unhurt	,,	EP238	DW–D	Cat B dam
610	FL P. D. Poole		P	Killed	,,	EP235	DW–F	Lost Cat E
610	Sgt J. G. Leech		P	Killed	,,	EP342	DW–S	Lost Cat E
611	FS A. P. F. Vilboux	Fr	P	Killed	Spitfire IX	BS179		Lost Cat E
	FL J. E. Scott		P	WIA	,,			
614	Sgt W. Johnson		OB	Killed	Blenheim IV	V6526		S/off Cat E
	FS G. R. Gifkins		AG	Killed				
616	Sgt N. G. Welch	Rhod	P	Unhurt	Spitfire VI	BR255		Cat B dam
616	Sgt N. W. J. Coldray		P	Killed	,,			Lost Cat E
616	FL J. S. Fifield		P	Unhurt (baled)	,,			Lost Cat E
616	Sgt Rogers		P	Unhurt	,,	BR563		Cat AC dam

APPENDIX G

Luftwaffe Fighter Pilot Casualties

Jagdesgeschwader 2

Staff Staffel	Oblt Erich Leie	Kommodore I/JG2, wounded and baled out
Staff Staffel	Stfw Erwin Kley[1]	Killed in combat with Spitfire
1st Staffel	Uffz Kurt Epsiger	Missing 2 km south of Dover after collision with a Spitfire
2nd Staffel	Ltn Reinhart Bohm	Missing
2nd Staffel	Ofw Karl Schweikart	Missing
3rd Staffel	Uffz Gunter Brietz	Missing 4 km north of Dieppe after shooting down a Spitfire hit by flak and disintegrated
3rd Staffel	Uffz Rudolf Roebbers	Wounded
4th Staffel	Gefr Siegfried Eimers	Killed in combat with Spitfire
4th Staffel	Uffz Werner Urben	Wounded in combat with Spitfire
4th Staffel	Uffz Heinz Schulze	Wounded in combat with Spitfire
4th Staffel	Ltn Ludwig Spinner[2]	Wounded in combat with Spitfire
6th Staffel	Ltn Franz Sommer	Missing after combat with Spitfire
6th Staffel	Uffz Gunther Gegunds	Missing after combat with Spitfire
9th Staffel	Fw Heinrich Pfeffer	Wounded and baled out
9th Staffel	Uffz Wilhelm Gunther	Wounded, shot down during ground attack

[1] Stabsfeldwebel Kley was credited with 13 victories.
[2] Leutnant Spinner was killed 6 September 1942.

Jagdesgeschwader 26

2nd Staffel	Ofw Paul Czwilinski	Killed in action
5th Staffel	Ofw Werner Gerhardt[3]	Killed in action
5th Staffel	Uffz Hans Rieder	Killed in action
9th Staffel	Fw August Golub	Killed in action
10th Staffel	Uffz Heinrich von Berg	Killed in accident
11th Staffel	Oblt Johannes Schmidt[4]	Killed in action

[3] Oberfeldwebel Gerhardt was credited with 13 victories.

[4] Oberleutnant Schmidt, credited with 12 victories, was Staffelkapitän of II/JG26.

Royal Air Force Fighter Claims 19 August 1942

Pilot	Rank	Squadron	Destroyed	Probable	Damaged
Henderson, J.	PO	19		FW190	
Bradley, C. F.	FL	19		FW190	FW190
Davies, P. B. G.	SL ⎱				
Mundy, I. M.	Sgt ⎰	19			FW190
Mundy, I. M.	Sgt	19			FW190
Imbert, A.	Sgt	41			FW190
Stepp, M. L.	FL	41			FW190
Kingaby, D. E.	FL	64	Do217		
Duncan-Smith, W. G. G.	SL	64	2 Do217s		
Duncan-Smith, W. G. G.	SL ⎱				
Batchelor, W. J.	FS ⎰	64	Do217		
Thomas, C.	FL	64	FW190		Me109E
Mason, G. A.	FS	64			FW190
Withy, H. F.	PO	64			Do217
Tinsey, T. D.	Sgt	65	Do217		
Biggs, K. A.	Sgt ⎱				
Brown, R.	Sgt ⎰	65	Do217		
McMullen, D. A. P.	SL	65			Do217
Strickland, H. H.	PO	71			FW190
Peterson, C. G.	SL	71	Ju88		Ju88
Coen, O. H.	FL ⎱				
McPharlin, M. G.	FO ⎰	71		Ju88	
Anderson, S. M.	PO	71			Ju88
Anson, P. J.	PO	81		FW190	
Vancl, F.	FL ⎱				
Spranger, B. A. C.	Sgt ⎰	111			Do217
Baraldi, F. H. R.	FL	111			Do217
Henrichson, Y.	Sgt	111			Do217
Gale, B. E.	PO	111			FW190

Pilot	Rank	Squadron	Destroyed	Probable	Damaged
Shepherd, J. B.	FL				
Stewart, I. G.	FO				
Watson, S. A.	FS	118	Do217		
129 Sqdn pilot	—				
DeCourcey, T. J.	Sgt				
Gibbs, P.	WC	118	Do217		
Edner, S. R.	FL	121	FW190		
Halsey, G. O.	PO	121		FW190	
Blanding, L. M.	Sgt	121		FW190	
Smith, F. D.	PO	121			FW190
Griffiths, L. P.	FL				
Bland, B. J.	PO	122			Do217
Kilian, J. R. C.	SL				
Peet, W. W.	Sgt				
Collingnon, L. C.	PO	122	Do217		
Williams, A.	Sgt				
Mercer, D.	Sgt	122			Do127
Gregson, W.	FL	124	FW190		FW190
Durnford, P. E. G.	FS	124	Do127	FW190	
Kilburn, M. P.	PO	124		FW190	
Hull, B. J.	PO	124	FW190	Ju88	FW190
Russell, A. G.	PO	124			FW190
Gregson, W.	FL	124			FW190
Reeves, R. L.	Sgt	129		FW190	
Shillitoe, J. B.	PO	129			FW190
Ingram, B.	FL	129	$\frac{1}{4}$ Do217		
Thomas, R. H.	SL	129			Do217
Blake, M. V.	WC	130	FW190		
Snell	Sgt	130		FW190	
Braybrooke, A. W.	Sgt	130			Ju88
LeBlond, R. P.	PO	130		FW190	
Harries, R. H.	FL	131	FW190		
Harries, R. H.	FL				
Wilson, N. S.	FO				
Eckert, A.	PO	131	Do217		
Bower, A. W.	Sgt				
Pedley, M. G. F.	WC				
Copeland, H. G.	PO				
Thorogood, J. D.	Sgt	131	Do217		
Davidson, J. L.	Sgt				
Copeland, H. G.	PO	131			Do217
Pedley, M. G. F.	WC				
Jackson, H. S.	FO	131	Ju88		
Copeland, H. G.	PO				

Pilot	Rank	Squadron	Destroyed	Probable	Damaged
Doll, J. C. S.	FL				
Jackson, H. S.	FO				
Williams, E. A. J.	PO	131		Do217	
Crawford, I. K.	PO				
Allen, R. H.	SL	131			Do217
Blakeslee, D. J. M.	FL	133	FW190		Do217
„	„	133			FW190
Alexander, R. L.	FS	133	Do217	FW190	FW190
Baker, W. H.	PO	133	FW190		FW190
Beaty, R. N.	PO	133			FW190
„	„	133			Do217
Brettell, E. G.	FL	133	FW190		
Doorly, E.	FO	133			Do217
Gentile, D. S.	PO	133	FW190		
Gudmandsen, D. D.	PO	133			Do217
Nelson, J. C.	FO	133			Do217
Wright, G. G.	PO	133			FW190
Cleo, R. O.	Sgt				
Grant, G.	Sgt	141	Ju88		
Carlson, D. C.	SL				
Harrison, G. A.	FL				
Davies, M.	PO				
Turnbull, A. S.	FO				
Chambers, H. W.	PO	154	Do217		
Flote, F. J.	Sgt				
Buiron, J. G.	WO				
Whaley, J. S.	Sgt				
Garrett, I. T.	PO				
Hallowes, H. J. L.	SL	165	Do217		Do217
Colquhoun, E. W.	FL				
Pederson, H. L.	PO				
Warren, B.	PO	165	Do217		
Warren, D.	PO				
Disney, L. R.	PO				
Richardson, H. C.	PO	165			Ju88
Disney, L. R.	PO	165			Do217
Meredith, J. E.	FL	175	He111		
Peters, R. A.	PO	175		FW190	FW190
Dawson, R. H. L.	FL	266	Do217		
Munro	PO	266			FW190
Gillam, D. E.	WC	266			FW190
Harris, R. F. F.	PO				
Adamson, J.	PO	277			Me109

Pilot	Rank	Squadron	Destroyed	Probable	Damaged
Zumbach, J.	SL	303	FW190	FW190	
Kelecki, T.	PO	303	Ju88		
Socha, S.	PO	303	FW190		
,,	,,		Ju88		
Marciniak, J.	FL	303		FW190	
Glowacki, A.	PO	303	FW190		
Giermer, W.	FS	303		FW190	
Karczmarz, J.	Sgt	303		FW190	
Stasik, S.	Sgt	303	FW190		
Popek, M.	FS	303	½ FW190		
Horbaczewski, E.	FO	303	FW190		
Zumbach, J.	SL	303	He111		
Whisonant, W. B.	Lt	307th		FW190	
White, J. H.	Lt	307th		FW190	
Hill, F. A.	Capt	308th		FW190	
Junkin, S., Jr.	Lt	309th	FW190		
Thyng, H. R.	Maj	309th			FW190
Thorsen, J. S.	Capt	309th			Do217
Dolezal, F.	SL	310		Do217	FW190
Foit, E. A.	FL	310		Do217	Do217
Popelka, V	Sgt	310		Do217	Do217
Kimlicka, B.	FL	310			Do217
Hartman, J.	PO	310			2 Do217s
Doucha, J.	PO	310			Do217
Fornusek, A.	WO	310			Do217
Stivar, J.	Sgt	310			Do217
Skach, A.	Sgt	310			FW190
Motycka, T.	FS	312		FW190	
Ruprecht, V.	PO	312		FW190	
Smolik, V.	PO	312			FW190
Keprt, J.	FO	312	Do217		
Liskutin, J.	Sgt	312	½ Do217		
Pipa, J.	FS	312			Do217
Rutkowski, K.	FL	317	Do217		
,,	,,		He111		
Maciejowski, M. K.	PO	317	Ju88		
,,	,,		FW190		
Powlowski, W.	Sgt	317			FW190
Brzeski, S.	PO	317	He111		
Lukaszewicz, S.	FO	317	FW190		
Maciejowski, M. K.	PO	⎰			

Pilot	Rank	Squadron	Destroyed	Probable	Damaged
Kolczynski, A.	Sgt	317	Do217		
Stramko, K.	FS	317	½ He111		
Scott-Malden, F. D. S.	WC	—	Do217		
Mehre, H.	Maj	331	FW190	FW190	
Birksted, K.	Capt	331	FW190		
Birksted, K.	Capt }				
Fearnley, F. S.	Sgt }	331			Me109
Sem-Olsen, E.	Lt }				
Owren, G. P.	Sgt }	331			FW190
Berg, R. A.	Lt }				
Grundt-Spang, H.	Sgt }	331			FW109
Hagerup, A. C.	Capt }				
Sognnes, H.	2/Lt }	331	Do217		
Fearnley, F. S.	Sgt	331		Do217	
Sem-Olsen, E.	Lt	331			Do217
Weisteen, T.	Lt	331			Do217
Ree, M.	Lt	331			Do217
Grundt-Spang, H.	Sgt	331	FW190		FW190
Hegland, S.	2/Lt	331	FW190		
Berg, R. A.	Lt	331	FW190		FW190
Sem-Olsen, E.	Lt }				
Fossum, E. P.	Sgt }	331			Do217
From, R.	Capt	332	FW190		FW190
Erickson, M.	Sgt	332	Do217		Do217
„	„		FW190		FW190
Lofsgaard, J.	Sgt	332	FW190		Do217
Thorsager, F.	Capt	332	Do217		2 FW190s
Djonne, O.	Sgt	332	Do217		
Kristiansen, O.	Lt }				
Ullerstad, O.	Lt }	332			Do217
Christie, W.	2/Lt	332	½ Do217		
Rygg, J.	Lt	332	Do217		
Boudier, M.	2/Lt	340			FW190
Labouchere, F. de	Capt	340	2 Do217		
Laureys, P.	2/Lt	340	Do217		
Bechoff	Capt	340			Do217
deMonceau, I. G.	FL	350	FW190		FW190
Picard, H. A.	PO }				
Plas, E. J.	PO }	350	FW190		FW190
Flohimont	Sgt	350			2 FW190s
Venesoen, F. A.	PO	350	2 FW190s		

Pilot	Rank	Squadron	Destroyed	Probable	Damaged
Smets, H. J.	PO	350	½JU88		
Boussa, A. L.	FL	350	FW190		FW190
Seydel, G. M.	PO				
Boute, F. E.	Sgt	350	½JU88		2 FW190s
Alexandre, R. A.	Sgt	350		FW190	3 FW190s
Plisnier, A. M.	PO	350	FW190		
"	"		½JU 88		
Seydel, G. M.	PO	350			FW190
Vanterberge	Sgt	350	½JU88		Do217
Zobell, B. M.	FS	401			Do217
"	"				FW190
Hodson, K. L. B.	SL	401			Do217
Coburn, S.	FS	401			Do217
Morrison, D. R.	PO	401	FW190		
Murray, G. B.	PO	401		FW190	FW190
Westhaver, H.	PO	401			FW190
Whitham, J.	FL	401		FW190	FW190
Bretz, N. H.	SL	402			FW190
Bland, E. A.	FL	402			FW190
Keith, G. N.	PO	402			FW190
Hill, G. U.	FL	403	FW190		
Hill, G. U.	FL				FW190
Fletcher, M. K.	Sgt	403	FW190		FW190
Murphy, H. J.	PO	403	Me109F		
Ford, L. S.	SL	403	2 FW190s		
O'Leary, P. T.	FL	403			FW190
Newton, R. B.	SL	411	½ FW190		
McNair, R. W.	FL	411		FW190	
Newton, R. B.	SL				
Matheson	FS	411			Do217
Hills, H. H.	FO	414	FW190		
Russell, H.	FL	416	FW190		
Buckham, R. A.	FO	416	FW190		Ju88
Phillip, J. D.	FS	416	FW190		
McKendy, J. S.	PO	416			Ju88
					FW190
"	"				
Chadburn, L. V.	SL	416		Ju88	Ju88
Boulton, F.	FL	416			Ju88
Rae, J. A.	PO	416			Ju88
McDonald, H.	FS	416			Ju88
Jameson, P. G.	WC	—	FW190		

Pilot	*Rank*	*Squadron*	*Destroyed*	*Probable*	*Damaged*
Chrystall, C.	PO	485	FW190		
Black, L. S.	FO	485			FW190
Baker, R. W.	FL	485			Do217
Stanbury, P. J.	FL	501			FW190
Brothers, P. M.	SL	602			FW190
Marryshaw, J. A.	Sgt	602			FW190
Sampson, R. W. F.	PO	602	FW190		2 Do217s
Bocock, E. P. W.	FL	602	Do217		FW190
Hauser, P. L.	Sgt	602	Do217		
Rippon, E. D. M.	FO	602			Ju88
"	"				Do217
Niven, J. B.	FL	602			Do217
Loud, W. W. J.	Sgt	}			
Caldecott, W. E.	Sgt	} 602	Do217	Do217	Do217
Lethbridge, W. V.	Sgt	602			Do217
Johnson, J. E.	SL	610	FW190		
Johnson, J. E.	SL	}			
Smith, L. A.	PO	} 610	Me109F		
Creagh, S. C.	FS	}			
Smith, L. A.	PO	610			FW190
Hokem, L. E.	PO	610			FW190
Crowley-Milling, D.	FL	610	Me109F		FW190
Watkins, D. H.	SL	611	FW190		
Crawford-Compton, W.V.	FL	611			FW190
Manak	FL	611			FW190
Gaze, F. O. A.	FL	616	Do217		
Fifield, J. S.	FL	616			FW190
Maclachlan, G. B.	FO	616			FW190
Smithson, J. H.	PO	616			2 FW190s
Cooper, M.	Sgt	616			FW190
Large, R. G.	PO	616			FW190
Broadhurst, H.	GC	—	FW190		3 FW190s

APPENDIX I

Luftwaffe Fighter Claims 19 August 1942

Pilot	Rank	Unit	Claim	Victory No.	War total
Schopfel, Gerhard	Maj	Kdr JG26	2 Spitfires	39–40	40
Siefert, Johannes	Hpt	I/JG26	Spitfire	41	57
Christof, Ernst	Uffz	,,	Spitfire		9
Zink, Fuelbert	Oblt	,,	{ 2 Spitfires		
			Mustang	24–26	36
Adam, Heinz-G.	Fw	,,	Spitfire		7
Hermichen, Rolf	Oblt	3/JG26 {	Spitfire		
			Airacobra*	16–17	64
Scheyda, Erich	Uffz	I/JG26	Spitfire		20
Willius, Karl	Fw	,,	Spitfire	22	50
Babenz, Emil	Ofw	2/JG26	3 Spitfires	19–21	24
Schmidt, Johannes	Oblt	3/JG26	2 Spitfires	11–12	12
Galland, Wilhelm	Oblt	5/JG26	1 Spitfire	13	55
Bierwirth, Heinrich	Ofw	II/JG26	Spitfire		8
Kruska	Ofw	II/JG26	Mustang		
Meyer, Walter	Ofw	,,	Spitfire	16	18
Meyer	Fw	,,	Spitfire		
Prym	Ltn	,,	Spitfire		
Glunz, Adolf	Fw	,,	Spitfire	21	71
Roth, Willi	Ofw	,,	Spitfire	16	20
Philipp, Wilhelm	Ofw	4/JG26	2 Spitfires	17–18	81
Ebersberger, Kurt	Oblt	II/JG26	4 Spitfires	25–28	29
Stammberger, Otto	Ltn	III/JG26	Spitfire		7
Mietusch, Klaus	Hpt	7/JG26	Spitfire		72
Borris, Karl	Oblt	8/JG26	Spitfire		43
Ruppert	Hpt	III/JG26	Spitfire		
Leie, Erich	Oblt	Kdr JG2	Spitfire	43	118

* presumably either a Mustang or a Spitfire with the American Star insignia.

Pilot	Rank	Unit	Claim	Victory No.	War total
Mayer, Egon	Oblt	JG2	2 Spitfires	49–50	102
Wurmheller, Josef	Ofw	9/JG2	{ 6 Spitfires		
			1 Blenheim	55–61	102
Rudorffer, Erich	Oblt	6/JG2	2 Spitfires	44–45	222
Schnell, Siegfried	Oblt	JG2	5 Spitfires	66–70	93
Seeger, Gunther	Ltn	Stab/JG2	3 Spitfires	20–22	56
Brietz, Gunter	Uffz	JG2	Spitfire		
Epsiger, Kurt	Uffz	JG2	Spitfire		
Eicher	Ltn	JG2	Spitfire		
Hahn, Hans	Hpt	III/JG2	2 Spitfires	66–67	108
Bolz, Helmut	Oblt	II/JG2	Spitfire		
Geltzsch, Kurt	Ofw	5/JG2	2 Spitfires		43
Meimberg, Julius	Ltn	II/JG2	2 Spitfires		53
Buhligen, Kurt	Oblt	JG2	Spitfire		112
Godt	Ltn	JG2	Spitfire		

German ranks (abbr)		RAF equivalent
Maj	— Major	Squadron Leader
Hpt	— Hauptmann	Flight Lieutenant
Oblt	— Oberleutnant	Flying Officer
Ltn	— Leutnant	Pilot Officer
Fw	— Feldwebel	Warrant Officer
Ofw	— Oberfeldwebel	Senior Warrant Officer
Uffz	— Unteroffizier	Sergeant
Gefr	— Gefreiter	Leading Aircraftsman

This list is incomplete. Total Luftwaffe claims for 19 August 112 but not all at Dieppe. The two Jagdesgeschwaders made the following claims:

JG2   —   59 confirmed, plus 7 probables

JG26   —   38 confirmed

—

97

Bombers claimed 6 and flak claimed several more.

Bibliography

Dieppe—August 19th 1942, Eric Maguire, Jonathan Cape Ltd 1963

Green Beach, James Leasor, William Heinemann Ltd 1975

The Battle of the Narrow Seas, Peter Scott, Country Life Ltd 1945

Aces High, C. F. Shores and C. Williams, Spearman 1966

2 Group RAF, M. J. F. Bowyer, Faber & Faber 1974

The RCAF Overseas (The First 4 Years), Oxford University Press 1944

New Zealander with the RAF, Vol 1 W/C H. L. Thompson, Oxford University Press 1953

Air War Against Germany and Italy, John Herington, Canberra, Australian War Memorial 1954

Horrido, T. J. Constable and R. F. Toliver, Arthur Barker Ltd 1968

Wing Leader, J. E. Johnson, Chatto & Windus 1956

History of the Polish Air Force 1918–68, J. B. Cynk, Osprey Publishing Ltd 1972

The Mouchotte Diaries, Ed. André Dezarrois, Staples Press Ltd 1956

War Eagles, James S. Childers, William Heinemann Ltd 1943

Mustang at War, Roger A. Freeman, Ian Allen 1974

Fighter Squadrons of the RAF, John Rawlings, Macdonald & Janes 1969

Exemplary Justice, Allen Andrews, George Harrap & Co, Ltd 1976

Haerens og Marinens flyvapen 1912–1945, Fredrik Meyer, Gyldendal Norsk Forlag 1977

After the Battle Magazine, Number 5

The Focke Wulf FW190, G. Swanborough and W. Green, David & Charles 1976

Index

252   *Index*